Praise for
pajama school

"*Pajama School* is a unique book in the sense that very few books chronicle a school experience beginning as early as the fourth grade. But this book is much more than the story of a school girl progressing through school with all the trials, fun, and games. This book is about a family, and how God blessed this family because of their simple faith that what He says He will do. It will be a tremendous encouragement for any family who wants to obey God, but will especially bless the homeschool mom or child that needs a little encouragement to get through the day, the week, or even the school year. Natalie tells the story with brutal honesty and a refreshing prose. Without appearing to make an effort to lay down principles for living, with story after story, it's like reading one of the parables, but much easier to see the principle that is being taught. This book is for anyone that doesn't mind laughing, crying, and every other emotion—all in one page. The bottom line is that after you finish reading, you will say: 'Natalie, when are you going to write your next book? I can't wait.'"

Mike Smith
President, HSLDA

"Many books have been written about homeschooling and much advice has been given. However, the real experts are those who go through the process. That's what makes this book valuable. It provides perspectives that would help every parent and homeschool student."

Bill Gothard
Founder, Institute in Basic Life Principles

"*Pajama School* is one of those rare books which allows readers full and generous access to the thoughts and judgments of a girl becoming a woman. It's also a comprehensive record of 'Cornerstone School,' where Natalie, Nicole, Nadine, Noelle, Naomi, and Joey Wickham learned their ABC's and much else under the direction of their parents (and one another). Homeschooling takes many forms these days in America, but while the author is an eloquent advocate of her own experience, everyone who sets his or her own particular preference aside long enough to read *Pajama School* with an open mind will take real value from Miss Wickham's observations. You'll like this book, I feel certain."

John Taylor Gatto
Author, *Dumbing Us Down* and *Weapons of Mass Instruction*

"Natalie writes convincingly and cheerfully of the 'other' side of homeschooling—that of the student. I enjoyed the honest, inside look at a homeschooling family navigating through the turbulent waters of modern day life. But beyond the humor is Natalie's heart for living for the Lord as an adult. This book will be an inspirational resource for all those 'others' who, like Natalie, have finished homeschooling and are seeking God's will. This is a welcome addition to all the books on homeschooling!"

Jan Bloom
Veteran Homeschool Mom of 3
Author, *Who Should We Then Read?*

pajama school

pajama school

stories from the life of a homeschool graduate

by *natalie wickham*

to mom and dad for

praising my endeavors
putting up with my faults
pouring your lives into me
preparing me to be a mature adult
pondering questions and issues with me
passing on a legacy of godly faithfulness
prompting me to seek the Lord in everything
providing the life experiences that inspired me to write this book

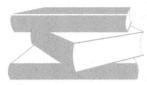

Contents

Dear reader

It was the end of 2006 and I was thinking and praying about goals for the next year. The words of Daniel 12:3 had been on my mind for the past several days, "And they that be wise shall shine as the brightness of the firmament; and they that turn many to righteousness as the stars for ever and ever." From this verse came forth two overarching goals for the following year—to grow in wisdom and to turn many to righteousness. I had some ideas of how I could grow in wisdom, but how could I turn many to righteousness? The idea flitted into my mind suddenly—I could write a book!

I reflected on the frequent conversations I have with homeschool families, or parents who are considering homeschooling their children. As soon as they learn that I graduated from high school as a homeschooler, the questions begin to flow. From what curriculum we used, to how we handled P.E., to what we did for socialization, at the heart of them all is the unspoken search for the assurance that if they homeschool their children they will turn out okay. I love encouraging weary Moms not to give up, and sharing with them the daily struggles we encountered as a homeschool family. I love answering the plethora of questions posed by curious Dads, and communicating to them my own Dad's vision for homeschooling. I love challenging children and teenagers to embrace these years of their life and make the most of their homeschool experience for the glory of God.

The more I contemplated the possibility of writing a book, the more excited I became. Books have played such a huge role in my life. I love reading stories of men and women whose lives have been changed by the Lord. I love catching glimpses into their struggles and triumphs. I love being challenged and inspired by the things they have learned and the experiences they have lived. So, with a desire to encourage the hearts of homeschool families, and a vision to record a legacy that can be passed on to future generations, I set out to write this book. I had no idea how hard it would be, and there is no explanation other than the grace of God as to how it ever got finished! My slow and feeble writing skills alone could never have done the job. But at long last you hold in your hands the culmination of hundreds of hours of thinking and writing (and deleting and re-writing!). This is my story. The story of our homeschool family through my eyes. It's not always what I wish it was, and in many ways it is a story that is still being written each day of our lives. But my prayer is that in it God will shine forth brilliantly and beautifully. And that He will use it to advance His kingdom and turn many to righteousness.

His servant~
~Natalie
January, 2009

Chapter 1

"Homeschoolers will be inspired, blessed, and encouraged as they read *Pajama School*. Natalie masterfully relates how homeschooling both provided her with and prepared her for real life experiences. In addition, she challenges the reader to walk closely with the Lord and follow His leading."

Kelly Adams

in the beginning

There we stood. Each of us three girls on one of the bottom stairs, dressed in our specially chosen outfits and posing for Mom as she positioned herself at the bottom of the stairs to take our picture. Today was a memorable day—the first day of school. It had always been our tradition to take a picture on the first day of school, but this year it was different. This year, we would be attending a different school. Homeschool.

I'm not sure any of us knew what they meant when Mom and Dad announced that they had decided to withdraw us from our beloved school and homeschool us. It was something akin to a death sentence. We had never heard of such a thing and we certainly didn't know any one else who did it. School was everything to us. Our little K-6 school was part of our church and we were a close-knit family. Each of our classes was comprised of twelve or so students and made up our network of friends. We went to school together. We went to church together. We went on field trips together. We celebrated birthdays together. We celebrated holidays together. We went through struggles together. We lived life together. But all of that was about to change.

We had cleared out our basement playroom and it had been transformed into a schoolroom. Dad put together Mom's new desk and placed it at one end of the room, facing her "class." Her class consisted of us three girls—me—9, Nicole—8, and Nadine—5. Three desks and their accompanying chairs sat facing the "teacher" and were filled with our school books for the year. Around the room, posters had been placed on the walls. At the back of the room, the Preamble to the Constitution and the Bill of Rights adorned the wall above our spare couch. The front wall of the room, behind the teacher's desk, was lined with bookshelves. Mom and Dad were already booklovers and this new homeschooling endeavor was the perfect excuse to add to their growing library.

The door into the schoolroom sported a little sign announcing the "Field Trip of the Month." Directly underneath it was a postcard of the local zoo, our first scheduled field trip. And above all of that was the official sign: Welcome to Cornerstone School. Cornerstone School. That was the name Mom and Dad had chosen for our homeschool. It felt so unreal. Like the grown-ups were joining us in our world of play, where we often set up our own classroom and took turns being the teacher. Now Mom was playing the part of the teacher, a role in which she never would have imagined herself. But God knew what He was doing. Long before the doors of Cornerstone School were officially opened, God was directing the steps of our family, preparing us to walk this path...

After being stationed for nine years at Ellsworth Air Force Base (AFB) in Rapid City, South Dakota (where he met and married Mom and where Nicole and I were born), Dad received orders to go to Germany. He was to be stationed at Hahn Air Base. With their one and two-year old children in tow, along with a fluffy white Great Pyrenees and a black and white Cocker Spaniel, Mom and Dad packed up and made the move overseas to a little village called Schwarzen. Schwarzen was roughly 5 miles from the base and boasted a population of about 120. If they were to spend four years living in another country, Mom and Dad wanted to take full advantage of the opportunity to get to know the people, learn the language, and experience the culture.

Two years into our time in Germany, we were blessed with the addition of girl #3—Nadine, the name inspired and shared by one of our neighbor friends. Once we were old enough, Nicole and I began attending a German Kindergarten. Mom tearfully walked me to the bus stop the day I was to begin school and waved me off, armed with the one essential German phrase she thought I needed to know: Wo ist die Toilette? (Where is the toilet?) Nicole and I quickly learned to speak German fluently and were often mistaken for natives. I remember my Kindergarten teacher calling me over to her desk one day. I nervously complied, wondering what I had done wrong. I was relieved to discover that I was not in trouble, but that an American boy had been enrolled as a new student in our class and she needed me to translate for him.

Nicole and I were employed as translators on more than one occasion. On the weekends, Dad would often take us girls to one of the German towns where a volksmarch was being held. Volkssports (literally "people's sports" or "sports for all people") originated in Germany in 1972 as non-competitive sporting events in which all participants could receive awards. The most popular of the sports is volksmarching ("people walking"). It quickly grew in popularity and any given weekend might find several cities holding events with thousands of people participating. Dad faithfully logged every event in our record books and we collected many medals (and an occasional beer stein!) commemorating the location of each event. Walking hundreds of miles of the German countryside and towns gave us an appreciation for God's magnificent creation and afforded us many opportunities to spend time together and make lasting memories.

Many Americans were introduced to volksmarching while serving overseas and regularly participated in the events. At one walk in which we participated, the Germans at the registration table were having trouble communicating with the Americans and asked Nicole and me to serve as translators. We readily agreed and were even compensated with a coke for each of us at the end of the day.

As we entered our final year of Dad's assignment at Hahn AFB, Mom was concerned that I would be behind in school when we moved back to the States. She set about to lay an academic foundation for me, but was at a loss to know what to do. This was due, in part, to the fact that she had been part of the failed academic experiment that sought to eliminate phonics training in the classroom. She forged ahead, though, and did her best to prepare me for my years of school in America. Little did she know that God was also preparing her for an aspect of her own life calling that was yet to be revealed. And revealed it was! Dad was transferred to McConnell AFB in Wichita, Kansas in 1987. Three years later, even in light of the wonderful experience at our little Christian school, Mom and Dad came to the understanding that the Lord had placed on them the responsibility of educating their children.

And so it was that we came to be standing on our basement stairs that first day of school in September of 1990. After the picture-taking was complete, we made our way into the schoolroom to begin our day the only way we knew how. We each stood at attention beside our desks, hands placed reverently over our hearts as we recited the words of the pledge—first to the American flag, then to the Christian flag, and finally to the Bible. That was the way we began each day when we went to "real" school, so if we wanted to do this right we figured we had better follow suit.

We slowly established a routine and became accustomed to the odd-feeling of going to school in our basement. Mom tried her best to plan our daily lessons and the three of us girls tried our best to stay on task. We tried not to get angry and yell at each other. We tried not to make faces at and distract each other while we were supposed to be doing our schoolwork.

We tried not to get frustrated because we couldn't figure out the answers to our math problems and Mom couldn't explain them and Dad's explanations were more confusing than helpful. We tried not to answer the phone during school hours. We tried not to divert Mom's attention so that she would forget to tell us to go back to the schoolroom and do our work...okay, maybe not on that last one. But we tried to be a good homeschool family. Whatever that was. And then, the inevitable happened.

We were all gathered in the family room for a family meeting called by Dad. I don't remember if he indicated a particular reason at the outset or not. I do remember Dad asking Nadine, who was five at the time, what she might like for her birthday the following July. He seemed quite pleased when she responded that she would like a baby doll. It couldn't have played out more perfectly if he had planned it himself. "What would you think if you got a real baby instead?" After a moment of letting his question sink in, it hit us! Mom was going to have a baby! We were ecstatic! After six years of naturally preventing the conception of children, Mom and Dad had been enlightened by verses like Psalm 127:3: "Lo, children are an heritage of the LORD: and the fruit of the womb is his reward." They began to view children as God's blessing and decided to allow Him to determine their family size. Almost immediately, God graciously blessed Mom with the pregnancy of their fourth child. And that's when our little homeschool began to fall apart. Or at least that's what it felt like to us.

We said good-bye to the schoolroom. Oh, not officially. It remained tucked away in a corner of the basement. We just found that the kitchen table was a convenient substitute for the desks we had eagerly looked forward to using at the beginning of the year. The reality of our different personalities and weaknesses hit us full-force as we were forced to work together, and often erupted in tears. Every phone call prompted spontaneous dismissal for recess and, more often than not, marked the end of school for that day. There were some days that we didn't do school at all, and others when Mom would wearily implore us to please at least do our math lesson for the day. Other times she threatened to send us all back to school if we didn't get along and do our work. Lunch regularly consisted of a drive across town to McDonald's, where we were on a first name basis with most of the employees, and was often followed by an excursion to Wal-Mart, where we came up with all sorts of creative reasons to explain to the questioning clerks why we weren't in school.

In the midst of our struggles and short-comings, God was shifting our paradigm. We had automatically adopted the methods and practices of society's educational institutions as the model for our own. We were trying to pattern our school after what we had always known school to be...and we were failing miserably. Without realizing it, we had allowed the world to define education for us instead of looking to God and to His Word for a true definition of education. God was determined to break us away from this faulty mold and the sand on which it was founded and lead us to the Rock that would never be moved and from which we could never be shaken. We were beginning to understand that school was not to be our life, but that life would be our school.

Chapter 2

"Having also started our homeschooling journey with the chalkboard in the front of the room, and the kindergartner ready for a three hour school session, this book has real life comic relief. If families can find the delicate balance between the 'life education' that we offer as we teach our children and the book learning that we know they need to learn, we will all be more successful in our endeavors. May *Pajama School* be a blessing to all who begin this journey. And may you laugh along the way!"

Cynthia Barger

the family that
*sc**h**ools* together...

The questions would begin flowing the moment any of us informed a friend or acquaintance that we were being homeschooled. "Do you get to go to school in your pajamas?" topped the chart as the number one question that I fielded for many years. And close behind were others of equally profound importance, "Do you still have to do school when it snows?" "Do you get off of school on your birthday?" "Do you get to have recess?" And then, there was the quintessential homeschool question, "But what about friends?" Or, as stated in a more sophisticated manner by many an adult, "But aren't you concerned about your children's socialization?" Perhaps such questions were formed from images conjured up in the mind of the questioner of houses fortified with locks on the doors and bars across the windows. From behind the bars peer the faces of helpless little boys and girls as they are relegated to a life of isolation from the rest of the world. On rare occasions they are permitted an outside excursion, of course with as minimal interaction with other human beings as possible before being readmitted to their academic cell.

Having never been on the questioning side of such an exchange, I cannot say for sure what images in reality prompt such questions, nor what mentalities promote the view of homeschooling as an exercise in social isolation, but I do know that socialization was certainly not neglected in our family.

That's not to say that I was particularly thrilled with Mom and Dad's view of social priorities. They had adopted this idea that my family, especially my sisters, should be my best friends. Always before I had looked primarily to my classmates for friendship. But now my sisters were my classmates. Surely Mom and Dad didn't really expect us to be friends! Why, we didn't even get along with each other. Apparently that was the point.

Somewhere in this whole mix of life changes inflicted by Mom and Dad, the after-school cartoons got cut too. No more *Chip 'n Dale's Rescue Rangers*. No more *Duck Tales*. No more shows like *The Brady Bunch* and *Highway to Heaven*. The only show we were allowed to watch now was the daily episode of *Little House on the Prairie*, which we did religiously. Other than that, however, we were on our own for entertainment.

After we had finished school, most days found us setting up offices in our basement family room so we could conduct business with our imaginary customers. We opened a doctor's office and donned our "scrubs" before operating on deathly ill patients (a.k.a. any dolls lying around), often accompanied by an irate "mother." We kept meticulous records for all of our patients, recording their ailments and the procedures we performed before filing their charts away until their next visit.

We set up a fabric store and taped yard sticks to the surface of our cupboards so we could accurately measure out the yardage requested by our "customers."

We also practiced dentistry and creatively concocted ways of emulating the adjustable patient chair while arranging the lamps just right to shine glaringly in the eyes of our poor subject. We enjoyed putting to use the little long-handled mirrors we had found and used paper clips re-formed to replicate the sharp metal tool used by dentists to scrape tartar from between the teeth.

We loved hanging sheets and fabric from the ceiling and walls to create romantic settings for little restaurants, complete with candles and soft music. On more than one occasion, we made use of our toy kitchenette

and assortment of cooking utensils, combined with the necessary ingredients supplied by Mom, to cook and serve dinner to our invited patrons
(a.k.a. Mom and Dad). We proudly presented them with our hand-designed
menus and donned our aprons to take, prepare, and serve their orders. They
were always such well-mannered guests—never complaining (too much!)
about the cold or undercooked food.

Eventually we found a business that suited us very well and we stuck
with it longer than any of the others—a travel agency. We became zeal-
ous travel agents, sending in cards from magazines for information about
particular states, regions or countries. We called Convention and Visitors
Bureaus requesting information to assist us in making our travel plans. We
were constantly on the lookout for any leads that might generate additional
travel information for our agency. In addition to acquiring and updating
our file cabinet full of maps, brochures, and magazines, we kept busy with
the day-to-day operation of our thriving little "business."

We typed up travel itineraries on our old MS DOS computer, consult-
ed with clients by phone, greeted walk-in customers, produced passports
and other forms of identification, and processed payments. Our offices
were spread throughout the basement, so it became necessary, for the sake
of efficiency, to implement a messaging system whereby we could attach
hand-written messages to a pulley device and send them across the room
to our "colleagues" without having to leave our offices and work untended
in order to deliver the message. We were quite pleased with our clever in-
vention and put it to frequent use. We were constantly on the lookout
for new supplies to assist us in the operation of our business and often
scoured garage sales in hopes of finding something that would elevate our
own office a step above either of the other two sisters' offices.

I felt like I had struck gold the day I spotted a credit card machine at a
garage sale down the street. You know, the old kind where you placed the
credit card on the metal plate with the carbon receipt over top of it and
had to slide the top part of the machine over it to impress the credit card
information on the receipt? I didn't hesitate a moment before snatching

up the coveted machine and the box of carbonated receipts and handing the seller the $10 amount listed on its price sticker. She quizzed me for several moments before ultimately consenting to allow me to purchase her machine. Apparently she thought I didn't know what I was buying. But I most certainly did know! I pedaled home on my bike as fast as my legs would allow, anxious to put this newly acquired piece of equipment to use. Now the envy of my sisters/business partners, I was careful to allow them to use the machine only under the strictest guidelines and with constant supervision and oversight provided by myself.

When we weren't absorbed in our work "responsibilities," many days found us girls riding our bikes all over town, often accompanied by one or more neighbor kids after they got home from school. Over the years, we earned the privilege of riding our bikes to Taco Bell for lunch, making trips to the grocery store to pick up miscellaneous goods for Mom, and visiting the library to check out books or movies.

As much as we might have rejected the idea at the time, Mom and Dad's plan was working—little by little my sisters were becoming my friends. Homeschooling was giving us something for which there is no substitute—time. We were with each other all the time. We did school together. We played together. We ate lunch together. We worked together. We talked together. We made memories together. We lived life together. And yes...we still fought together.

Somehow that worst side of us always seemed to come out at piano lessons. None of us particularly enjoyed piano lessons. But Mom and Dad had started me in them as soon as we moved back to the States. Nicole started shortly after me and we both dreaded our weekly trip to the house of our teacher. More than anything musical, my memories of those years of lessons include my teacher's poodles and fish. Neither Nicole nor I were especially fond of either, but our teacher always reserved for us the privilege of feeding her fish each week. We even tried to act sympathetic the week that our teacher sadly relayed the news that one of her pet poodles had choked on a piece of cheese and died. In spite of these rather morbid and unpleasant memories, our strict and dedicated teacher provided us with a solid musical foundation upon which we would continue to build for years to come. And the handful of composer busts I collected by earning points at my weekly lessons now make their home on top of a set of shelves in my studio.

By the time we started homeschooling, our first teacher had moved and Nicole and I had transferred to another teacher, who was unlike the first in every way—except in her ownership of a dog who was often present at our lessons. We continued to dread going to our weekly lesson, even more so once we were required to ride our bikes there at 7:00 in the morning on the scheduled day. Our dread was compounded by the fact that we had rarely completed our assigned theory prior to the lesson and whoever went first would have to confess as much to our teacher. In light of this, we argued weekly over whose turn it was to go first. Our poor teacher tried to devise a workable rotation, but we did our best to confuse her each week so that we would not be forced to go first.

Once Nadine started taking lessons, the rivalry increased. When it was not our lesson time we were allowed to use the computer in a room down the hall from the piano. Since there were two of us not taking a lesson and only one computer available, the fight continued as to who got to use the computer. The unlucky one to have not taken possession of the chair at the computer first would devise all sorts of torturous tactics to compel the other to relinquish the seat and the computer time. But more often than not, this would result in the victimized sister stomping out of the room and tattling on the other. At this point our poor teacher was again forced to be the arbiter in our sisterly squabbles. I didn't keep track, but I'm sure she has a nice collection of apology letters that we had to write over the years as a result of Mom finding out about our behavior, usually from the sister who hadn't been involved in that week's ordeal.

And yet, in spite of the ongoing struggles and obvious character deficiencies in each of us, God was drawing us closer together. We were becoming more than classmates. We were becoming best friends.

Chapter 3

"Natalie is a perfect example of a homeschooling success story and the kind of woman you want your daughter to grow up to be like. As a former member of the 'Derby Group' and a homeschooling Mom myself, so many of the things Natalie has written hit home for me! Homeschooling isn't an easy choice, but if God leads you to do it, He will bless your efforts."

Erin Strange

winds of change

If we thought our world had been turned upside down when we started homeschooling, by the end of our first year we felt like we were living in a completely different world. One change after another invaded our lives and left us groping for something, anything, to hold onto that would again provide some semblance of stability. But it was not to be.

Within a year of when we began to homeschool, Mom and Dad made the very difficult and painful decision to leave our church and look for a new one. Countryside Christian Church was the only church I could remember attending and it was the only remaining link to the friends I had left behind the year before when we began homeschooling. In many ways, it was the spiritual foundation of my life. That was where I had learned the timeless stories of the great men and women of the Bible. I vividly recall crawling through the dark tunnel affixed to a classroom door to listen to "Daniel" as he told the story of God closing the lions' mouths when he was thrown into the den. I remember dropping my jaw in awe as I beheld the beauty adorning the "palace" where Esther was made queen and used by God to save her people from annihilation. I remember singing the words "I'm in-right-out-right-up-right-down-right happy all the time" while jumping around giddy and carefree in the pews of our little junior church room. I remember raising my hand expectantly, hoping I would be picked for the favorite job of holding the "Giving Tree"—a hand-crafted construction paper tree on which were adorned little slips of paper that eager students were chosen to pick off the tree. Each slip of paper contained a special task that the student would then be allowed to perform. I remember fervently studying the book of Revelation, trying to anticipate what questions would be asked each Sunday night so that I could amass the coveted one-dollar bills, awarded to the first to answer each question correctly. I remember regularly stuffing a change of clothes into a little bag and trying to persuade one of my friends to invite me over after church on Sunday mornings. And I remember being glad that even though I would no longer be going to school with my friends, at least I would still get to see them on Sundays at church. Or so I thought.

I didn't fully understand what had happened, but Mom and Dad were confident that God was leading our family elsewhere. Although they were committed to maintaining friendships with the other families we had grown to love during our time together at the church and school, we knew it would never be quite the same. In fact, we did continue to meet with a core group of families for many years, often celebrating holidays and special occasions together. But God led each of our families down a different path. Our path led to First Christian Church in Derby.

When we arrived, we were the only homeschool family attending the church. Within weeks after we made the switch, Noelle was born. The fourth girl. That also made us the largest family attending the church at the time. We developed friendships and grew to love the people that made up our new church family. It was different than before, though. At our other church we often spent an hour or more visiting with others after the service before leaving for home. At our new church, we noticed right away that within ten minutes of the conclusion of the service, the lobby was cleared and the halls were empty. Our new friendships felt similar—we talked and spent time together on Sunday mornings, but our paths rarely crossed during the week. Very few friendships extended beyond the doors of the building.

Sunday School and Youth Group were comprised primarily of students that attended school together during the week. Even those who didn't attend the same school had in common that they attended public school. No other person in my grade or class was homeschooled. Although I tried to be friendly, and everyone was friendly to me, I didn't feel like I fit in. The truth was I didn't fit in. Of course, at the root many of the struggles and challenges we faced were the same, but they looked nothing alike on the surface. We were in completely different environments, dealing with different issues and situations day in and day out.

For a while we regularly attended Sunday School and youth programs and tried to get "plugged in" to the various activities and ministries the church offered. Summer was quickly upon us and we participated in VBS. Nicole and I traveled to summer camp with our designated age groups. We were slowly becoming settled in our new church home.

The spring of 1991 paved the way into what has now gone down in history as the *Summer of Mercy* in Wichita, Kansas. Pro-life leaders from across the nation converged on our city to publicly decry the horror of abortion and to enlist and equip churches and individuals to fight the battle for the lives of unborn children. Dad became very involved in these efforts and many days spent his lunch hour praying outside of one of the abortion clinics. Nicole, Nadine, and I spent many hours with Dad, either at the abortion clinic, attending one of the numerous rallies, or sitting outside of meeting rooms doing school work while he and other key leaders prayed and strategized.

One afternoon Nadine was outside the clinic with Dad and a number of the abortion clinic escorts were taunting and ridiculing the sidewalk counselors and others who were gathered to pray and protest. At one point they grew very obnoxious and Nadine looked up at Dad and asked in all seriousness, "Can I just stick my tongue out at them?" Such was the tender and merciful heart of Nadine, who was always quick to rise to the defense of the less fortunate and had a strong desire to see justice carried out.

I remember one incident from that summer like it was yesterday. A large group of pro-life men and women were going to be staging a protest outside of the infamous George Tiller abortion clinic. They were going to sit in rows one-by-one across the driveway, blocking access into the clinic. It was the evening before the protest was to be held and I had asked Dad if I could go and sit with him. He had said yes, but when he told Mom, she was adamantly opposed to it. That night marks the only time I can recall Mom and Dad getting into a heated argument and raising their voices in anger toward each other. Mom was crying and would not hear of her 10-year old daughter participating in an event where it was probable that every protestor would be arrested.

By the next morning, the decision had been made that I would not go with Dad; I was heartbroken and upset. I was aware of the consequences and was willing to risk being arrested in order to take a stand for the innocent little children being murdered en mass right in my home town. But it was no use objecting. There would be no reconsideration of the decision. Dad did go sit in front of the abortion clinic that day. We prayed all day and watched the news that night. He was arrested, along with numerous others and was taken to a local school gymnasium, where they were held until they were released "on their own recognizance" about eight hours later.

Dad continued his lunch time prayer vigils outside the abortion clinic almost every day. Usually he changed into his civilian clothes, but one day in particular he didn't have enough time to do so, so he wore his uniform. That day was one of the most tense he ever experienced at the clinic. A riot broke out when several protestors scaled the fence and tried to get inside the abortion clinic. There was media coverage of the ordeal and people on both sides were videotaping and taking pictures. One of the abortion clinic workers sent a copy of a picture with Dad in it to the base. As soon as Dad returned, his boss told him that the Colonel wanted to see him. He received an administrative punishment that remained in effect until his retirement. As a result, he received no retirement ceremony.

Dad has always maintained that if he was a part of something that resulted in babies' lives being saved, an administrative punishment and no retirement ceremony was a small price to pay. Those *Summer of Mercy* experiences and the years that followed propelled us into greater political involvement, and Dad's unwavering commitment to truth and principle would be seen many times over in the years ahead.

That summer also marked Mom and Dad's first trip to Knoxville, Tennessee. They had heard about a homeschool program called ATIA (Advanced Training Institute of America) and were very impressed by the educational philosophy of the organization. In order to join, they needed to attend a training seminar so that they could pick up our curriculum for the year and learn how to use it effectively.

We didn't know much about curriculum options and at that time there weren't very many resources available that were designed specifically for homeschoolers. So this ATIA curriculum seemed like a good option, albeit a very non-traditional approach to education. The curriculum was comprised of 54 *Wisdom Booklets*, each one based upon a verse from Jesus' Sermon on the Mount in Matthew 5-7. All of the subject areas included in each *Wisdom Booklet* were built on the key verse. The underlying philosophy of this unit-based approach was that Bible teaching should not just be another course taught alongside other school subjects, but that the Bible should be the foundation of all learning and the starting point for true education. Areas like Science, Law, History, Medicine, Greek, and Mathematics were developed within a biblical framework. Study of each subject reinforced the understanding that the Bible is not just a guide for spiritual matters, but that the truth and principles contained within it could and should be applied to every area of life. This type of schooling would require a major paradigm shift, but Mom and Dad were convinced that it was in line with God's design for education and that He would bless their decision.

Although this unit-based teaching style required a great deal more planning than a textbook approach, the Knoxville sessions had been inspiring and Mom was determined to do it right. She was convinced that this upcoming year of homeschooling would be a good one. She wouldn't be pregnant and we could focus more on school; we would get all of our work done; we would learn a lot.

Mom bought separate lesson assignment books for each of us older three girls and dutifully laid out our work for the year. She had high hopes for a productive year. At the beginning of each day, we met together to read aloud from the *Wisdom Booklets*. Mom wanted to involve all of us as much as possible, so she let us take turns reading. The only problem was that Nadine wasn't a very fast reader yet and neither Nicole nor I were inclined to wait patiently or encourage her efforts. Instead, while Nadine plodded laboriously through her sections, Nicole and I would quickly and silently read through it on our own as fast as we could and then interrupt to tell Mom that we had finished and ask if we could be excused to start on our other work. If she denied our request we tried to look as bored as possible and emitted loud sighs to make our exasperation obvious. On numerous occasions our tactic worked exactly as we hoped and Mom would give up and tell us to just leave. With not a hint of remorse we would be off, congratulating ourselves on our successful escape from the monotony of this imposed family reading time.

By this time in our homeschool journey we had become a part of two homeschool support groups—there were other homeschoolers in the world after all! Mom was already experiencing the difficulty of balancing her responsibilities to children in two different age groups. On one end of the spectrum she had three older children who could read and were quickly developing independence in their academic studies. On the other end of the spectrum she was readjusting to the early stages of motherhood, after almost six years of assuming that that part of her life was over. Not only that, but she was facing the prospect of having another student whom she would have to start from "square one." Could she really provide an adequate education from start to finish? Nicole, Nadine and I had received an excellent foundation in a traditional classroom with a trained teacher. How could she, an untrained Mom who had never really even had a desire to teach, provide such an education for Noelle? Would she fail completely? Would

Noelle ever learn to read well, let alone complete all the other advanced courses that would be necessary? These were the questions and fears that raced through Mom's mind on a regular basis and threatened to sabotage our homeschool. Our two support groups helped provide Mom with the confidence she needed to keep going.

We referred to our two support groups as "the Wichita group" and "the Derby group." Each one was unique in its makeup and provided us not only with educationally-rich opportunities and experiences, but also with friendships that we treasure to this day. The Wichita group was the more academic-oriented of the two and we participated in subjects as varied as Orienteering, Rocketeering, Geography Bees and Spelling Bees. We learned practical life skills like how to read a map and compass and chart a course. We enjoyed the competitive edge of the Bees and spent hours studying the European countries and their capitals so that we could respond instantaneously when drilled. We learned to work together as a team to accomplish various tasks and to appreciate the strengths and weaknesses of each person on the team. We found in the families of the group a love for the Lord and a common vision as we pursued this home-schooling lifestyle.

The Derby group was more the extra-curricular group. With them we participated in activities like P.E., Valentine's Day exchanges, craft project get-togethers, literary recitations and numerous field trips to places like health museums, old railway stations, the Old Cowtown Museum, the Cosmosphere, wildlife habitats and more. I remember doing school for a day in an old one-room schoolhouse. I remember getting up in front of a roomful of people, sporting a ball cap and carrying a baseball bat, and reciting the well-known *Casey at the Bat*. I remember having a group of younger girls over to our house to work on a festive wall-hanging that they could give to their mothers for Christmas. I remember competing against the boys on Friday mornings during P.E. class to see who could do the most push-ups. I remember spending hours creating my Valentine's box, hoping to win first prize in the contest for best design. I remember riding to a bug exhibit with another family and playing an animal-themed twenty questions with their 7-year old son and not even recognizing the names of half the animals he chose. I remember going to a Civil War Rendezvous and listening to costumed re-enactors tell stories that made history come alive.

These groups offered us far more than support in our homeschooling efforts. In many ways they became our extended family, sharing with us when times were good and when times were hard. Little did we know that by the end of our second year of homeschooling we were about to enter some of the hardest years of our lives.

Chapter 4

"Natalie never ceases to amaze me with her accomplishments and activities. We've discussed many topics, including how to live Christianity in politics, and had some very memorable experiences in the process! Eventually, we both came to understand that valuable change comes not from the influence of political power, but through Christ's transforming power in the hearts of men."

Alisa McCullough

a real *life*
civics education

In June of 1992 Dad retired from the Air Force and began working from home full-time. He already had an office in our basement, but now he would be doing his work from there. We would be able to see him any time of day we wanted! This adjustment was probably harder for Mom than anyone. She had been used to running the house during the day, setting the schedule, coming and going as she needed to. But now with Dad at home, he would have the final say and would largely be the one to determine the daily schedule. Along with that major adjustment would come another, even more difficult, one.

Dad received a call from his Mom's pastor, back in Baltimore, Maryland. Grandma had stopped taking her medication and was not doing well emotionally. She had bi-polar disorder and had suffered for years with depression and at least one near-escape from suicide. You would never have known it, though, and none of us kids did at the time. She had been widowed nine years earlier, but was one of the most happy, out-going people I knew. When we visited her in Baltimore, she would take us to her favorite restaurant, *Friendly's*, and buy us milkshakes. All the workers there knew her by name and would stop by our table to visit with her. It seemed like Grandma knew everyone and everyone loved her. But for some reason she was now refusing to take her medication. There was really only one course of action we could take. Dad traveled out east to get her and bring her back to live with us. We were thrilled when we were told that Grandma was coming to live with us! That excitement was short-lived.

The moment we saw Grandma get off the plane, we knew that something was wrong. Grandma was somber and unsmiling and her pleasant plumpness had been reduced to folds of skin now hanging from her bones. She was not the Grandma we knew and remembered. Dad made all the necessary arrangements, sold her house and most of its belongings, and traveled back to Kansas in her little red Honda with all her remaining earthly belongings. No more would we get to visit Grandma's old house on Krone Drive. No more would we get to climb up in her oddly-shaped closet and slide down the angled shelf. No more would we inhale the musty smell of the basement library where Grandpa had amassed hundreds of books and cataloged them all by hand. No more would we play office with his old adding machine—the kind with the rows of numbers and a lever on the side. No more would we explore the overgrown woods on the other side of the fence in her backyard. No more would we enjoy Grandma's delicious cooking the last day of our visits when she would fix each of us whatever we wanted to eat for breakfast. Grandma's house now belonged to someone else and we were left with only her beautiful set of China dishes, a few pieces of her gaudy costume jewelry and distant memories of the woman she used to be.

The guest room in the basement became Grandma's bedroom. Our overflowing toy closet in the corner would have to remain contained now, and we would have to go through Grandma's room in order to get to it. Some days Grandma was chipper and seemed almost like her old self. But most days she was listless and everything was a battle. We tried to be loving and kind, but sometimes she would suddenly lash out at one of us girls, yelling at us or accusing us. There was tension in the house almost constantly—between Mom and Grandma, between Mom and Dad, between

Dad and Grandma, between us girls and Grandma. We hated the fact that she had to go with us almost everywhere, because we couldn't leave her at home alone for long periods of time. We hated the fact that we often had to leave places early to get Grandma home or to get home to her if we had left her there. We hated the fact that everyone knew that our Grandma was such a mess.

In December of that year, we moved Grandma upstairs to Noelle's bedroom. Nicole, Nadine and I moved into the downstairs bedroom and Noelle moved into our old bedroom. It was in this upstairs bedroom that I mostly remember our years with Grandma. Many mornings she would lie in bed and refuse to get up until Mom forced her to get out of bed or Dad physically removed her from her bed. It was another battle to get her to put in her set of false teeth, to get her to eat, to get her to take her pills. She was living a miserable existence and was making our lives miserable too. Occasionally still, there were short periods of time when she would be her lively self. At those times, we could convince her to participate in activities at the local Senior Center; we would enjoy going on outings with her; she would help out around the house. But those good times became fewer and farther between. Although she had extensive emotional problems, her physical health was excellent and Mom sometimes commented that Grandma would probably outlive her. We were sure that this would be our lot in life forever.

We had thought maintaining structure was hard before, but now with a mentally ill Grandma living in the house, we seemed doomed to failure. Every day was unpredictable and we dreaded what it would bring. In spite of the constant trial we faced at home, though, we tried to carry on as best we could. Nicole and I started volunteering at our local library, preparing for and assisting with the children's storytime, re-shelving books, laminating materials in one of those old pocket laminators, and generally doing whatever needed to be done. We gained valuable skills, learned to interact with people of all ages and had many opportunities to develop a strong work ethic as we performed menial and mundane jobs. We enjoyed being involved in community service and developed long-lasting relationships with many people.

For the first year or so, I primarily assisted in the children's storytimes—greeting the parents and children, helping them feel comfortable, taking them to the bathroom, answering questions, etc. I really wanted to do some of the reading, but just waited for the opportunity to present itself. Finally the day came. The storytime leader asked if I would like to read one of the books that day. I jumped at the chance and was determined to do a good job. The book was one of my favorites: *Going on a Bear Hunt*. I put all my energy into that story, dramatizing every action and getting the kids on their feet to be a part of the bear hunt. We loved every minute of it. And from that day on, I was allowed to read at least one of the books during each storytime.

As soon as I turned twelve I began my babysitting "career." I loved children and was excited about the prospect of spending time with them and making money in the process. Mom and Dad required me to take the Red Cross babysitting course so that I would be better trained to handle my responsibilities and any emergencies that might arise. Thankfully I never had to deal with any of the horrible situations they covered in the class—like performing the Heimlich maneuver or doing CPR on a child—but I had plenty of other experiences that helped prepare me for life and made those years memorable.

I excitedly put together a special babysitting bag that included a variety of necessary supplies—craft projects, coloring pencils, crayons, stickers, emergency phone numbers and more. And the calls started pouring in! Well, that may be a bit of an exaggeration. However, as soon as people found out that I was homeschooled and was available to babysit during the day, word spread quickly. As I got older I was accepting babysitting jobs every day of the week, sometimes two and three different jobs a day. Eventually it got out of hand and Mom and Dad had to put a limit on my babysitting schedule. I had to have some time to get my schoolwork done! The new rules stipulated that I was not allowed to babysit before 3:00 in the afternoon and could only accept three jobs a week. This definitely put a damper on my "career" (and my income flow!), but Mom and Dad were very wise in implementing this change.

1992 marked a significant change in the political climate of Kansas. The *Summer of Mercy* the year before had prompted many people in the Wichita area to run for office on both a local and state level and we jumped on board several of the campaigns—Todd Tiahrt's campaign for a State Senate seat and Don Myers' campaign for State Representative. We donned t-shirts and walked in parades. We collated pieces of literature into bags and walked door-to-door through Derby neighborhoods hanging the bags on every door. We walked the neighborhoods as a family. We recruited friends and walked the neighborhoods some more. We attended rallies and listened to the candidates speak. We volunteered at the campaign offices. In fact, as we worked at Tiahrt's campaign office one afternoon we were made aware of a dilemma. They were having a banquet that evening with a lot of the big contributors to the campaign and had no one to make the name tags. They had been praying for someone who could write the names in calligraphy. Well, it just so happened that Nicole and I had taken a calligraphy class earlier that year and could do a decent job writing the names. We spent the remainder of the afternoon doing our best calligraphy on the couple hundred name tags of the banquet attendees. The office workers were thrilled and we were excited to see how the Lord had used us to answer their prayer, even in a seemingly small and insignificant matter.

We attended our first election night parties that November and waited in suspense as polling numbers started to trickle in. We visited with friends while munching on snacks and keeping our eyes and ears on the big screen TV in the corner of the room. It was tense and some of the races were close, but by the end of the night we had tasted the sweetness of victory. The two candidates we fought for the hardest had won and would now be representing us in Topeka. All of our efforts had been well worth it!

These first steps into the world of politics were exciting and fun. They gave each of us in the family a desire to stay abreast of current events, and a willingness to work hard on behalf of good candidates. We saw the importance of electing godly people to represent us and to help preserve the freedoms we enjoyed—not just as United States citizens, but as a homeschool family as well. Homeschooling was becoming more and more widely accepted, but we could never take for granted those freedoms that others before us fought to secure. Now it was in our hands to continue the battle for the sake of the generations to come.

With an increased interest in the political world, Mom and Dad made arrangements for me to serve as a page for one day at the state capitol in Topeka. I got up early in the morning one weekday and was picked up by Donna and her son Chris, who was also going to serve as a page for Don Myers. We arrived at the building just as the activities were getting under way and I spent the day running up and down stairs, trying not to get lost in the symmetrical hallways of the building, and performing all sorts of tasks for various legislators. It was thrilling! The work itself was mostly routine office work, but being in the halls of our state's capitol infused me with excitement. I could hardly wait to do it again!

The next legislative session, I recruited Nicole and several friends to go with me to page for Don Myers again, and then I went back with another friend a month later to page for our State Senator, Nancey Harrington. I managed to go a couple times each year for the next few years and grew familiar with the layout of the building and the general placement of the offices. I loved sitting in the room when the legislature was in session and watching the representatives or senators as they discussed and voted on various bills. On one occasion, I was asked to sit in on a committee meeting to be available for any needs that might arise. It was all fascinating and gave me a first-hand understanding of the workings of our state government. Eventually I grew past the age limit for day pages and had to discontinue my semi-annual trips to Topeka. But my fascination with the political world remained.

Years later, after extensive involvement in grassroots politics, I took my first step into party politics by assuming the role of Precinct Committeewoman to replace the vacancy left by Nicole when she got married. Shortly thereafter, my friend Alisa invited me to attend the annual Kansas Days event in Topeka. After several weeks of planning and putting together outfits to wear to the formal banquets held each night, we piled into the car on Friday afternoon and made the two hour drive in the cold, snowy weather to the state capital. I had made arrangements to stay with Michelle, a lady I knew in the area, so when we arrived in town we quickly drove by her house to make sure we could identify it later that night when we were done with the day's festivities. We noted the location and then journeyed through town to the Capitol Plaza Hotel where we spent the remainder of the afternoon attending receptions for state office holders and getting to know other people from across the state that were in town for the event.

That evening, we attended a banquet and heard a timely message from David Limbaugh on the persecution taking place toward outspoken Christians right in America. We enjoyed conversing with the others at our table and I loved asking questions and learning as much as I could from these people who were involved in all levels of local, state and federal government. We concluded the evening by attending a social gathering and then made our way back across town to Michelle's house.

As we pulled up in the driveway, Alisa noted the handicap license tag on the car and asked if my friend was handicapped. I was surprised, because I wasn't aware of any handicap, but reasoned that she might have a health problem that qualified her to receive the tag. We pulled our bags from the trunk and lugged them through the snow-covered lawn to the front porch. Michelle had told us that she would probably be in bed by the time we got there, but that she would leave the front door unlocked for us. I tiptoed across the porch so as not to make too much noise and reached for the door knob. It wouldn't turn. I repositioned myself and tried again to no avail. The door was locked. I whispered the news to Alisa and then explained that Michelle must have forgotten to leave the door unlocked after all. I turned back to the door and tried again while we debated what to do. I started to lightly tap the door as Alisa walked back into the yard and looked up above the garage and then over at the street sign. Then came the realization—we were at the wrong house!

As fast as we could, we plunged back through the snow to our car, threw the bags into the backseat and sped out of the driveway and over to the next street. There we confirmed the address (it was 32nd Street, not 32nd Terrace!), then double-checked it and were quite relieved when we found the front door unlocked and the room awaiting our arrival. It was a fiasco that will be long-remembered since we shared it with several people the following day and they have never let us live it down!

Saturday morning began bright and early with a breakfast sponsored by Kansans for Life. The day continued with numerous meetings and a chance to hear directly from our State Legislators and U.S. Congressmen about how things were going and what issues were the most pressing. The culminating event was the State Committee meeting where new party leadership was elected. I later learned that it had been a years-long process to reach this point. The change had to start from the "bottom up," by electing new Precinct Committee people, who in turn elected the leadership at the county level and the delegates to the district meeting. Those delegates then elected the district leadership and the delegates to the State Committee. The new State Committee delegates then elected the new party leadership.

It was an education in itself to attend the State Committee meeting and observe the proceedings. I finally began to understand the underlying structure of the party in the state. Even having served as a Precinct Committeewoman for a short period of time by that point, I was mostly ignorant of what it really entailed. It was at this meeting that I also got my first taste of what I refer to as the "Gospel of Party Politics." It was very different from my memories of grassroots politics, but it would take two more years before I could put my finger on what exactly it was that was so different.

For the next two years, Alisa and I traveled together to Kansas Days and each time I found myself peppering her with questions about why the party leadership did certain things or wouldn't do other things. We had many good discussions about the things we observed, and it was so helpful to have a like-minded friend with whom to hash through these issues! I discovered that things weren't as simple as I once perceived them to be. The more I asked questions of those in leadership (or those running for leadership positions), the more frustrated I became. It was apparent that I just didn't "get" politics.

It wasn't until after a social event for one of the State Party Chairman candidates one year that I finally comprehended the difference between grassroots politics and party politics. Grassroots politics was all about the candidate. We, on the outside, saw a good candidate and threw our energy and support into getting him elected. Party politics was all about the network. Those on the inside handpicked promising, upcoming, loyal party members and groomed them for positions they wanted them to fill. Then they would wield their positions of influence and networks of friends to get those people elected. An attitude of elitism permeated the party and I experienced firsthand on more than one occasion the efforts of those in leadership to suppress information in order to manipulate votes or garner support.

I became increasingly disillusioned as I observed those in the party treating people in a manner equivalent to that which they vehemently decried in their opponents. It was appalling. My spirit was conflicted as I saw those I respected and admired acting as players in the game of politics. After one particularly ugly experience, I sought counsel from Bev, a wise woman who had been involved in the political arena for many years. Her words of insight gave me an incredible boost and helped redefine my own purposes for remaining involved in the field. She explained the importance of viewing the political arena like any other mission field—a place full of people who need to know the love of Jesus Christ. She looked forward to opportunities to develop relationships with even the most "unreachable" people and share the gospel with them. Her heart for the souls of people reminded me that lasting change in society is achieved not through political processes, but through the transforming power of Jesus Christ in the lives of individuals. Not through political ideals, but through the application of the Word of God to every area of our lives. Bev's counsel was so refreshing and enabled me to achieve a more balanced understanding of the role politics should play in my life.

I began to understand what party politics does to most people. Instead of seeing people as individuals, it immediately labels them with an identity of political construction—Democrat, Republican; Liberal, Conservative; etc. Those with an opposing label are seen as enemies who must be subdued under "our" form of government. I realized that I was allowing my political affiliation to determine my identity and the way I related to those around me. After a time of intense soul-searching and seeking direction from the Lord and Mom and Dad, I stepped back and determined not to become more deeply involved in political work for the party. While my interest in politics and desire to stay informed and abreast of current issues remains, I have had enough of a taste of the inside workings of the political world to satisfy me for now. At the same time, I am grateful for the experiences I've had that have given me a greater understanding of the structure of our government and a greater appreciation for the godly leadership of the men who had the vision and wisdom to establish such a government in our nation. And I am equally grateful for those who have devoted their lives to helping preserve the principles and freedoms upon which our nation was founded. More than ever, I realize the importance of supporting, encouraging, and praying for those families whom God has called to enter the trenches of the political arena and fight on our behalf.

The Lord has a way of using the right people at the right time to teach me, counsel me, and help me understand different areas of life from His perspective. That's an education far above and beyond what I could have ever learned from a textbook!

It was during our early years of political involvement that we garnered a reputation of sorts in the community for being the place to drive by if you needed to know which candidates to vote for. This

was due to our location on a well-traveled street and the fact that we were not above placing numerous political signs in our yard. During one relatively low-key year politically we had only a sign for a County Commissioner candidate in our yard. One of the children of our new neighbors, whom we had befriended, along with her sister, and with whom we spent quite a bit of time playing, asked what the sign was for. Nicole lowered her voice and sadly told her that it was to mark the place where we had buried our uncle. The girl looked at her in horror and slight disbelief. She questioned why the sign said County Commissioner. Again with a lowered voice Nicole explained that that was his job when he died and it was very important to him and his family. Nicole finished her tale by warning the girl not to tell anyone else, because we didn't want people to know we had buried someone in our front yard. The girl nodded solemnly and we resumed our playing for the day. It wasn't until several weeks later that the girl came running across the street and exclaimed, "My Dad said that that is not your uncle buried in the front yard!"

Chapter 5

"Natalie shares her homeschool experience, but not from the teacher's side of the desk (OK, homeschoolers don't always use desks, but you get the idea). Homeschoolers are often criticized for sheltering their children from the 'real world.' Natalie's story reveals how practical and enriching the 'real world' of homeschooling can be."

Brian Middleton

stepping into the bigger world of
homeschooling

Life was picking up speed and we found out firsthand that home-schooling was far from the isolationist lifestyle that some propound. While we continued with our daily schoolwork responsibilities, each day also presented a host of other experiences and opportunities. It rarely took more than several hours a day to complete all of our assignments, so we were able to devote time and energy to many other pursuits as well.

As our conviction and passion for homeschooling grew, Mom and Dad were asked to join the Board of the Teaching Parents Association (TPA), the Wichita-area homeschool support network. We became responsible for organizing the annual Used Book Sale and Dad spent countless hours thinking through the most efficient way to conduct the sale and developing various systems and spreadsheets toward this end. In the early years of the sale, we took all the table reservations from sellers by phone. We had a spiral notebook in the kitchen to record the information and without fail we would begin getting phone calls a week or more prior to the published first day for sellers to make table reservations. The first year we organized the sale, the day we were to begin accepting reservations arrived and we were awakened before 6:00 in the morning by the first caller who was determined to secure one of the much-in-demand tables.

Dad took the call and kindly asked the lady to call back at 8:00!

Calls continued to pour in the rest of the day and week until all the available tables were reserved. Our whole family worked together to take table reservations from sellers, recruit volunteers, collect tables from their numerous borrowed locations, and set them all up on-site the night before. They had to be wiped down and labeled and positioned exactly according to Dad's detailed diagram. If we were off at all, Dad was sure to notice and would have to reposition the tables and chairs according to his precise specifications.

After we were done setting up the tables, we took turns rolling each other around on the big table carts and exploring the dark, musty "caverns" under the stage at one end of the gymnasium, where the tables were kept when not in use. We hauled big pieces of equipment out of the area and cleared off junky surfaces to make the way clear for the many buyers and sellers who would fill the building the following day. Then we would unload all the boxes of soda pop, juice, water, candy, pretzels, hot dogs and whatever other bargains Mom and Dad had snagged for the concession stand that would be run by us girls.

We took pride in organizing everything in the most efficient way possible. The refrigeration system was a good 15 feet from the concession window and we worked out who would take the orders and handle the money, who would fix the pretzels, who would run and grab the items from the refrigerator, and who would wheel the cart around the sale area to generate additional sales from those who wouldn't otherwise make it over to the window. The plan was set and we were eager to put to work all those business skills we had been developing for years in our own home-based "offices." We recruited a few friends to help manage the stand in exchange for a couple of free items. They jumped at the chance. After all, doesn't every child want to be the one behind the counter acting all grown up and taking orders from the customers?

Sale Day arrived bright and early and the line of buyers began to form long before the scheduled opening time. There were bargains to be had and everyone was anxious to be the one to find them! We were allowed to look at the offerings before the doors opened since we would be too busy to do so after the sale was underway. But we weren't actually allowed to buy them yet...just find the ones we wanted and ask the seller to set them to the side for us. Being an avid reader and book lover, I was on the lookout for bargains too! The only problem was that I loved visiting with the sellers as much as I loved looking through the books, so I rarely made it to all the tables. Regardless, I was always pleased with the few treasures I was able to add to my collection. Then it was back to my post behind the concession stand window so that I could supply shoppers with their desired sustenance.

A fast three hours later the sale would be over, sellers would start giving away their books, concession items would be marked half-price, and tear-down would commence. Many friends pitched in to help and the gymnasium was emptied, the floor swept and the tables returned to their various locales in time for all of us to go eat lunch at a local pizza place. We enjoyed lively conversation, developed close friendships, and made lots of memories that would be treasured for years to come. And so the Used Book Sale continued for many years, occasionally experiencing changes in location to accommodate growing needs and avoid scheduling conflicts. Still it contained all the same elements that made it more than just an event, but a tradition enjoyed and anticipated each year by our family and many others alike.

That's what the world of homeschooling is like. It stretches far beyond the boundaries of a single family, a community, or one local church. It is comprised of all sorts of people, from varied backgrounds and different walks of life, but who are united in a common goal—to take seriously the upbringing of their children and provide them with the best education possible. That will mean different things for different people. But that's the beauty of homeschooling. Stereotyped as we may be, no two homeschool families are exactly alike. A peek into any homeschool will quickly reveal that. But still, there persists a familial bond of sorts as we are brought together as part of a bigger community for events such as these.

While the Used Book Sale felt like a reunion each year, it paled in comparison with the annual convention. My earliest memories of the convention are from when it was held in a large church building on the west side of town. A big tent would be set up in the back parking lot for the exhibitors. I remember helping with set-up the day before. This included arranging tables, transporting chairs, tearing apart perforated name tags for the pre-registered attendees, and spending hours alphabetizing them since every year, without fail, the printer had messed up the order and printed them randomly instead of alphabetically. These were then placed in the designated index card boxes according to last name so that attendees could retrieve their name tags without having to wait in line. Once the set-up was complete, the rest of the evening was spent with children of the other TPA Board members, having fun together exploring the huge building.

Bright and early Friday morning Nicole and I found ourselves behind the registration tables again, this time greeting the parents as they arrived, giving them directions, answering questions, or registering them for the workshops. We loved our "job"! I because of all the people I got to meet and talk to, and Nicole because she could help keep everything organized and running efficiently. We wouldn't have put it in those words back then, but looking back now that we've learned more about our different personalities and characteristics, we can see how perfectly God placed us so that we could work together as a team. At the time, though, we were just helping out and having fun!

After registration had closed one year I was walking through the foyer and noticed that the booth where the taping company was located was overwhelmed with customers. The couple running the booth looked frazzled, as did my friend Emily who was helping them. I jumped in to give them a hand. As things calmed down introductions were made and I was given a crash course in how to run the duplication machines, how the cassettes were organized on the tables, and what to tell customers inquiring about specific sessions. I continued helping for the remainder of the convention and the grateful couple even paid me at the end of the day. When they asked me to help the following year I eagerly agreed to do so. Thus began my distinguished career as a worker for the taping company. At least I felt awfully distinguished working with all that machinery and taking orders from the customers!

A couple of years later, the convention moved downtown to the Century II Convention Center. Homeschooling was growing more and more every year and the TPA Board was committed to providing the best convention possible. I always loved the weekend of the homeschool convention. In addition to helping with registration and working at the taping booth I loved walking through the exhibit hall and perusing all the books and curricula, visiting with old friends, making new friends, and meeting the speakers and their families. For years the TPA Board had a tradition of letting each family on the board sign up to take the keynote speakers out for meals throughout the weekend. This was always a highlight! I have fond memories of getting to meet and share a meal with incredible home-schooling heroes like Mike and Vickie Farris, Mike and Elizabeth Smith, Chris Klicka, Inge Cannon, Doug Phillips, the Grimes family, Jim and Anne Ryun, the Boyer family, Dean and Karen Andreola and others.

I remember a humorous incident from one year when Doug Phillips was one of our keynote speakers. I was walking through the exhibitor hall and had stopped at his booth to peruse some of the books on the table. After a moment he came over and pointed out a new book they had on the topic of family worship. He went on to share about it in more detail and encouraged me to consider it for my family. By the time he was finished, I decided to just smile and thank him for his recommendation. I left the booth, but a short time later Dad, Nicole and I met up with him since we had arranged to take him out for lunch. He looked at me in surprise when Dad introduced me as his 17-year old daughter and explained that he had thought I was a homeschool Mom. I laughed and confessed that I was often mistaken for someone much older. Most people thought I looked around 25 at the time. He laughed at his own error, but then made a statement I have never forgotten. He said that he thought it would be wonderful if all young women would carry themselves with such dignity and poise. It was just a little side comment, but it infused me with a new sense of vision. I wasn't just destined to look old; instead I could be a young woman of dignity and poise. What a wonderful thought!

As the four of us ate lunch together at the Spaghetti Warehouse, we spent time discussing several topics. Most notably, though, I remember Mr. Phillips explaining his thoughts on marriage and the belief that people should get married while they are still young if possible. He said the only thing he regretted about his marriage was that he hadn't married his wife sooner. I confess I had never heard such a philosophy before, having been primarily exposed to teaching that young people should remain single as long as possible before pursuing or settling into marriage. In fact, the topic had developed in our conversation because I shared of a commitment I had made the previous year to remain unmarried for the next four years so that I could focus without distraction on my relationship with the Lord. I had made the commitment with my Dad's blessing and was already experiencing incredible freedom and joy in it. However, Mr. Phillips' gracious disagreement with this practice gave me much food for thought and an appreciation for his own ministry and his careful study of God's Word. Years later, the long-lasting impact of this conversation would be felt even more fully in my life.

And so we continued, year after year, enjoying every facet of the annual homeschool convention. Little did we realize how much bigger God's vision was for the convention than we had even thought to think! In a few short years, He would lead us down uncharted territory into a brand new...adventure.

Chapter 6

"We are encouraged by Natalie's illustrations of God's faithfulness and provision through His people in the midst of the storm. That is the ultimate homeschool lesson!"

The Steve Kientz Family

cheaper by the...
half dozen

We all pulled out our chairs and took our seats for dinner at the dining room table. But before we bowed our heads to pray, Dad walked around the table, placing a slip of white paper face-down on each plate. He gave us strict instructions not to turn it over until he gave the directive to do so. Once all the papers had been deposited, he gave the word to turn them over. In big bold letters across the top of the slip were the words, "BABY CONTEST." Just below them were separate categories followed by a blank: Birthdate, Height, Weight. Our momentary confusion quickly gave way to the realization of what this meant—Mom was going to have another baby! Excitement erupted around the table as we all comprehended the news. Mom informed us that the baby was due in July. We could hardly wait!

The previous year, on Christmas Eve, as we all prepared to attend our church's annual Christmas Eve service, Mom said she wasn't feeling well and opted to stay home. We found out later that she had been in the first trimester of a pregnancy and had undergone a miscarriage. We all felt sad at the loss, but I think only Mom ever experienced the full breadth of emotion associated with losing a child she had been carrying. Now it was with reserved hope that Mom and Dad announced another pregnancy and asked us to pray for the life and health of the baby. Mom made it past the first trimester and we all grew more and more excited as we anticipated the birth of a new little one.

In early June of 1994, Dad and the three of us older girls made plans to attend the annual ATI conference in Knoxville, Tennessee (at this point the organization had become international and changed its name to just Advance Training Institute). It was too close to Mom's due date for her to make such a long trip, so she planned to stay at home with Noelle. On the morning of our departure, we loaded up the van and said our goodbyes to a very tearful mother. She and Dad kept going off to the side and talking amongst themselves, but we had no idea what was going on. Finally, Dad was in the driver's seat and we were backing out of the driveway when Mom broke down and asked Dad to stay. Her water had just broken and she felt the need to go to the hospital, even though it was still a month until her due date. We piled back out of the van and spent the rest of the day at home while Mom and Dad sat at the hospital, biding their time since the little baby refused to come out. By evening, Mom's labor still hadn't progressed, so the doctor sent them back home. It was the middle of the night before the intensity of the contractions finally escalated and propelled Mom and Dad back to the hospital. Shortly after 6:00 the next morning, the baby arrived. Another girl! There had been a long debate between all of us over what to name her, but now Mom and Dad settled on their favorite—Naomi Anne.

Due to her premature birth, Naomi's lungs were not fully developed and she was rushed into the Neo-Natal Intensive Care Unit (NICU) where she spent the next 10 days of her life. She was kept in a small glass tube and we were only allowed to look at her from a distance. We were excited to have a new little sister, but according to the doctors, there was a chance she might not survive. We prayed fervently for her life, begging God to develop her little lungs and grant her good health.

The morning after Dad brought Mom home from the hospital, he was brushing his teeth when his back suddenly gave out. He collapsed to the floor and was rendered incapable of moving without experiencing excruciating pain. We prepared a bed of blankets on the floor at the end of their bedroom, where Dad was relegated to lay and nurse his injury. Our whole family felt helpless. Mom hadn't recovered enough from labor yet to drive; Dad could barely move; I was still too young to drive; and, less than a week old, Naomi was all alone in the hospital. It was during this time that we experienced the outpouring of love from numerous friends and church members as they prepared meals for us, provided transportation, made arrangements to get a diagnosis and care for Dad's back, and lifted us up in prayer before the throne of God.

The details of those days are nothing more than a blur in my mind, except for the striking image of a group of men passing Dad through the back window of the house on a stretcher and loading him into a van to take him to the office of a chiropractor to receive treatment. It is during such times that I think of the familiar *Footprints in the Sand* poem and the revelation that there is only one set of footprints during the hardest struggles of life because it is then that God carries us. Indeed, as I look back on those days following Naomi's birth, I do not recall my part in all that happened. I only recall that through the love and support of many dear friends, God saw us through, brought healing to Dad, and breathed life into Naomi. After her ten days in NICU, Naomi was released from the hospital and officially introduced to her sisters and given a tour of her new home.

Due to complications from her premature birth, Naomi was born with cerebral palsy, which affected the entire left side of her body. Particularly her left hand and foot were disabled and she would be unable to develop fine motor skills on her left side. Naomi quickly recovered from her traumatic entry into the world, though, and soon upheld the Wickham baby tradition by becoming a chubby, healthy, happy little girl. We adored her and continued to be referred to by most as "the Wickham girls."

Naomi's disability introduced a new dynamic into our family life and daily schedule. Mom found herself running to appointments several days a week, getting advice, and taking Naomi to physical and occupational therapists for treatments and exercises. At home, Mom showed us exercises we could do with Naomi during the day and she encouraged us to help her develop movement in her left hand and foot. Naomi learned quickly and her cerebral palsy didn't seem to slow her down a bit. We all treated her like a normal little girl and challenged her to try harder when she experienced frustrations and obstacles. Her physical disability was soon overshadowed by a sharp mind, an intense personality, and a depth of character unmatched by most able-bodied persons. She put us all to shame with her determination and perseverance. We all concluded that God must have some pretty amazing plans in store for this little lady!

Needless to say, our school schedule was becoming even less structured than before (if that's possible!). We were often left on our own to get our work done while Mom and Naomi were at the doctor's office. We had our list of assignments that had to be completed, but beyond that, it was up to us to schedule our day and make sure we got them done. If we were feeling particularly motivated, we would activate our "high gear" mode and finish up all of our assignments by mid-morning. Occasionally, I would even do a whole week's worth of a particular subject on Monday just so I wouldn't have to do it the rest of the week. If we were feeling less motivated, we would take it upon ourselves to postpone some of our work until the next day and then engage in some more exciting activity, like working on a craft project, baking cookies, or playing a game outside.

Mom found it even harder to keep up with all the teaching and grading, household responsibilities, caring for a new baby, and dealing with numerous doctors' appointments each week. It was time for us girls to take on more responsibility. Mom gave us the teacher's books for some of our school subjects and assigned us the job of grading our own work once we finished it. She delegated more of the household duties and we took turns doing laundry, ironing, dusting, vacuuming, planning meals, and cooking. We had always had chores, but now those same tasks took on new meaning as we recognized the importance of all of us working together to contribute to a well-run household. It was actually exciting and definitely one step up from our days of playing house with our fake food and toy kitchenette!

Life was good. Almost. Grandma was still living with us and the situation became increasingly tense. It was a battle most days to get her out of bed and dressed and she would often refuse to get up, even to use the bathroom. This resulted in an almost daily ritual of removing all of the sheets and blankets from her bed and washing them, adding to the already full laundry schedule. She became more and more despondent and nothing we could do or say seemed able to bring her out of it. On two occasions she left the house in the middle of the day to take a walk and was later returned by the police who had found her wandering aimlessly in another neighborhood. Grandma was nothing but skin and bones, but a physical check-up in the fall of 1996 indicated that she was in excellent physical health.

In December of that year, just after Christmas, Dad and the four of us oldest girls were getting ready to take another trip. Mom was now expecting another baby, due in March, and decided to stay home, partly for her own health, and partly because we didn't have anyone who could watch Grandma. Mark and Lexie Day, a godly couple who had a significant influence on Mom and Dad during their early years as committed Christians, had invited us to the wedding of their oldest daughter. We had visited them once before at Texas A&M, where they had been on staff with the Navigators for years, and we were looking forward to another visit. We all piled into the van and waved our goodbyes to Mom before embarking on the nine-hour drive. This time there was no unexpected premature labor, so we made it to College Station, Texas right on schedule that evening and checked into the condo where we would be staying for the week. Dad had decided that since we were traveling so far, we might as well make a vacation out of it and take a week to sightsee in the area as well.

We made it over to the church in time for the wedding that evening and stayed through the reception and until the bride and groom departed. On our way back to the condo, we stopped at a grocery store and bought all the groceries for the week. Nicole and Nadine and I had planned the menu and prepared the shopping lists and we would be overseeing the meals for the week. After a long day, we were all glad to arrive back at the condo and grabbed a bag of groceries on our way up to the front door. When we reached the door, there was a sticky note posted on it that said, "John—call home immediately." We were all duly alarmed and Dad quickly unlocked the door and made his way to the phone on the end table. The four of us girls listened with somber faces to Dad's side of the conversation. It soon became apparent why Mom had called. Grandma had died.

Dad consoled Mom the best he could from over 500 miles away and gave her some further counsel about what to do. Then he hung up and relayed the news to us. Grandma had been taking a bath and when Mom went in to get her out, she was dead. Her head was above water, so it was unlikely that she had drowned, but the cause of her death was uncertain. Mom immediately called one of the pastors from our church and he arrived at the house within minutes of her call and took over the situation. Other church members quickly rallied around Mom to offer support and comfort. Mom was doing okay, but of course we would need to return home right away. It was too late to make the trip that night, but Dad informed us that first thing in the morning we would be heading out.

I was in shock. Grandma's death was completely unexpected and I was totally unprepared for it. I had tried to talk to her several times about her relationship with the Lord. Sometimes she had been receptive. Other times she had been cold and unresponsive. I had no idea if she knew Jesus as her Savior and if she would spend eternity in heaven with Him. My thoughts left me numb. There was nothing I could do now. She was gone. Forever. I cried myself to sleep that night, trying to come to grips with the reality of the situation. It still seemed so unreal.

We arose early the next morning, packed all of our bags and our recently purchased groceries into the van, and began the day's journey back to Derby. It was long and mostly quiet as we all sat lost in our thoughts and emotions, and only occasionally discussing the situation amongst ourselves.

Once we were back home, planning for Grandma's funeral and burial began. Our whole family attended the meeting with the mortician and discussed which casket and vault to purchase and how the service would be conducted. We selected the songs for the service and collected pictures of Grandma to use in the photo montage. I had never experienced death so closely before, so the entire process was unfamiliar and uncomfortable. I wanted to curl up in my bed and spend several days processing and dealing with my emotions and the reality of what had happened, but instead we were forced to make decisions about morbid details that I didn't even want to think about. But it was good to confront death in the context of our family and deal together with the permanence of this change and what it would mean for all of us.

Grandma's funeral service was held the following week at the mortuary and many of our close friends came to support and comfort us during our time of grieving. Nadine and I each played one of Grandma's favorite hymns for the service and we were touched by the loving message our pastor shared. Our church family continued to provide meals for us for the next week as we learned to adjust to Grandma's absence and redefine how our family would function without her. Although her death was sad and difficult, there was an element of relief as we anticipated a more "normal" family life in the days ahead. In a few short months, the hole left by Grandma's death was replaced with the next addition to our family.

After doing some research, talking with a local midwife, and going through a childbirth class, Mom and Dad decided to deliver this baby at home. About a month before the due date we had the midwife, Kathy, over for dinner, along with her daughters Brandi and Holli and her apprentice, Wendy. We enjoyed visiting with them over dinner and then they took time to walk us through the process of how the birth would go (ideally) and what we needed to do to prepare for it. Nicole and I were given permission to observe the birth if we wanted to and we were excited about the possibility of seeing our next sibling make his or her grand entrance into this world!

The evening of March 25th rolled around and Mom's contractions became very intense. We began timing them and it seemed certain that the baby's birth was imminent. We called Kathy. She and the three young ladies made their way to our house. By the time they arrived, Mom was in the early stages of labor. They encouraged her to continue walking around as long as possible and then when she couldn't stand the pain anymore, she positioned herself on the beanbag chair we had placed in her room for this purpose. Each of the midwives and Dad filled their roles by giving Mom directives, encouraging her, or quoting passages of Scripture to comfort her and give her strength. Meanwhile Mom, always the server, in between labor sequences kept asking the midwives if they needed something to eat, or a glass of water...or anything else!

It was awesome to be part of this momentous occasion and it was absolutely thrilling to see my new sibling's head push its way into the waiting hands of the midwife. At long last, the labor was over and Kathy proudly announced that it was a boy. Dad, ever in good humor, told her to check again just to be sure. A second inspection confirmed that the baby was indeed a boy. Joseph Hosea had made his grand entrance into a world of sisters!

Although he was dressed in his fair share of girl's clothes as a toddler and even had his nails painted on one occasion, there was no mistaking that Joey (as he quickly came to be called) was all-boy. As soon as he was old enough to use his imagination and make noises, he was treating spoons and pretzel sticks like guns, and building blocks were employed as fighter jets. But as soon as Joey was walking confidently, we started training him to hold the door open for us girls. Whenever we got home from somewhere, we would open the front storm door and position him in front of it, instructing him to stay there while we walked through. If we were carrying a heavy load, we would give him a few items that we knew he could handle and ask him to carry them for us. When we were approaching the door of another building, we would stand a few feet in front of it and wait to walk through until he opened it for us. By the time he was five, he was a perfect gentleman—opening and holding doors of his own volition and eagerly offering to carry items for us. He adored all of his big sisters and we adored him.

One of Nadine's favorite pastimes was getting Joey dressed up in different outfits, gelling his hair and then posing him in locations all around the house and yard to take pictures. Nicole and I had done the same thing with Noelle six years before, obsessing over her and teaching her to model for all of our glamour shots. Now Nadine was taking up the role of photographer with Joey and he played his part perfectly. Perhaps it was an exercise in vanity, but we had fun doing it and it certainly saved our family from being in the category of families whose oldest children get all the attention and pictures and then the younger ones are hard-pressed to document each year of their life by the time they graduate from high school!

We didn't know it at the time, but it soon became clear that Joey was the final addition to our family—finishing us out at an even half-dozen. Mom was 44 when she gave birth to Joey and although she and Dad were willing to accept any more blessings that the Lord would bestow on them in the way of children, God had filled their "quiver" and entrusted them with six "arrows."

Chapter 7

"Knowing how to manage one's money and exercise financial finesse is a crucial life skill, a life skill Natalie has learned well. Natalie and I serve together on the convention committee for our local homeschool board. She is conscientious about her spending and is constantly finding ways to achieve more with less cost. On more than one occasion, I have heard her say, 'Just tell me my budget, and I'll stay within it.' What a testimony to the financial education her parents gave her!"

Lori Beckstrom

how I learned that money doesn't
grow on trees

An unfamiliar face opened the front door of the house and greeted us warmly. Our family was strewn in varying positions between the vehicle and the door, our arms loaded with luggage as we tripped up the walkway. Dad was standing on the doorstep and made a sweeping motion with his arm as he introduced us to the family who had graciously agreed to host us for the night. We squeezed into the entryway just in time to hear our host, David Barfield, offer that we could just toss our bags into the living room until we had everything unloaded and were ready to be shown to our rooms. Much to our horror, Dad heaved his bag and literally threw it halfway across the floor. I wanted to crawl into a hole and never show my face again. But after a brief moment of stunned surprise, David broke into laughter at the realization that Dad was just taking him up on his suggestion to "toss" our bags into the living room.

We found ourselves the overnight guests of the Barfield family because we were traveling to Lawrence to participate in a track meet and Dad, ever averse to spending any money unnecessarily (i.e. lodging in hotels), had looked up homeschool families in the area. David was the chairman of the Christian Home Educators Confederation of Kansas (CHECK) and their family lived in Lawrence, so Dad called him to see if they knew of a family in the area who would be willing to put all of us up for the night. He and his wife, Cathy, and their three daughters kindly opened their home to us and thus began a long friendship between our two families.

As strange as this practice might have seemed at first, it soon became customary during our family travels. If we were traveling to a destination that required more than a day of driving we would either connect with friends or family along the way or make new friends for the occasion! I quickly came to enjoy the prospect of meeting new people wherever we went and often follow the model Dad established for our family when I travel on my own or with friends. It is a wonderful way to enjoy fellowship with other families and save a significant amount of money in the process. Which was always an important factor for Dad.

Some might call him stingy, but Dad has always preferred the term, "frugal." From the time we were young, Dad thought it was essential that we learn financial responsibility. Instead of just giving us an allowance, Dad developed a points system whereby we would receive monetary compensation according to our consistency in fulfilling our daily responsibilities. There were approximately twelve line items for each day of the week. Things like: Arise Promptly, Make Bed, Brush Teeth, Wash Face and Hands, Quiet Time, Memory Verses, Exercise and Run, Table/Dishwasher/Trash, and Other (so that he and Mom could award additional points at their discretion). We recorded one point for each day that we completed the item listed and at the end of the week we tallied the points and turned in the chart to Dad. At the end of each month, Dad totaled the points from all the weeks that month and gave us three cents per point. If we received more than a specified number of points in a given week, he would also include a bonus payment for that week.

At the beginning of each month, we would wake up one morning to find stacks of money on the kitchen table, with a sheet of paper above them indicating how much each of us earned—right down to the penny. After counting up our money to make sure we got the right stack, each of us would pull our pink metal bank down from its home on top of the refrigerator and deposit our money. Inside the bank, between the coin tray and the section that held the bills, were four pieces of cardstock, designed and printed by Dad and cut to size to fit inside our banks. Each one was a different color and displayed a different title. The cards resembled a checkbook register, with a column for the date, entry description, amount and running balance. On the INCOME card, we recorded all income that we received. The GIVING card was where we listed our monthly deposit that was equivalent to 10% of the income received that month. This card was supposed to be zeroed out each month when we transferred the money from our little banks to the offering plate at church. On the SAVINGS card, we recorded another 10% of our gross income and any additional amount we wanted to reserve for savings. Once we had amassed a significant amount, Mom or Dad would take us to the bank, where we each had our own savings account, to deposit our accumulated savings. Finally, the EXPENSES card was where we recorded any other purchases made throughout the month.

We didn't keep up with the system perfectly, but every one of us kids began to learn from an early age the value of a dollar and the importance of budgeting and using our money wisely. Mom and Dad instilled in us the value of hard work and made sure that we never grew accustomed to handouts. If Mom took us out to lunch during the day, we were often responsible to pay for our own food. If we wanted a higher priced item like a camera, a CD player, or some office gadget, we had to wait until we had saved up enough money to buy it ourselves. We understood that Mom and Dad didn't have a lot of money and they used what they had to provide for the daily necessities of running a household and raising a family. There are a few instances, however, when I think Dad might have gone a little "over the top" in his financial expectations of us kids!

Occasionally one of us would entertain the notion of ordering pizza for dinner and would convince the others that we should ask Dad for permission to do so. Of course, we would present this as diplomatically as possible, usually prefacing it with extreme appreciation for Mom and all her hard work cooking meals for us every night. This would be such a nice way to thank her and give her a night off, wouldn't it? After discussing the plan in great detail amongst us kids, inevitably I would be elected to present our proposal to Dad. My heart would beat a little faster as I played through each carefully chosen word in my mind and approached the door to Dad's office. A light knock secured Dad's response, "Come in." I would peer into his room and then approach his desk with a smile on my face. After quickly surmising whether I thought his mood was conducive to a favorable response, I would launch into my spiel and conclude with another smile, anxiously awaiting his response. And then it would come, "And who's going to pay for this pizza?"

We had already anticipated the response and I answered with a tentative, "Uh...you?" Without any further consideration, usually Dad would respond, "No, not tonight." Again, my carefully planned response, "Well, what if us kids paid for it?" Ah, now that elicited a more promising look from Dad! He would carefully weigh the finished proposition and finally conclude, "I guess we could do that." I would quickly escape from his office, running into Nicole and Nadine on my way out, since they were positioned outside his door, straining to hear the words of our conversation. The three of us would run upstairs and advise Mom of our dinner plan. We would shrug off her protest that we shouldn't have to pay for dinner for the family and make our way to the kitchen to scour the coupon drawer for the best deal. We were just thrilled to get to "eat out" and it didn't bother us a bit to spend our hard-earned money to indulge in that rare pleasure!

Mom was always on the lookout for ways to earn a little bit of money on the side, and at one point she and us kids got a job delivering papers for Pennypower, a weekly shopper that was distributed throughout the area. The pay was decent and it was something we could all work on together. We delivered several different routes and spent Tuesday evenings bagging up the papers and then Wednesday mornings delivering them to our assigned neighborhoods. Mom drove us to certain drop-off points and we would race up and down the streets, hanging papers on every door. We never said so out loud, but inwardly we all knew it was a race to see who could finish their streets and get back to the car first. This worked quite well and allowed us to make quick progress. Until we got assigned to a neighborhood with lots of loose dogs. We tolerated it until the day that I was approaching a house where a huge German Shepherd lived. Apparently he was in a particularly bad mood that day, because as I walked toward the door, he took a running leap and cleared the 6-foot wooden privacy fence that surrounded the yard. I heard Mom panic and scream my name from inside the van. I'm sure I panicked, too, but not one to scream, I stood affixed to my spot on the ground, unable to move. The dog never actually attacked me, thank the Lord, so I made it safely back to the van. From that point on, we drove the neighborhood and reached through the car windows to place the papers next to the mailbox for each house.

I was put in charge of keeping track of all of our earnings and making sure that we tithed on it. The rest of it was set aside as a special savings for joint purchases for the benefit of all of us. I deposited all of the earnings into my account and just tracked it in a separate register. Some of the money was spent on supplies for other business ventures, some was spent on rubber stamping supplies when we all took up the art of making our own cards, and a significant portion of it was spent on our "new" computer. Dad was ready to upgrade his computer and offered to sell us his old one for $500. After discussing it at great length amongst ourselves, Nicole, Nadine and I decided to take him up on his offer. The old MS DOS computer we had used for years served well for our imaginary business needs, but now that we were getting older, we saw that it would be valuable to have our own up-to-date computer with software programs that we could learn and use for everyday purposes.

As I entered my teenage years, Dad decided to take me a step further in my financial understanding by going through the Crown Ministries Financial Study for Teens. Mom and Dad had participated in and led a number of Crown Financial Studies for adults over the years, and after retiring Dad began working part-time for Crown Ministries in Wichita. Eventually, he joined forces with his friend, Peter DeGraaf, to provide financial counseling for couples and families in distress through their own organization—Shepherd's Staff Ministries. Having been instrumental in helping other families recover from massive amounts of debt, teaching them to budget, and encouraging them to develop better spending habits, Dad wanted to make sure that he helped his children avoid many of the common financial pitfalls he observed. The two of us met weekly for our study and discussed what the Bible says about money and how to apply those biblical teachings and principles in our lives. He helped me set a budget and taught me to live within my means. He taught me to set financial goals and kept me accountable as I worked to achieve them. He went with me to set up a checking account when I turned fourteen, and taught me how to balance my checkbook each month.

Shortly after I turned fourteen, Mom took me to get my Instruction Permit, which allowed me to drive with an adult in the front passenger's seat. (Dad's philosophy is that teaching us to drive at the age of fourteen gives us a full two years of practice with him or Mom in the car before we can get a full license at the age of sixteen.) Since my addition to the insurance policy once I turned sixteen caused an increase in the premium, Dad devised a plan for gradually working me into paying for my insurance. For the first 6-month period, I would be required to pay 25% of the increased amount. For the next 6-month period, 50%, then 75% and finally, 100%. This way, by the time I turned eighteen, I was paying the full amount of my insurance. This was the first monthly bill I ever had to pay, and I learned how to budget that amount into my monthly expenses. Since we had acquired a third vehicle when Grandma came to live with us, her little Honda Civic became my primary mode of transportation. I had to take responsibility for filling it with gas when the tank was empty, and keeping it maintained.

By the time I had my license, Nicole had started driving as well, so Mom talked to Randy, a friend of ours who was known to do a lot of maintenance work on bicycles and vehicles. He agreed to teach a beginning car care class for us and our friends Julia and Ian. For several months, we attended his weekly class and learned all about cars and how to properly maintain them. He taught us how to check the fluids and change the oil. He explained the different parts of a car and gave us a "tour" under the hood. He walked us through how to change a flat tire and jumpstart a dead battery. It was an excellent class and was the perfect introduction to our new responsibilities on the road.

Several years later, Nadine was added to the roster of drivers in our family and with the increase in busyness between all of our schedules, Dad encouraged me to consider purchasing a car. I will always be grateful that he and Mom established an investment account for me when I was born and faithfully deposited money into it as long as they could afford to do so. Once I started generating my own income, I took up responsibility for the account and made deposits from my savings account whenever it reached a certain level. The balance of the account was enough to pay cash for my first car. The only problem was that I didn't know nearly enough to purchase a car. Dad gave me the number for an acquaintance of his who was a car broker. He had purchased our suburban for us at an auction several years earlier and the experience had been very positive. So I called him up, told him my price range and what features I wanted the vehicle to have, and then prayed that the Lord would help him find the right car.

The following Tuesday morning, he called and told me he was looking at a particular car at the auction that was very nice, but was higher than the price range I had given him. He said the cars were going for more than he had anticipated and thought I should go with this one. I debated for a moment, but knew that the price range I had given him was the top amount that I wanted to pay for a car. I reaffirmed my position over the phone and he hung up, still committed to finding something for me. Less than an hour later, the phone rang again. There was another car on the auction block that looked really nice. He was convinced it was exactly what I wanted, but again the price was higher than I had specified. He said if I would just be willing to pay about $1,000 more, he could purchase this car for me. I thanked him for his persistence, but remained firm in my price. As I hung up the phone from that call, I dropped to my knees. I knew I couldn't keep dealing with the stress and pressure of these phone calls. I cried out to God, acknowledging that He knew better than I did what kind of car would be good for me. I asked him to oversee the remainder of the process on my behalf and help the car broker find the right vehicle.

Almost as soon as I rose to my feet, the phone rang a third time. I answered with a measure of uncertainty. The first words I heard were, "Do you like the color blue?" He went on to describe in great detail the Saturn Coupe he had just purchased off the auction block for me. He was amazed at what a great deal he had gotten and kept reiterating all the great little extras about the car. I was overjoyed! When I went in to pick up the car the following week, I was able to share with him how God had answered my prayer through him. As much as I had learned the importance of handling my finances wisely and being a good steward of the things God entrusted to my care, I experienced another important lesson that day. Ultimately God was the One who would meet my needs and provide peace and stability in a constantly fluctuating world. As long as my trust and confidence remained in Him and not in my own financial savvy, I knew I would be just fine.

The lessons learned since childhood proved invaluable as I opened the doors of my piano studio business and had to deal with increasing business and financial demands. Tax reporting became more complicated, but Dad walked me through what he could and challenged me to study and learn what I needed to know beyond that. I found out that my friend, Alisa, and her sister were leading a financial study group, so I began attending the weekly meetings and was excited to discover a wealth of information about topics I had never explored before. We read books about retirement, investing, business structures, and leadership skills. As we studied each topic, a panel of people would be brought in for a question and answer session so that we could learn from those who were experts in the areas we were studying.

In addition to weekly assignments, we set individual financial goals for ourselves and each week shared one action step we were taking to meet those goals. The following week, we would give an update on our progress and hold each other accountable as we worked toward those goals. We began each class by reading portions of Scripture and discussing how it applied to our lives and finances. Periodically, we would meet for a night of dinner and playing Cashflow—the educational game developed by Robert Kiyosaki—after which we would go around and each share something that we learned about finances. The atmosphere was always one of encouragement and eagerness to learn new things. As we acquired knowledge in particular areas from our own experiences or studies, we shared it with the group. If we had questions, we presented them for discussion and those with more expertise or experience gave helpful advice.

The class was a natural continuation of the things Mom and Dad had been teaching me for years and the structure of the class was a natural transition from the self-directed studying I had done through high school and beyond. I have been amazed to realize the excellent educational opportunities that exist in so many venues, and the fields that can be explored even just by gathering with a group of like-minded families and individuals to engage in in-depth studies. Once we experience a paradigm shift and understand that true education is not relegated to the confines of a classroom, the possibilities truly are limitless!

Chapter 8

"Natalie captures profound truths that can transform anyone who is willing to learn. Her journey is one of hope, humility, and experiencing God's amazing grace in her life."

Robert Greenlaw

the path to good character

The Institute in Basic Life Principles Seminar (often shortened to just "Basic Seminar") was first held in 1965 when Wheaton College invited Bill Gothard to design and teach a course based on his work with youth. Since then hundreds of thousands of people have attended and experienced life transformation as they've applied the Biblical principles presented in the week-long seminar. I attended the Wichita Basic Seminar for the first time in 1995 and was thoroughly overwhelmed with the amount of information that was presented! The following year, we received word that they would be holding a Children's Institute (CI) in conjunction with the seminar. I wasn't familiar with it, but I loved working with children, so I sent in my application to help with the program. My application was accepted and I arrived Monday afternoon for the first day of teacher training. After being handed our curriculum, the next several hours were spent training and equipping all of us volunteers to teach the children that would arrive later that evening. I was assigned a position as an assistant to a girl who had traveled from Oklahoma to teach at the Children's Institute. It would be our responsibility to teach a group of 15 children throughout the week.

Each evening, our time was divided between large group assemblies and small group sessions. In the large group assemblies we learned Bible verses and songs and watched entertaining skits. In the small group sessions we taught the lessons, made crafts, played games, and generally oversaw our students. Each night of the seminar, the children were learning the same biblical principle as their parents, just in a way that was more fun and age appropriate. Even though I had been working with children for several years by this point in my life, it was a new experience planning out detailed lesson plans and teaching them on a spiritual level. The teacher I was assisting was the one primarily responsible for the teaching, while I was primarily responsible for keeping our team booth organized and craft materials ready for each session. I loved getting to know each of the children on our team, and by the end of the week found myself wishing that I could be the one doing the teaching. I wanted more than anything to make a difference in the lives of those children.

I made lots of new friends among the other teachers, and toward the end of the week people began asking if I was going to be teaching at the CI in Oklahoma City. I didn't understand what they meant at first, but soon learned that these CIs were held throughout the country and young people like me could apply to work at CIs in other cities. What an exciting opportunity that would be! I didn't waste any time informing Mom and Dad of what I had learned and securing their permission to apply to work at the Oklahoma City CI. I sent in my application, and this time indicated that I wanted to be assigned a role as a teacher, not an assistant. Time could hardly go fast enough as I anticipated my trip to Oklahoma City.

Shortly before the October seminar arrived, I received a letter from a man named Larry Guthrie, informing me that a character curriculum was being developed for use in the public schools. They planned to conduct training during the Oklahoma City CI and implement a nine-week pilot project in eight Oklahoma City schools that fall. They were looking for volunteers to receive training and go into the schools to teach character to the children. I was practically trembling as I read the letter. What an amazing opportunity this would be! I had only dreamed of doing such things, but now I was being invited to do it for real. Again I sought permission from Mom and Dad and sent in an application to be considered for this project. Several weeks later I was packed and on my way to Oklahoma City, having been sent under the authority and with the blessing of our church elders.

My time at the Oklahoma City CI was a stretching experience. I was assigned to be a team assistant, much to my dismay. To make it worse, the team leader I was assisting was not a very good teacher. I can remember complaining to my Dad about this arrangement and have never forgotten the counsel he gave me. He said, "Sometimes we learn the most from those who are not good leaders." I took his words to heart and made every effort to identify and develop the qualities that I saw lacking in the leader so that I would be a more effective leader in the future. In spite of some of these trials of selfishness that I was facing, the Lord was beginning to work in my heart in a big way. As I prepared to teach biblical principles like Design—recognizing the unchangeable characteristics in my life and accepting the way God made me, Authority—having an attitude of submission and obedience toward those God had placed over me, trusting that He would direct me through those authorities, and Ownership—acknowledging that everything I have has been given to me by God and I have no right to be selfish with my possessions; I became more and more aware of how much these principles were lacking in my own life. Little by little I began to see that God was calling me to approach life from a new perspective, a perspective firmly founded in the Word and ways of God.

As it turned out, the Pilot Project for teaching the character program in Oklahoma City was postponed until the following February. Due to a divine set of circumstances, I was unable to be involved. I was heartbroken. This was my heart, my passion; but the Lord had closed the door for reasons I could not understand. At the same time, the Lord planted a seed in my heart. I began to dream about the possibility of starting a character program in the schools right in our hometown of Derby. The thought sent shivers of excitement down my spine and I began to pray that somehow the Lord would turn my dream into a reality.

That year I saw a significant expansion in my education. My sophomore year was in full swing, but I found myself focusing less on academics and more on pursuing life experiences and developing relational skills. When I was at home I continued my math studies and other areas I was interested in—Greek, history, writing and piano. But I also traveled and taught at CIs in Tulsa, Fort Worth, Dallas and Oklahoma City. That summer, I attended a Character First! Education (CF!E) training in Oklahoma City. The Pilot Project had been completed and was an overwhelming success. Plans were underway to continue curriculum development and train additional volunteers to present and implement the program in their own cities. Nicole and I, along with a handful of friends from the Wichita area, went through the training together. Part of the training included mock presentations that we had to give to "school officials" who grilled us with questions about the program. After an intense week of training and practicum, I received the official document certifying me as a Character Coach. At the end of the week we headed home, anxious to see how God would open the doors in our area now that we had been through the training.

The next spring, at Dad's suggestion, Nicole and I presented the CF!E materials to the Children's Minister at our church and asked him about the possibility of putting together a program for the children at the church based on the materials. He loved the idea! The first curriculum series consisted of nine character qualities, and we decided to spend one week focusing on each one. Each character quality would be taught and reinforced through stories from nature, the Bible, and various object lessons, crafts and games. We recruited 6th graders to lead teams of children and planned a day of training to familiarize them with the curriculum and explain how the program would work. Several high school guys from our church were willing to tell stories. We asked several other young men who had gone through the training with us to fill in as guest storytellers on the other weeks. We had done everything we knew to do to prepare and could only pray and wait to see whether the endeavor would be a success or not.

The first day of the new program arrived and the children filed into the classroom. We began by assigning the children to their teams, which were named after the various animals we would be studying. The format was completely different than what they had been used to. Our family had begun to question the practice, initiated by the government school system and adopted by most churches, of placing students into age-segregated classes. We observed that most family members, upon arriving at the church building on Sunday morning, were ushered in different directions rather than being encouraged to worship and fellowship together as a family. God had obviously designed the family as a unit and we wanted to promote the idea of families working and serving together, and students learning in age-integrated environments. Although Nicole and I assumed the primary responsibility of implementing the program, the rest of the family jumped in to help with preparations and assisted in numerous ways during the class time.

The students adapted surprisingly well to the new format. We kept things moving at a fast pace so that we could cover everything within our allotted time. All of our training was put to the test as Nicole and I stood in front of the children and applied the steps we had learned to generate enthusiasm in the students. Our excitement grew as we led them in memorizing Bible verses and helped them understand how to apply the character quality we were studying in their daily lives.

By God's grace, the program was a huge success! The children loved it and the parents were amazed at how smoothly everything ran and how well-behaved the children were for the duration of the hour and a half program each week. Our numbers grew more and more as word spread and others wanted to be a part of what was taking place in the children's ministry. We had a blast working with the student teachers and children, and my desire to see CF!E implemented in the Derby schools continued to grow. I prayed continually that God would open the door for us to go forward with that idea, but still He did not lead in that direction.

Fall of 1998 arrived and Nicole traveled with me to teach at a CI in

Dallas. I was assigned the role of teacher and Nicole was my assistant. We hadn't necessarily planned to be on the same team and had actually been hoping to work with other people. But this was our assignment and we began the week with high hopes. However, the Lord saw fit to populate our team with a group of very challenging children. We found ourselves increasingly frustrated with their behavior and found it almost impossible to get through the lessons we were supposed to be teaching. Tensions mounted between Nicole and me as the week wore on. It would be hard to pinpoint the specific cause of our irritations, but the differences in our personalities and spiritual gifts were becoming more prominent under the mounting pressure. Nicole is a gifted organizer and is very alert to details. She recognizes what needs to be done and is systematic in approaching and meeting those needs. I, on the other hand, am more of a visionary—seeing the big picture and approaching situations with a desire to help other people grow. I can quickly come up with brilliant ideas that are completely impractical and I have a tendency to delve into things before considering what's really involved. These were some of the personality traits that began to cause tension between us. But more fundamentally, God was bringing to the surface my controlling, self-centered, nature.

One of the very things that I was teaching the children in my group—the principle of yielding their own rights and preferring their siblings or friends over themselves—was sadly lacking in my life. I had a serious anger problem and was known to frequently blow up over little infractions committed by my sisters. I was the domineering older sister who cowed my sisters into catering to my whims. Recently, this anger problem in my life had become more evident to me, but I didn't know how to get rid of it. And of course, anger is not something that can just be gotten rid of once and for all in a single act! But God was at work on me, taking me through the process of humbling me and teaching me how to resolve my anger.

Just as I taught the children under my care, God taught me that anger rising up within me was a sign that I was holding onto a personal "right." If one of my sisters borrowed a shirt without asking and I became angry with her, it was because I had a "right" to my clothes and to determine who could or could not wear them. According to the Bible, "The earth is the LORD's, and the fulness thereof; the world, and they that dwell therein" (Psalm 24:1). My clothes ultimately belonged to God, not to me. This was a new concept for me. Well, I'm sure Mom and Dad had said something of the sort before, but now I was hearing, as if for the first time, the truth of God in contrast to the selfish philosophy I had adopted. Indeed, everything I had belonged to God and He was fully capable of taking care of His things. I had to realign my thinking so that it was in harmony with God's thinking. If my clothes belonged to Him, then I figured it would be fine with Him if any of us girls wore them. Plus, I'm sure He was just as capable of keeping a shirt free from ruin on one of my sisters as He was on me! As I began to apply this principle to all of the possessions in my life, I experienced a new and incredible sense of freedom. As new possessions were acquired, I would go through a deliberate process of acknowledging that they belonged to God and that He could do with them whatever He thought was best.

As I think back to those years of my life, I am reminded of a message I once heard where the speaker explained the process of refining silver. When silver is placed under the fire, all the impurities rise to the surface and the silversmith scrapes them off. This results in a substance of silver that is 99% pure. The process can be repeated numerous times, each time with additional impurities being raised to the surface and scraped off by the silversmith. The Lord was allowing me to face situations that were causing the impurities of my life to be brought to the surface, plainly visible for all to see—especially myself. And it was not pretty. I wasn't nearly as good of a person as I had convinced myself I was. Now I looked even worse than the unruly children on our team!

A few months later, Nicole and I were in Oklahoma City where we found ourselves once again assigned to lead a CI team together, much to our chagrin. We had some wonderful children on our team that we both adored, but they were overshadowed almost immediately by several very unlikable children. It was extremely hard not to show favoritism, and we tried to treat each of the children with love. Again, Nicole and I grew frustrated and impatient with one another to the point that both of us hated working with the other one. If only they had placed us with someone else instead of each other! I could be a much godlier young lady when I wasn't being impeded in my spiritual endeavors by my sister. At one point, as we were preparing for the lesson that evening, we were extremely angry with one another and were casting daggers with our eyes and speaking in harsh whispers to convey exactly how we felt about each other (we didn't want to be overheard by any of the other young people). Just then, the female staff leader, Rebekah, approached our table with a big smile and an enthusiastic greeting, followed by a sincere query as to how our preparations were going. Like good Christian homeschool girls, we smiled back and quickly assured her that everything was going wonderfully. After lingering a moment, she moved on to the next group, reminding us to pray together before the children arrived. Pray?! That was the last thing we wanted to do together! But pray we did. And somehow we made it through the night and the remainder of the week without one of us injuring the other. As I taught the lessons each night, I was laden with guilt. I was a hypocrite and I knew it. But try as I might, I could not be the good person I so much wanted to be. And that, I soon discovered, was the problem.

As I had my quiet time one morning, I was looking up some of the words from a particular Bible verse in the concordance. As I looked up the word "sin," and referenced the original Greek, I was reminded of the definition that I'd heard before, but never really pondered, "to miss the mark." God's standard of perfect goodness was the "mark" and all my attempts toward goodness were the "miss." None of my attempts would ever hit God's mark. I would never be good enough for God. It hit me like a heavy blow. Sure I had heard people talk about sin before and our need for God, but all of a sudden it was personal. It was then that it occurred to me that Jesus, through His sinless life, had perfectly hit the mark...on my behalf. Romans 8:3-4 became crystal clear to me, "For what the law could not do, in that it was weak through the flesh, God sending his own Son in the likeness of sinful flesh, and for sin, condemned sin in the flesh: That the righteousness of the law might be fulfilled in us, who walk not after the flesh, but after the Spirit."

The fact that I was a Christian did not mean that now I could somehow hit the mark of God's perfect goodness. In fact, it made me more painfully aware of how incapable I was of ever hitting the mark. I got on my knees and wept before God as I confessed my sins—my many, many attempts and subsequent failings to hit His mark of goodness. I acknowledged my desperate need for Jesus Christ, not just for salvation from my sins, but for the ability to live each day in a way that was pleasing to God and that was in harmony with His Word. I had tried for too long to live a good, godly life by my own effort. Now that I had a proper understanding of my own sinful nature, I reveled in the joy and peace of knowing that Jesus Christ had already accomplished this on my behalf. My life need not be dictated by rules and regulations, but rather by a vibrant and close relationship with Him. For the more that He was in me and in control of my life, the more my life would line up with God's holy standards.

By God's grace I had journeyed through the same process as the apostle Paul to finally reach a solution for my embattled efforts to overcome the sinful nature of doing evil when I wanted to do good, and not doing good even though I had an inward desire to do good. The solution had nothing to do with me and my measly efforts, but everything to do with Jesus Christ and His life, death and resurrection on my behalf. This was the necessary foundation that God needed to pour in my life so that He could build upon it in the years to come.

Chapter 9

"We can see in Natalie the reason she is so qualified to write this book. She is a successful homeschool graduate who has excelled in academics. But more importantly, her desire is to know and do the will of God above all else. That, in any parent's eyes, is truly a successful education."

Richard and Susan Neu

giving up & my dreams

An unquenchable hunger and thirst for the Word of God had been birthed in my heart. God's Word was no longer a dry spiritual guidebook. It was a living, life-changing, God-revealing Book. I loved spending time in the mornings reading and studying it, digging into the passages I read and exploring the original languages for deeper meanings. One of the beauties of homeschooling during these years was that I could dedicate such large chunks of time to Bible study and prayer. I was constantly challenged by the things that I read, and as I grew closer to the Lord and began to apply the things I read in my life, I sensed that the Lord was transforming me and molding me into a different person. I wanted more than anything to please Him, to serve Him, to go anywhere and do anything for Him. Just as the psalmist wrote many years before, I experienced personally that God was showing me the path of life; in His presence was fullness of joy and at His right hand were pleasures for evermore (see Psalm 16:11).

The big dilemma now was knowing what to do. There were so many opportunities, so many needs, so many people who did not know the Lord. But where should I go? What should I do? I prayed earnestly for clear direction from the Lord. I needed to know His calling for me. I needed a way to navigate through the endless possibilities and determine with confidence that I was heading the direction He wanted me to go. One morning as I read through Ezekiel in my regular Bible reading, I was drawn to the calling God gave him: "For thou art not sent to a people of a strange speech and of an hard language, but to the house of Israel; Not to many people of a strange speech and of an hard language, whose words thou canst not understand. Surely, had I sent thee to them, they would have hearkened unto thee. But the house of Israel will not hearken unto thee; for they will not hearken unto me: for all the house of Israel are impudent and hardhearted. Behold, I have made thy face strong against their faces, and thy forehead strong against their foreheads. As an adamant harder than flint have I made thy forehead: fear them not, neither be dismayed at their looks, though they be a rebellious house" (Ezekiel 3:5-9). Even though the specific calling was given to another person for another time, at that moment it was as if the Lord was whispering similar words to my heart. This was it. This was God's direction for me. God had not called me to go to a foreign country. He had called me to America, to the people right around me. He confirmed this to me in the following days through other passages, and I experienced an overwhelming sense of purpose and direction for my life. Even though I didn't know any more specifically than before exactly what I should do, I knew that this would provide a helpful measuring rod by which I could evaluate the opportunities that presented themselves to me.

By now I was in my senior year of high school and graduation was approaching. Mom and Dad didn't give me any specific requirements in order to complete high school, but I continued my attempt to finish Algebra 2 while working on various other projects that were of interest to me or that Mom or Dad had assigned to me. There had been no talk of college and I began contemplating what I should do after graduation. Again I sought the Lord. What did He want me to do? Should I go to college? What should I study? What direction should I head with my life? Again, He provided direction. It came during my time of Bible reading one morning. This time I was challenged by three short verses in Proverbs 4:25-27, "Let thine eyes look right on, and let thine eyelids look straight before thee. Ponder the path of thy feet, and let all thy ways be established. Turn not to the right hand nor to the left: remove thy foot from evil."

All around me peers, extended family members, friends, (and even a few strangers who felt compelled to express their concern on occasion) were anticipating the next step in my education, namely—college. If I didn't follow that path, what would people think? But as I studied the caution in Proverbs I became far more concerned about what would happen to me if I blindly followed along a path that God had not established or confirmed for me. I needed to ponder, to think, to contemplate carefully the path that I should take. And the path I should take would be the one clearly directed by God. So far, college didn't appear to be part of God's plan.

About this same time I was approached by Susan Neu, a good friend who was helping coordinate the next CI in Wichita. She asked if I would consider being the stage leader for the week of the seminar. The stage leader was the one who led the assemblies, helping the children learn the verses and songs and the coordinating hand motions. Did she know that this had been my dream? I had taught at many other CIs by this time and had dreamed of the day when perhaps I could be the one on the stage leading the assemblies. I knew it was a position that was attained only by invitation from the seminar leadership and I thought that perhaps if I kept teaching at enough CIs, eventually I would be asked to serve in this role. Now I could hardly contain myself! The position was being offered to me and I was ready to jump at the chance. With the admonition from Proverbs fresh in my mind, though, I told her that I would need to pray about it and get back to her with my final answer. I began praying about it, but I already had in mind what God's answer would be. He had to say yes. This was the opportunity I had been waiting for and it was a perfect way to carry out the calling He had given me. But as I stubbornly pressed ahead, peace eluded me. There was a hesitation in my spirit and I couldn't understand why.

Several weeks later as I sat in church on a Sunday morning, our pastor preached a sermon. I don't remember what the topic was, but I remember with perfect clarity the point he made that grabbed my attention. He spoke of the Israelite army and how they had sent the spies into the land of Canaan. Following the bad report by the majority, they decided, contrary to God's command, not to try to possess the land. God issued His judgment upon the people, declaring that they would be relegated to the wilderness for 40 years. The next morning, the people regretted their disobedience and determined to go into the land and defeat their enemies. God tells them that if they go now, in opposition to Him, He will not go with them and they will be defeated. They ignore His warning and go into battle and are soundly defeated. Very clearly, the Lord communicated the same message to me through that illustration. It was not His will for me to be the stage leader at the Children's Institute and if I persisted, I would be on my own. I didn't want to believe that this was really the Lord directing me. It wasn't the direction I wanted.

Another couple of weeks passed and it was the day before a prayer meeting was scheduled for all those assisting with the Basic Seminar. I knew Mrs. Neu would be there and she would want an answer from me. I wasn't prepared to give her one. Not yet. I still needed something more clearly from the Lord. Or so I convinced myself. In reality I just wanted God's answer to line up with what I wanted. I petitioned the Lord that morning for a word from Him. Being the patient, loving Father that He is, He gave me a very clear word from Proverbs 21:30-31, "There is no wisdom nor understanding nor counsel against the LORD. The horse is prepared against the day of battle: but safety is of the LORD." The words stopped me dead in my tracks. What? Again the Lord was saying, "No." If I was to proceed with my desires, it would be in opposition to Him. Deep within my heart, the battle began to rage more fiercely than ever.

The next day dawned and I awoke in turmoil. The brunch meeting to which I would have normally looked forward, I was now dreading.

Thoughts swirled continuously through my mind. *Perhaps I'm misunderstanding God.* The words of the tempter filtered in amongst the others. *Did God really say...?* My own desires burned passionately within my heart. *Why would God say no to something that I want to do for Him?* Dad and I drove together to the meeting and greeted the others once we arrived. I smiled on the outside, but I was a wreck on the inside. Just as I had anticipated, as soon as we were standing next to each other in the buffet line for the brunch, Mrs. Neu asked me if I had made a decision. I hesitated. She said that she had come up with another girl who could do the job if I decided not to. She had already spoken with her about the possibility and she was willing to do it. "NO!" I screamed in my heart. "I want to do it!" And in my ugly pride I quickly reasoned that I would do a much better job than this other girl would in the position. Somehow I managed to calmly reply that I would give her my decision before we left the meeting.

I am surprised I didn't fall to the floor, the wrestling within me was so intense. God had said no. He had said it twice. And I knew it. But I didn't like His answer. I wanted Him to give me a different answer. Instead, He flooded my mind with the following promise that had long been committed to memory, "Trust in the LORD with all thine heart; and lean not unto thine own understanding. In all thy ways acknowledge him, and he shall direct thy paths" (Proverb 3:5-6). Trust in the Lord. Lean not on my own understanding. I didn't understand. It didn't make any sense to me. But I knew without a doubt now what I had to do. I made my way back over to Mrs. Neu and explained that after considerable prayer, I had decided that it was not the Lord's will for me to serve as the stage leader. She expressed disappointment and understanding and thanked me for letting her know. She had no idea the battle that had taken place that led to the answer I gave her that morning. No one knew. No one but God.

As Dad and I drove home, I sat at the wheel while he dozed off in the passenger's seat. I could no longer contain myself and broke down. I wept uncontrollably before the Lord. My dream...was gone. I am sure God was looking down with tender compassion upon this stubborn child who was learning what it really meant to trust Him. And I wouldn't be surprised if the corner of His lip turned up in an eager smile because only He knew what was just around the corner.

Chapter 10

"Strength and ductility are two important qualities in steel. Character is like steel. There must be standards (strength) that one lives by, but without love, humor, and creativity (ductility) to diffuse difficult situations, the standards give way to legalism. Natalie has shown by her example the quality of the character that God has molded in her life. She is a testimony to the faithfulness of God when we are faithful to wait, listen, and obey."

Chase and Tiffany Hiebsch

going to public school

The next morning was Graduation Sunday at church. All the graduates were asked to come forward and we each received a handmade wooden Bible holder in the shape of a cross, made by a gentleman from the church. A brief picture presentation was shown and we were applauded by the congregation. Following the service, a lady named Sherry stopped me to ask what my plans were now that I had graduated. We talked briefly about some things I was doing and then she asked what had ever come of the CF!E program. One of her sons had participated in the program when Nicole and I taught it at our church and she knew I had thought at one time about using it in the schools. She wondered whether I had made any plans in that direction. Only a short time before, I had actually given up on ever pursuing this idea. After nearly two years of praying for an open door, I told the Lord that I wasn't going to bug Him anymore about it. If He wanted it to be done, He would have to throw the door wide open. I told Sherry that I was just waiting to see if God would open the door for us to start the program. She suggested that I talk with Chris Showalter, another lady who was a member of our church and was also a fourth grade teacher at one of the elementary schools. I thanked her for the suggestion, amazed at God's timing in bringing this up again after the emotionally trying events of the day before. I wondered if perhaps, not unlike Abraham, God was testing me to see if I was willing to lay down the greatest desire of my heart for His sake so that He could then pour out upon me a far greater blessing than I could have ever imagined.

Later that night our family attended a reception for one of my fellow graduates and I had a chance to talk with Mrs. Showalter and share a little about the CF!E program with her. She was somewhat familiar with it from when we had implemented it at church and was excited about the possibility of incorporating it into her classroom. We arranged a meeting date for several weeks later and I dug out my materials and reviewed all that I'd learned about presenting the program to a prospective teacher. In one day the Lord had brought about the fruition of two years of dreaming, preparing and praying. I was in awe and moved ahead with complete confidence that this was the will of God.

With curriculum in hand and posters under my arm I walked up the sidewalk to the front door of Mrs. Showalter's house. The day of our meeting had come! She invited me in and we sat in her living room where I displayed all the materials and gave her an idea of how the program could work in her classroom. We would focus on one character quality a month. I would recruit and train the volunteers to plan and conduct the lessons and she would reinforce and remind the students of the concepts throughout the course of the school day. The only cost to the school would be the purchase of the teacher's curriculum, a set of character cards for each student, and posters to hang up in the classroom. We would cover the cost of all the other supplies and materials we used for the lessons. She could hardly believe it. As we discussed the details, our enthusiasm continued to grow. She felt there was a definite need for character education in her classroom and this program appeared to be one that would do the job well. I left her house with her promising to discuss this idea with the school principal and arrange a time for me to meet with him and the other two fourth grade teachers at the school.

A little over a month later I received a call from Mrs. Showalter. CF!E was approved for use by all three fourth grade classes at Derby Hills Elementary School. We were both ecstatic. The following week I went to the school and met with the other two fourth grade teachers to discuss logistics. We set the schedule for the year and I placed an order for all the program materials. Our team of volunteer character coaches would spend every other Monday morning at the school, teaching the lessons, working with the students, and providing whatever other service the teachers needed during our time in their classrooms. This was a new approach for the teachers and entirely new territory for me. Prior to our meeting that day, the only other time I had been in our local public schools was to vote. The same would be true for most of our other volunteer character coaches.

I had already alerted a number of people as to what was transpiring in Derby with CF!E and they were committed to being a part of this ground-breaking opportunity. Now I contacted each of them to let them know that it was a go. I scheduled a meeting at our house for two weeks later so that all of us could meet together, pray and plan for the year ahead. As thrilled as I was, those two weeks were filled with feelings of trepidation and inadequacy. I felt keenly my dependence on the Lord and found strength in His Word. During my quiet time one morning, the Lord led me to Nahum 1:7, "The LORD is good, a stronghold in the day of trouble; and he knoweth them that trust in him."

As I pondered this verse, I pictured a great big city with a wall 30 feet wide surrounding the boundary of the city. At the gate is the city guard. A man approaches the gate and tells the guard that he wants to come in because an enemy is after him. Yet as he speaks, he mutters under his breath that the city probably won't offer much protection; he reasons that he will be just as safe on his own. The guard, understandably, is baffled. How ridiculous to assume that equal protection will be afforded outside the walled city! The guard invites the man into the city, but he turns away, assuring him that he'll be fine on his own.

In the same way, I imagined myself running to the Lord and telling Him of all my problems, but as soon as He offered the invitation for me to "come in" and trust in His protection, I turned away and attempted to manage on my own. When viewed in that light, my position seemed ridiculous. God had offered me a fortified place to dwell, free of fear; but it would require trust. Trust was what the Lord used to bring me to this point and that's what would be required in order to faithfully walk the path the Lord had now set before me.

During this time my passion for reaching children with the hope of Jesus Christ was also renewed. For years I had been drawn to the hurting, lonely children who live their lives everyday with no word or act of kindness or love. I knew cities all across the country were filled with such children. But how could I, a white female from a middle class family, living in a nice suburb, hope to be able to reach these children? I was optimistic that perhaps through CF!E the Lord would begin to take me down this path. I was always looking toward the future, always wanting to do more, to go different places, to reach different people. But for now, God was teaching me to serve Him right where I was; to be faithful in that which was least; to make the most of every minute and every opportunity.

At long last the day arrived. The day I had prayed and waited for for the past two and a half years. September 13, 1999. I arose early in the morning, and after getting dressed and gathering the supplies I would need for the day, I slipped onto the front porch with my Bible and journal. The sun was just peeking up over the horizon and I gazed at it while inhaling the cool fall air. My heart was flooded with a torrent of emotions. Apprehension. Excitement. Curiosity. What would the day hold? How would the students respond? What would the teachers think? How would we do teaching the lessons? As my mind overflowed with these questions and thoughts, I cried out to God, asking His blessing on the day. I knew that apart from Him we would utterly fail.

By 8:00 that morning, the rest of the team had arrived at our house, spent time in prayer, discussed final details and loaded up to make the short drive to Derby Hills Elementary School. Our team consisted of Kendra, Chad, David, Staci, Cal, Chase, Steve, Daniel, Nicole and me. We had a well-trained, experienced team, but only God could have fully prepared us for the things that would be required of us in the days, months and years that followed that first morning. As soon as we arrived at the school we were greeted by the principal, Dr. Silvertooth. He was all smiles and immediately told us of his support for what we were doing and shared with us about some of the character initiatives that he had already implemented in the school. One of his favorites was the morning broadcast given over the school speaker system. It always concluded with a reminder to all the students to demonstrate good character in their behavior throughout the day.

We split up into the classroom teams we would maintain for the year—David, Staci, Chad and Nicole would be in Mrs. Showalter's classroom; Daniel, Steve and Kendra would be in Mrs. Crowe's classroom; and Cal, Chase and I would be in Mrs. Rush's classroom. The girls on each team were responsible for leading the song or memory work with hand motions. The guys on the team were responsible for memorizing and telling the stories. Once a month, David donned his tall hat and black coat and made the rounds to each classroom as "Abraham Lincoln," sharing stories from his life with the students and encouraging them to identify how he demonstrated the character quality they were studying in each particular story that he shared.

We had set aside three hours of the morning to be in the classroom, but only used one hour for our character presentation. This allowed us to spend the additional two hours working with the students one-on-one or in groups as requested by the teacher. Throughout the year we all developed close relationships with the teachers and students in our class-room. We played with them at recess, ate with them at lunch, went on a field trip with them, participated with them in their field day...we became a part of their lives. And we loved it.

We were shocked to discover how many of the students in this middle class neighborhood came from broken homes. The teachers often told us of some of the difficult situations the students in their class were facing. Mrs. Rush once commented to me that she had on more than one occasion been frustrated with one student or another for various reasons. She couldn't understand why they were being so difficult and why she was having so much trouble with them. Then she would hold a parent-teacher conference and would find herself amazed that the student was doing as well as they were based on what she observed and experienced during her time with the parents.

The students gravitated to us like magnets. They were starved for attention, for love. At the time we always thought it peculiar how attached especially the girls would become to the male character coaches. But years of working in the classroom showed us how hungry these girls were for the love and acceptance of a man. Very few had fathers who filled that role in their lives. And so, in a very real sense, our male character coaches became a father figure to these students—and they set a high standard of love and respect, treating each one equally and behaving toward them like true gentlemen. We received numerous cards and letters from the students expressing their appreciation for us and for CF!E. They loved us and we loved them.

Before we knew it, the end of the school year had arrived and we said our farewells, with the students begging us to come back the next year. We assured them that if it was up to us we would be back. Little did we know that God had an even bigger plan in mind for the next year! Some of the other classroom teachers at Derby Hills had observed the CF!E program from a distance and began inquiring as to how they could get us to implement it in their classrooms as well. I met with Dr. Silvertooth and discussed the possibility of expanding the program to some of the other grades. He was all for it, as were most of the teachers. The school increased the character education line item in the budget so that the following year all the 2nd–5th grade classes could purchase the curriculum and sets of character cards for their students. Dr. Silvertooth left the decision to participate up to the individual teachers and only one 2nd grade teacher opted out. She was very antagonistic toward anything she perceived as religious and was concerned about the influence we would have on her students.

Since we were almost quadrupling the number of classrooms we'd be working with, we decided to incorporate assemblies as part of our teaching. All the students would gather for an assembly at the beginning of the day where we could introduce the character quality, learn the memory work or song, and tell the story. Then we would spend the rest of the morning going into each of the classrooms and reinforcing the lesson with hands-on projects, object lessons and games. We added more character coaches to our team of volunteers the second year in order to effectively handle the increased number of classrooms. It was challenging to work out the logistics with more classes, since we had to try to work with each teacher's classroom schedule and all the other activities already scheduled into the day. Eventually, with some flexibility and after making some adjustments, we had our master schedule for the year.

Since there were P.E. classes being held in the gymnasium at the same time we would be conducting our assemblies, we had to hold the assemblies in the lunchroom. This was far from an ideal set-up, with awkward seating arrangements for the students and numerous distractions associated with the lunch time preparations. Although the children loved the content of the assemblies, the negatives soon outweighed the positive benefit derived from them. Although we stuck with it for the duration of the year, the teachers voted unanimously at the end of the year to go back to just teaching the lessons in a classroom setting.

The third year saw the expansion of the program to include all grade levels in the school. Even the Kindergarten teachers wanted to try it in their classrooms. With the increased number of classrooms and the decision to drop the assemblies, CF!E had become an all-day operation. Word spread among the homeschool community of what we were doing, and the Lord provided more volunteers who received training and became a part of the program. We had three teams of three or four people each. Each team was responsible for planning their own lessons, securing their own supplies, and memorizing the stories and memory work with hand motions. After each day at the school, time was set aside for teams to do lesson planning for the following session. They were required to submit an outline to me of the lesson plan and a description of which team member was responsible for which part of the lesson. Following our time at the school, each team gave a report of what went well and anything that didn't go well. They also filled out a written report from the day. All of these were stored in a binder with the lesson plans for future reference, should we have need of them.

Since we were at the school all day, we often played at recess with the students, ate lunch with them, accompanied them to other classes and talked with them in the hallway during breaks. We loved being a part of their classrooms and, by extension, their lives. Sometimes we were even invited to birthday parties or other special events. Often I would be walking down an aisle at the store and hear an excited voice call out, "Miss Natalie! Miss Natalie!" I would then get the chance to meet and visit with their parent and explain how we knew each other. In a small community like ours, those of us who lived in Derby often crossed paths with students from one of our CF!E classes. It was exciting to realize that in a small way, God was allowing us to impact the next generation—to build relationships with the children of today and inspire them to be the leaders of tomorrow. And not just any leaders, but leaders of character and integrity.

Through my work with CF!E in the schools I was interviewed by both local newspapers, the larger Wichita paper, and several times by the school district newsletter staff. I was asked to give a presentation to our local Board of Education to provide them an overview of the program and share the results we had seen from it. I also had the opportunity to travel to Topeka one year as part of the homeschool "Day Under the Dome" where I gave an interactive presentation about the character education efforts in the Derby schools. I had never taken an official public speaking class, but the training I received from the Children's Institutes and Character Training Institute, in addition to the life experience I had gained leading assemblies and teaching in the classrooms, was excellent preparation for the opportunities that began coming my way.

And come my way they did! Several churches in the area heard about CF!E and became interested in using it as part of their children's program. After presenting the materials to them in greater detail, they scheduled me to come in and provide training for their children's ministry staff and workers. One of our local homeschool basketball teams decided to start a character program for their younger players, led by the varsity players. They asked me to travel with them to one of their tournaments and conduct training for the high school students to help prepare them for their responsibilities. Also, the coordinator for a Children's Ministry conference contacted me and asked me to give a workshop for the attendees on why and how to implement a character education program in their church. Shortly thereafter, a community group in an outlying city requested that I provide training for them so that they could use the program in an after-school program that they were going to be organizing for students in their city.

It was one thing to plan lessons for a group of fun-loving grade-schoolers, but it was a whole new experience coming up with creative ways to effectively train adults to teach the children in their programs. I felt very inadequate for these tasks and constantly sought the Lord and searched Scripture. I needed guidance on how to teach effectively and what to share with those whom I was training. Each situation was different. Each group of trainees was different and came with different levels of experience and even different levels of interest in learning to teach. It was challenging to know how to reach each person I was responsible to train. I wanted to both equip them for their responsibilities and somehow infuse them with a vision and enthusiasm for the impact they could have on the children they were teaching.

The fourth year of CF!E in the Derby schools was approaching and

Gayle, the Media Specialist at El Paso Elementary, contacted me. She had been involved in a training I gave at her church and invited me to present the program to the principal and teachers at her school. A couple of the other character coaches and I made the presentation, showed a brief introductory video, and answered questions. After consulting the principal and teachers at Derby Hills, they made the decision to implement the program school-wide the first year. The character assemblies were given priority in the morning with the principal, Sharon, being actively involved in them. This contributed in large part to the success of the assemblies, and we found it to be a very effective way of presenting the character quality each week.

Again, more character coaches were recruited and trained to handle our growing responsibilities. I was on the team that went to El Paso to oversee the implementation of our first year there, and one of the other character coaches, my good friend Tiffany, became the school leader at Derby Hills. She was to oversee the responsibilities specific to that school and be available to handle questions or any other problems that might arise throughout the day. We continued to meet at our house on Friday mornings to spend time in prayer before carpooling to the schools where we would spend the rest of the day.

At El Paso we experienced the additional challenge of working in an open classroom environment. Rather than each class having a separate classroom, all the classes of a particular grade level were in one large space, with only short sets of bookshelves artificially dividing the room into sections. We learned through trial and error, and the helpful instruction of the teachers, how to teach more effectively in a classroom layout especially prone to distraction. We synchronized our activities as much as possible and combined the classes, when feasible, to work together on projects. During the time we were not teaching in the classrooms, the teachers regularly used us to assist them with other classroom duties or to work with students individually or in groups. This provided opportunities for us to get to know the students better and talk with them on a more personal level.

It was during one such occasion that I gathered with some 5th graders to be a part of their reading group.

We were each given a copy of the book and took turns reading one page at a time. The book we were reading was the story of the history of writing. It began with information from "prehistoric" times and the early cavemen and how they communicated with each other, and continued on to present times. The book was clearly based on evolutionary presuppositions. As we read, I looked around the circle of students and observed that they were all unresponsive and unquestioning. Once we finished, before the students rejoined the rest of their class, I asked them what they thought of the book and if they thought it was true. They looked at me with blank stares. It had never even occurred to them to question the accuracy of this "historical" account. I asked them several other questions and we discussed ways to discern whether something you read is true or not. One of the students suggested asking their teacher. I agreed that this was one way that could be utilized and suggested that they do so when we went back into the classroom. We finished our time discussing the importance of truth and of having an absolute and unchanging standard by which all information could be measured. The students were eager to hear what their teacher would say when they asked her, and I was glad to know that this particular teacher was a Christian. However, she was apparently preoccupied with some other responsibilities when one of the boys asked her whether the book was true or not and she quickly brushed him away, telling him that yes it was true and could he please put the books away and head over to his desk.

I was even more disappointed than the students were with the teacher's response. I realized how much the environment in a public school setting pressures teachers to focus on maintaining structure and measuring results, while at the same time squelching opportunities for sincere academic inquiry and intellectual discussion. The students had been challenged, perhaps for the first time, to think through the implications of what they read and to try to discern what was true and what was not rather than mindlessly accepting everything they read or were taught. But in less than a minute, this newly awakened sensitivity had been snuffed out as the students were forced to conform to the mold that required them to be passive learners rather than creative thinkers.

I can remember vividly one other experience that forever changed my perception of the government education system. Our focus was on the character quality of initiative and we were encouraging the students to look for ways to be leaders among their peers. I suggested that perhaps sometimes they could spend extra time after lunch or during recess reading a book instead of playing. Immediately one of the students piped up, "Oh, no, we're not allowed to have books in the lunchroom or at recess." There were other rules that prohibited them from staying inside during recess unless they had a legitimate reason or were in trouble. Immediately the thought crossed my mind, "this is like a kid prison." While individuality is touted as being of prime importance in education, in reality it is tolerated only so long as the students still cooperate with the established system. The "good" students were the ones who didn't question or break the rules. The "bad" students were the ones who pushed the boundaries—who brought books out to recess, or got out of their seats without permission, or laughed too loud in the lunchroom. In order to maintain order and meet state and federal standards, such behavior could not be tolerated.

I wonder how many amazing inventions will never make it onto paper because their would-be inventors spent too many hours sitting in a "time-out" chair in the corner of their classroom? I wonder how many great speeches will never be made because their would-be orators were sentenced to silence for talking too loudly in the lunchroom? I wonder how many timeless works of art will never be created because their would-be creators were reprimanded for doodling when they were supposed to be paying attention in class? The realization hit me full force. The government school system in America does not promote creativity or character; it emphasizes conformity and test performance. In a sense I began to feel like we were working against the whole system in our efforts to incorporate character education in our schools.

Still, the Lord led the way and we continued to follow. The next year I was contacted by Chris, the principal from Pleasantview, another Derby elementary school. She was Sharon's friend and was interested in implementing CF!E at her school. We scheduled a meeting date and I met with her and several other key teachers at the school who were exploring various character and bullying prevention programs for use in their school. I showed them the materials and explained that I thought character education was more effective than a bullying prevention program because it addressed behavioral issues from a positive angle and told the students how they were expected to act, rather than emphasizing how they should not act. The teachers agreed and several days later I received word that they had decided to use the CF!E materials. I was thrilled! One step at a time God was leading us. I had learned from the very beginning not to try to make things happen on my own, but just to wait on the Lord to open the doors and expand the program in His time. Now He had opened the door to Pleasantview and, with a larger team of character coaches than ever before, we began the 2003-2004 school year.

Again, I went with the team to our new school to start the program and assigned school leaders to the other two schools. At Pleasantview we experienced a heightened level of support for the CF!E program. Not only the principal and classroom teachers participated, but the P.E. and music teachers also took an active role in the implementation of the program. The music teacher designed programs for each of the grades that centered on the character quality of the month and taught them the songs. The P.E. teacher sat in on the assemblies and helped make them successful. The whole atmosphere of the school was charged and the older students took seriously their responsibility to be leaders and good examples for the younger students. Our team had an absolute blast getting to know and work with the students and teachers at Pleasantview!

Toward the middle of April that school year, I was spending time with the Lord and praying for direction for the future of CF!E. I was reading in Ezra and stopped short when I came to chapter 4, verse 24, "Then ceased the work of the house of God which is at Jerusalem. So it ceased unto the second year of the reign of Darius king of Persia." God had started the great rebuilding effort in Israel's history and then He had halted the work for a time. It seemed as though the Lord was letting me know that the work of CF!E would cease, at least for now. In the case of the Israelites God later resumed the work on the wall under different leadership. I had no idea if that would be the case in my situation, but I felt certain that God was preparing me for the end of my part in CF!E in the Derby schools. The thought broke my heart. How could I give up something that had filled my heart and my life now for five years? I had finally seen the Lord bring the fulfillment of my years of dreaming and praying...and now, five years later, it was all going to end? And yet, in the midst of my uncertainties and questions, the Lord filled my heart with peace. He reminded me that CF!E was never my program. It was always His. He had led the way. He had opened the doors. He was still leading the way. But now He was closing the doors. I didn't understand. But God didn't ask me to understand. He just wanted me to trust Him. So that morning I firmly resolved to trust God and let Him continue to lead the way.

Sure enough, a couple of weeks later Chris called me into her office and explained that the school district had been exploring various options for a district-wide character focus and had selected another program that they would be implementing the following year. They would no longer need our "support" for their character education. This was a district-wide decision and would be implemented in every school. So we would no longer be needed at El Paso or Derby Hills either. I asked her what criteria were used for determining which program to use. She listed three criteria:

- *Non-intrusiveness*—a program that wouldn't extract time from the regular classroom schedule
- *Low Cost*
- *Ability to be implemented district-wide*

Because of increasing pressure placed on teachers and schools for students to perform up to state and national standards, teachers felt very protective of the time they had with their students. Many found it difficult enough to include the mandatory reading and math periods in their schedule without carving out additional time for a character lesson, the results of which could not be easily measured on a standardized test. Although positive character development in students is often reflected in greater classroom efficiency and higher test scores, to successfully incorporate character education requires a paradigm shift by the teacher. It also takes an administration that is willing, if necessary, to buck the educational practices that leave teachers feeling robbed of creativity and enthusiasm. Unfortunately, most teachers and administrators have become slaves to an educational system that, while trying to uphold minimum academic standards, is raising generations of children who have little or no moral bearing to guide them in the realities of life.

I often wrestled with the question of how I could justify teaching character apart from any mention of Christ, the source of all true character. How could I challenge children to be obedient and truthful and virtuous without directing them to the Lord for the motivation and power to live out those qualities? My heart's desire was not just to create better citizens, but to proclaim the Gospel of Christ and advance God's kingdom. How could I do that if I couldn't openly speak the name of Christ or direct them to His Word, something which is now prohibited in our government schools?

The Lord did give us opportunities occasionally to enter into deeper spiritual discussions when prompted by a student-initiated question. But by and large we clung to the hope that Christ would bear fruit in us and through us as we abided in Him and faithfully served Him in our community. I also prayed often that the Lord would use these character lessons to plant seeds of truth in the hearts of the students. That they would recognize that there were absolute standards of right and wrong. That this would become the basis for them recognizing their own sinful nature and eventually turning to Jesus Christ for salvation. While the restricted position in which we found ourselves was far from ideal, God used CF!E to accomplish much more than I could have ever imagined!

Although our goal as character coaches was to teach character to the children in the schools, it is amazing now to look back and see how God was using those experiences to develop character and skills in each of us and to build amongst us deep friendships that were forged through our years of co-laboring for the Lord in service to our community. I have many lasting memories of our years of service together. I remember exploding an experiment in a fifth grade classroom and having students point out the mark it made on the ceiling for the rest of the year. I remember sharing reports of students throwing up after eating our "disobedient" brownie recipe (we had to adjust that object lesson a bit after that!). I remember donning sunglasses, long coats, and walkie talkies and posing as secret agents to introduce a special project to our students. I remember going to lunch with our team one day and taking our old blue Toyota van. The sliding door came off its track and Chase had to stand and literally hold the door for us girls while we stepped out. I'm sure any observers were laughing hysterically as Chase tried to reattach the door to the side of the van. I remember hearing reports of character coaches getting in trouble at recess for chasing the students because the principal explained that such actions cause "emotionality."

Just as vividly, I remember watching in amazement as God worked in special ways and taught me to trust Him, not just in spiritual or philosophical issues, but to provide for my daily needs. It was my custom each year to begin with a day of training and fellowship for the character coaches. One year I had sent letters to all the character coaches with the details for the day and told them that I would provide pizza for dinner at the end of the training. The only problem was that with the training day falling at the end of summer, and with many of my students taking off a good portion of the summer from piano lessons (my primary source of income), I didn't have enough money to order the pizza. I could have easily changed dinner plans or borrowed money from Mom and Dad, but instead I asked God to provide for that need. The day of training approached and I continued to pray fervently that God would provide the money for me to order pizzas. I couldn't imagine where the money would come from, but I knew God was in control of unlimited resources and could perform what seemed impossible to me.

The week before the training, I received a phone call from Janelle, a young lady I had met when I was overseeing a CF!E booth at a local seminar. She was an elementary school teacher in Wichita and had been using the curriculum with her students. We had become somewhat acquainted with each other, but had been out of touch for quite a while. However, since I was the local contact person for CF!E, she was calling to see if she could order character cards (a set of baseball card-sized collector cards that correspond to the curriculum) for her students for the following year. She already had the curriculum, but just needed 24 sets of cards. It just so happened that I had some extra sets of character cards that I no longer needed, so I ran down to my room, pulled out the notebook that contained them and counted to see how many complete sets I had. As I got to the last sleeve in my notebook, my jaw dropped. 24. I was in shock! I excitedly told Janelle that I had exactly the number of cards she needed and would be able to sell them to her at cost with no shipping charge. She was thrilled and we arranged a day later that week for her to stop by our house and pick them up. At our training day that weekend, I had enough money to order pizzas, but more importantly, I had an incredible story to share of God's provision on our behalf.

Many more memories live on in the hearts of each of us who were a part of CF!E in Derby and I'm sure there are more stories that only God knows. We were a group of homeschoolers, but for five years of our life we went to school together. And boy did we get an education!

Chapter 11

"As difficult as it is for our earth-dwelling hearts to grasp, life is not about the here and the now, about marriage or singleness. It is about glorifying God, giving all we are to Him—starting today, and spilling into all of eternity. That is the heart of Natalie's message."

Jennifer Neef

the journey of my heart

When I was in 2nd grade, I remember "liking" a boy in the 1st grade class. Most of my classmates had their own romantic interests as well. Although it was mostly a topic reserved for whispered conversations, occasionally someone would "leak" the information and the news would quickly spread among the rest of the classmates. This always created an awkward situation and an element of suspense until we found out if the feeling was mutual. If the resulting word was affirmative we breathed a sigh of relief and carried on as normal, relishing the thought that someone "liked" us back. Such knowledge gave a considerable amount of security to our childish hearts, and I found great personal satisfaction in being considered one of the popular ones in the class.

When Mom and Dad began homeschooling us, things began to change. For starters, there were no boys in my class (obviously!). It was just my sisters and me. Even once we became a part of several homeschool support groups, the atmosphere was not very conducive to these games of romance. The activities were more family-oriented in nature. Even if all of us kids were playing as a group, the parents were usually just a room away and the group was comprised of a wide variety of ages. I was one of the older children and was expected to set a good example for the younger ones in the group. I had been accused more than once of being the "teacher's pet" when I was in school, and my desire to present a good image and receive the approval of those in authority had not changed. Even though those authorities now consisted primarily of the moms of the other children in the group, I always strived to make a good impression on them.

Despite the fact that my situation changed outwardly, my romantic little heart was still beating strong within me. Natasha, a girl at our new church whose family joined the church shortly after us, and I quickly became friends. She attended the local Christian school, but her Mom was homeschooling her younger brother and we had a lot in common. I felt like she was the first real friend I had at our new church. At the time we both subscribed to Brio Magazine, a publication of Focus on the Family for teen girls. We spent many nights at each other's houses and wiled away our time taking quizzes to find out what kind of guys we liked or how well we understood members of the opposite sex, reading survey responses guys had given to what they liked in girls, etc. Once the night grew dark, we would hole ourselves up in the bedroom with the lights off and lie in our beds and share the secrets of our heart under the cloak of dark. For some reason, things we might be embarrassed to say in the light of day, we felt safe disclosing when the lights were out. With such pleasant thoughts swirling around in my mind I would eventually drift off to sleep, dreaming, hoping that someday the longings I experienced with such fervency would come true for me.

Over the next couple of years, I went through some emotional struggles. I slowly lost contact with my old friends from school and church, and never connected with most of the kids my age at our new church. Several other families at our new church began homeschooling, but each of them left our church shortly thereafter. Most of them went to another church in town—a church that was filled with homeschool families and even had its own homeschool support group. A girl I knew who attended that church invited me one week to the "bring a friend" night at their AWANA program. Mom and Dad gave me permission to attend with her, and after that Nicole and I both started attending regularly. We loved the competition of memorizing verses and quoting them each week for prizes. Dad had started us on a program of Scripture memorization when we were younger and we had already memorized many verses and passages. Since the rewards were all performance-based and we were good at memorizing quickly, we routinely passed 20 or more sections each night of AWANA. I began the program in my final year—6th grade—and Nicole in 5th grade, so once we finished the books for our respective grades, we were given permission to go back and work through books from the previous years. We both completed all the other books and by the end of the year I had earned the Excellence and the Timothy Awards for completing 4 books. Nicole had to wait until the following year since she wasn't allowed to go ahead. By the end of that year, she had earned both awards as well.

Although we became very involved in the youth programs at that church and shared much in common with the other homeschooled students, at that time we were never fully accepted or allowed to be a part of certain activities since we were not members of the church. On several occasions a couple of my close friends had parties or other get-togethers and then asked me why I had not attended. Then they would recall apologetically that they hadn't invited me. While on the outside I was friendly and cheerful, inwardly I felt rejected and alone. I had no friends. No real friends. Only people who called themselves my friends and then did things to hurt me.

Whenever I was included in a girls' sleepover, though, or hosted one at our house, without fail the topic of conversation would come up and we would discuss in hushed voices "who liked who." Usually information of that nature was traded for a price—an agreement to share equally "juicy" information—and was only given with the strict instructions to not tell anyone else. We always agreed to the arrangement. But of course, at a future date, if we needed a bargaining chip, we would readily renege on our word and trade the information in return for something else we really wanted to know.

The whole game was despicable, really, and I am quite sure that most of our parents had no clue the kinds of attitudes and behaviors that were propagated in such settings. Outwardly every one of us looked like innocent, pure-hearted girls. And by the world's standards, or compared to the things girls our age were being exposed to in a public school environment, we might have still been considered innocent. But we were not pure-hearted. I was not pure-hearted. I adhered to certain standards and didn't engage in certain behaviors, but my heart was far from God.

In spring of 1994 Dad, Nicole, and I traveled to Oklahoma City for a Regional Training Seminar that was being hosted by the ATI, our national homeschool organization. Lisa, a young single lady who was from our area, was traveling with the team of people who were conducting these seminars. She led a session on the importance of having a whole heart for the Lord. I do not remember many specifics, but I remember greatly admiring her, and a part of me longed to have what she had. There was something about her persona, about the way she carried herself, about her countenance that was so attractive. I didn't know any other older girls like that, but I determined that I wanted to be like her someday. This was the beginning of my change of heart. In the months that followed I continued to engage in our silly girlish conversations and I continued to daydream about this or that boy that I liked. But I felt a tug at my heart, an awareness that there was something more, something that I was missing.

The following year our family attended the annual training conference for ATI in Knoxville, Tennessee. Mom and Dad had attended before, but this would be the first time for the rest of the family to be a part of the conference. There were thousands of other homeschoolers there from all over the country! We spent the week sitting in sessions, listening to outstanding speakers like David Barton, Elisabeth Elliot, Roger Magnuson, Bill Gothard, Inge Cannon, and many others. I scribbled away furiously, trying to take good notes and absorb all the exciting messages I was hearing. My heart was burning within me, so to speak, as I heard the Scriptures opened and the truth proclaimed with power and clarity. My heart was being drawn more and more toward this Jesus that I had known of since childhood, and now I was beginning to understand more fully how His presence in my life could change me. Little by little I was falling in love with the One who first loved me.

In the afternoons, the teenagers were bused to a separate location on the university campus where we participated in choir and heard additional speakers. I heard the concept of courtship presented at this conference and a newly married couple shared the story of their own courtship. Rather than being involved in numerous dating relationships during the years leading up to marriage, we were encouraged to be content in our singleness and to spend our unmarried years seeking the Lord and serving Him. Then, at the right time, God would bring the right person and we would get married. In the interim, we (the teenage girls at the conference) were encouraged to entrust our heart to our Dad and let him protect us. If we were approached by interested guys, we could direct them to our Dad in order to receive his permission to court us.

We had never discussed relationship issues much at our house. It never really came up in conversation and bringing up such deep heart issues made me feel too vulnerable. Although the concept of courtship vs. dating and how it would play out in real life was still somewhat vague, I was challenged considerably by the exhortations to serve the Lord wholeheartedly. I left the conference inspired and ignited with a passion and desire to do great things for God. My focus was shifting away from the temporary pleasures of this life and I was getting a vision for doing things that would matter for eternity.

As soon as we returned home, the battle ensued. It was a battle fought deep in the recesses of my heart. And it was often fought in the blackness of the night as I lay upon my bed. The emotions and desires I had so willingly entertained before now paraded themselves into my mind and prepared to dwell there for my dreaming pleasure as I waited for sleep to come. I was tempted to think of this or that guy and to dream up some unrealistic scenario that would set us in the same place at the same time. He would somehow take notice of me or some terrible ill would befall me and he would come to my rescue and we would...like each other. I don't remember ever getting married in my fantasy world. I just wanted to experience the security and the emotional bliss that every girl I know longs for. Strong arms wrapped around me, piercing eyes gazing into my own, deep conversations while walking together—just the two of us. All the stuff of fairy tales and romance novels. Ah yes, romance novels. I was an avid reader and these were my books of choice. I had my favorite Christian authors and series' of books and would lose myself for hours at a time as I was transported to another world—a world where my fantasies were the stuff of reality. As the Lord began to change my heart and redirect my desires, it became apparent that this world of imaginary relationships had to go. But that was much easier said than done.

Nightly I wrestled, as my spirit longed to find rest in Jesus alone, and my flesh sought to pull me into its lustful thoughts. Only by the grace of God did I begin to experience victory as I cried out to Him for help and fought to set my mind instead upon the powerful truth of God's Word. I memorized and repeatedly quoted Colossians 3:2-3, "Set your affection on things above, not on things on the earth. For ye are dead and your life is hid with Christ in God." In fact, this became my "life verse," the motto by which I tried to live every day. In my fight for purity of heart and mind, I became convinced that it was critical for me to guard more zealously the input I was feeding myself. For this reason, I completely gave up reading any romance novels or historical fiction novels that incorporated elements of romance. I knew that those stories only fed my fleshly desires and did little to draw me closer to the Lord. I replaced those books with biographies of great Christian men and women like George Muller, Adoniram and Ann Judson, Jim and Elisabeth Elliot, Amy Carmichael, William Borden, and many others. These fed my growing hunger to know the Lord more fully and it was thrilling to see His hand at work in the lives of real people throughout history.

It was during this same time that the Lord saw fit to remove most of my friends from my life so that I felt like I had no close friend, no one in whom I could really confide or with whom I could share my secrets. My whole life I had been very peer-dependent. Even after we began homeschooling and spent more time at home as a family, I considered it very important to have friends—friends outside my family. I wanted to go to their houses and do stuff with them. I wanted to be invited to parties and to be considered popular. But now I found myself with no one. As hard and lonely as this was, it was exactly what I needed. I was learning that Jesus was my best friend, the One who would never leave me or forsake me, the One who was sufficient to meet all of my needs. He became the source of my fulfillment and joy. I learned, like Paul, that the secret of contentment is not found in a particular state of being, but in a very personal relationship with the Lord Jesus Christ.

In the fall of 1996 I helped work at the book table for Josh Harris' *New Attitude* conference in Wichita. Josh spoke boldly against the popular dating culture among young people and challenged us to find our identity in Christ and "die" to the things of the world. He gave both philosophical and practical ideas for dealing with relationship issues and I found myself more excited than ever to be part of this youth movement that was passionately seeking and serving the Lord. I began reading books on the topic of courtship, beginning with one by Ned and Drew Ryun called, *It's A Lifestyle*. And as soon as it came off the press, I devoured Josh Harris' *I Kissed Dating Goodbye*.

These were followed by many others—both books about courtship and relationships, and books by couples sharing the story of their own courtship. Eventually I felt like I had a good grasp of what courtship was (probably because I had exhausted every book then available on the subject!). But far more importantly, God had brought me to a point where I was experiencing firsthand the heart behind the whole concept of courtship. At this point in my life, it wasn't even about how I would handle romantic relationships or how I would find someone to marry. It was about loving the Lord with all my heart, with all my soul, with all my mind, and with all my strength. It was about being committed to Him and trusting Him fully to meet my deepest needs. It was about pouring my life out in service to Him from a heart overflowing with love for Him and all that He gave and did on my behalf. My life was literally being transformed. But it was just the beginning.

A year later Dad, Nicole, and I traveled to Indianapolis for a week-long seminar. In the course of the week, there were numerous speakers and various issues were addressed. But two things that week changed my life. The first was a session on "Loving Jesus." Whether it was taking walks with Jesus, writing Him love letters, or talking to others about Him, we were challenged to actively cultivate a relationship with Him. I found myself asking, "Do I really love Jesus more than anything else in my life?" "How do I express that love?" The rest of the week, I got up very early every morning, while the other girls in my room were still asleep, and I sat on the tile floor in the bathroom and spent time alone with Jesus. I was opening my heart to Him in a way I never had before. And He was opening Himself to me through the pages of Scripture in a way I had never experienced before. I began to see Him in every Scripture passage I read and my love for Him grew more and more.

As a result of the teaching I was receiving and the work the Lord was doing in my heart, I decided to make a commitment to remain unmarried for the following four years. I wanted to focus wholeheartedly on the Lord and invest my time and energy in service to Him. I shared this decision with Dad and he gave his approval and blessing. I won't pretend that it was an easy decision. After all, I was almost 17 and would be almost 21 by the time the four years had passed. Always before I had presumed that I would be married around the age of 20. But now I was setting aside that desire, giving it up for a season in order to be wholly devoted to Him. I had no idea what the next four years would hold, but there was no going back. I had made this commitment and I was determined, by the grace of God, to fulfill it.

There was one more thing the Lord needed to teach me that week in order to purify me and prepare me for a life of wholehearted service to Him. And it was without question the hardest thing I've ever been through in my spiritual life. But at the same time, it is the thing that has given me the most freedom, that has most contributed to my relationship with my parents and siblings, and that has given me the confidence to live boldly as a Christian. The teaching I received that changed my life was the principle of a clear conscience. One of the speakers at the seminar that week spoke on what it meant to have a clear conscience and the importance of maintaining a clear conscience before God and man. We were especially encouraged to make sure that we were not hiding things from our parents. God placed our parents in authority over us to protect us, and if we are moving out from under their authority by doing things we shouldn't do or hiding sinful behaviors from them, it will affect our relationship with the Lord. My heart burned within me as I heard these words. Immediately I thought of several things I had done when I was younger that were sinful and that I had hidden from my parents to avoid punishment or the shame associated with those behaviors. Now their memory was vivid in my mind and I felt the pressure of the Holy Spirit upon me, urging me to confess those sins.

I spent considerable time praying, asking the Lord for forgiveness and hoping that that would be enough to clear my conscience. But my feelings of guilt and conviction only grew stronger. I fought with every ounce of my flesh against it. Dad was just down the hall in his room, but I was sure I could never bring myself to tell him what I had done. What would he think of me? What would he say?

As I spent time with the Lord, though, it became apparent that I would not be able to experience true fellowship with Him as long as I continued to harbor these hidden sins in my prideful heart. That was what was really at stake here. My pride. It would take a huge dose of humility for me to confess these sins to Dad and ask for his forgiveness. And I was not a humble person. In fact, it was rare for me to ever even acknowledge if I made a mistake or was wrong. I was more apt to insist on my rightness in the face of obvious evidence to the contrary than admit that I was actually wrong. I wanted everyone to think the best of me, and to only praise me and the work I did. Criticism was never received graciously. God obviously saw these ugly character flaws in me and was at work to replace them with the humble and meek character of Jesus Christ. But I was resisting Him with all the strength I could muster.

Thankfully, though, God's grace is enough to overcome the hardest and most stubborn of hearts. You see, the Lord had birthed in me a desire so great to be close to Him and to enjoy an intimate, personal relationship with Him that ultimately I could not bear the thought of something dwelling between us and keeping us apart—and that something was my sin. Those secret sins that I had kept carefully and masterfully hidden for years. Now God was requiring me to bring them into the open, to lay them before Dad and to ask his forgiveness.

My resolve grew firm, and with a conflicted heart I made my way down the hall to Dad's room. I don't know how I made it there, or how I convinced my trembling hand to knock on his door, or how my voice uttered the words I had resolved to say, but that day will forever be etched in my mind. After I had poured out my wretched heart to Dad, he looked at me lovingly, said that of course he forgave me, and then gave me a hug. Tears were pouring down my face by this time as the emotional struggle within overflowed. Immediately my heart was flooded with peace; peace that comes only from the Lord, only from knowing that I had done what He required of me and that my fellowship with Him was restored. I breathed a sigh of relief and made my way back to my room where I collapsed in exhaustion on my bed. I felt very sure that a battle had been fought over my soul that day, and God had emerged the triumphant victor!

One of the most destructive sins I had been harboring was bitterness toward Dad. The seeds had been planted years ago in numerous ways—some sown by Dad, some by Mom, and some by myself. Ultimately, though, they were the seeds of Satan—seeds that were designed to kill and destroy. And that they had. They had destroyed my relationship with Dad. My heart was hard and unloving. I resented him and almost everything he did. I couldn't see any of his good qualities because I was too intent on everything I couldn't stand about him. My deep bitterness had clouded my vision and blown the truth way out of proportion. When I confessed this sin to Dad it was not out of a changed heart, but out of obedience. Having been completely unaware of this bitterness, Dad asked what he had done that had caused it. I was able to share some of my hurts with him—times when I felt like his priorities were wrong, or like he cared more about carrying out his own plans than developing a relationship with me. He responded graciously and took it all in without defending or excusing himself. His humble, loving response was the beginning of a new relationship between us. I began to pray fervently that God would cleanse me of my bitterness and replace it with a love for Dad. I began to pray *for* Dad—that he would be a godly spiritual leader in our family and that God would strengthen him in that role. Little by little my heart continued to change and the Lord began to turn my heart more and more toward Dad. Now I can say that I love him without reserve and am so incredibly grateful to have him not only as my earthly father, but also as my wise counselor and friend.

In the year that followed, the Lord took me through an intense time of gaining and maintaining a clear conscience. He brought other things to mind and I was compelled time after time to repeat the process of that day in Indianapolis. Mom and Dad both became the regular recipients of my confessions. While it was clear to me that this was not for the purpose of granting me forgiveness for these sins—that could be done only by the Lord—still the Lord impressed upon me the need for continuing this process. Looking back I see how vital that year was for imparting to me sensitivity to the Lord's direction so that I might act in accordance with His Word and ways. At the same time, He was teaching me the importance of humbling myself daily before Him. Plus, as I've often said since, there is no greater motivation to not sin willfully than knowing that if I do the Lord will make me confess it to someone and ask their forgiveness afterward! My poor family patiently endured with me during that year as I often found myself going back to them and asking their forgiveness for things that indeed seemed trivial. At times I think I would have rather been martyred for my faith, but this was the path God called me to walk and out of love for Him I pressed on.

It was these two areas—purifying my desires and affections, and gaining a clear conscience—that God used to transform my life from the inside out. Although the lessons were first learned in the context of vivid experiences, their impact was realized in the realities of daily life. I will never claim mastery this side of heaven, but I can attest to the incredible power of God at work within me, enabling me to conquer sinful behaviors that once mastered me. I find myself often echoing this quote of J. Hudson Taylor's:

"Oh, it is joy to feel Jesus living in you; to find your heart all taken up by Him; to be reminded of His love by His seeking communion with you at all times, not by your painful attempts to abide in Him. He is our life, our strength, our salvation...He is our power for service and fruit-bearing, and His bosom is our resting place now and forever."

Chapter 12

"The secular, feminist culture in which we live plagues most women with confusion and uncertainty about their role identities. Natalie is an exception to this phenomenon. Christ's Sovereign Lordship replaced a striving, competitive spirit with a contented heart that seeks to please the Lord and help make others successful. This process occurred over numerous years in a precious Christian homeschool family. Each of our family members are ever sharpened by Natalie's example to embrace her God-given roles with zeal, honor, and joyfulness. Her parents' lives challenge us to the same. *Pajama School* captures how the Lord graciously transforms His people within the lifestyle of a home educated family."

Sherri Hayden

confronting *feminism*

Mom grew up with a lot of feminist leanings. They weren't necessarily overt, but there was an underlying attitude of being able to do just as much as a man. And she was determined to prove it. She was on her way to becoming a doctor when she met and married Dad. And from there on out things began to change. I was born two years later and Mom became a full-time homemaker. Even though her status changed at once, it would be a much longer process for her heart to change. And in many ways it's a process that we have gone through together.

I was a tom-boy from an early age. Mom wasn't a big "doll person," so she never encouraged us girls to play with dolls either. Instead, our toy tubs were well-stocked with Legos, Lincoln Logs, cars and building blocks. We received a few dolls over the years, but they went largely uncared for, except for on those occasions when we had friends over who wanted to play dolls. By the time I started school I loved competition, and recess time found me on the soccer field with all the boys while the girls sat in the sand and built "nests" upon which they perched while waiting for their little ones to "hatch." The thought of joining them made me gag. Why would I do something silly like that when I could be playing soccer?

The boys and I (and occasionally another girl) would line up on the soccer field and appoint captains to choose the teams. I played as hard as I could during our games and took great satisfaction in being chosen before the boys. I always wanted to be the best. I always wanted to prove that I was just as good as the boys. Maybe even better. The competition was no less intense in the classroom as I competed to be not only the best, but also the fastest. But the competition was fierce. My small class of students was comprised entirely of firstborns and most of them were just as determined as me to prove that they were the best. To flaunt our success, whichever of us was the first to complete a particular assignment would loudly slam our pencil on the surface of our desk, causing the rest of the class to look up and see who had obviously finished their work first.

Once we started homeschooling, the outlet for this competitive streak became our support group activities. During our P.E. classes, Nicole and I were always competing against the boys in the group—seeing who could run the fastest, who could kick or hit the ball the farthest, or who could do the most push-ups. And when we won, we would rub it in and take great pride in our accomplishments. For some reason the boys never seemed as interested in competing against us as we were in competing with them. At the time we couldn't understand why.

During the years that we were part of a youth group, the guys and a few girls would gather before the meeting started and play basketball on a single rim at the back of the church parking lot. I didn't know a thing about how to play basketball and I've always been a terrible shot, but I was very aggressive and could often steal the ball. This earned me many compliments and slaps on the back. And that was what I lived for. I wanted to be accepted by the guys, and for them to think that I was just as good as them. I even went through a period of time where I hated the fact that I was a girl and wished repeatedly that God would have made me a boy. No matter how hard I wished, though, there was no changing who I was, so I pressed on in my determination to at least prove myself to the guys around me. Whether it was soccer, basketball, or football, the biggest compliment in my mind was if someone would say, "Wow, you play as good as a boy!"

I remember one of the highlights during this time of my life. I registered to attend camp with the youth group one summer and one of the guys initiated an arm-wrestling tournament that would take place on the way out there. It was a long bus ride to camp and the tournament would be conducted both on the buses as we traveled and at the places we stopped along the way. I loved arm-wrestling and could hardly wait! The day of our departure arrived and the tournament commenced. I slowly worked my way up the brackets in my division until finally I arrived at the top. There was one guy who was undefeated, and the two of us faced off. He was noticeably nervous, as was I. It was a hard-fought struggle, but in the end he won. Nevertheless, my name went down that summer as "the girl who almost beat Brock arm-wrestling." Surely now I would have the admiration of the guys, I surmised.

I think a number of factors contributed to this competitive, even feminist, spirit within me—Mom's own feminist leanings, Dad's competitive nature and his instillation of the same in us girls, the fact that since we were a family of girls we were frequently called upon to perform the tasks often reserved for the boys in the family, and the acceptance and encouragement of these competitive relationships between boys and girls in our peer groups. Perhaps there are other factors as well, but one thing I now know—it is certainly not a spirit promoted by the Bible.

This understanding of the differing roles between men and women is something that should have seemed perfectly normal and natural to me. After all, I've grown up in a conservative Christian family, attended church regularly all my life, sat through hours of sermons and seminar lectures, attended numerous conferences, and spent hours reading and studying the Bible. But somehow it all slipped through the cracks of my independent heart. I, albeit unconsciously, embraced egalitarianism and despised femininity. Because of my strong personality and take-charge attitude, I was often placed in positions of leadership. Sometimes I sought these out; other times they were bestowed upon me or I gradually assumed such a position. Instead of having a submissive and gracious spirit, I tried to control the people and details under my responsibility and "ran over" anyone who was uncooperative. Even in my godly desire to serve the Lord wholeheartedly, I was often driven by a desire to be the leader, the one who would change the world through all my heroic acts.

As I observed the beautiful and feminine lives of other godly women and became more aware of what the Bible had to say about His design for women, the Lord began to change my heart. Mom, too, made efforts to prepare us girls for the responsibilities of being wives and mothers someday. We had always had certain responsibilities around the house, but she expanded these to include doing meal planning and preparation, grocery shopping, cooking and cleaning. I actually loved ironing and spent hours ironing clothes while listening to messages on CDs. Mom trained us in the fine art of hospitality, primarily by example.

Our house has always been a constant flurry of activity. We live on a corner in a centrally located neighborhood and people stop by all the time for various reasons. Especially now, with both Dad and myself running small businesses from our house, we have people in and out all the time. Mom welcomes them all with warmth and friendliness, often setting aside her own work to visit with them and lend a listening ear. Young and old alike enjoy coming to our home, and many have commented on how much they love being there. I credit this to the great care Mom has taken to make it inviting and peaceful. She replaced her former dreams and aspirations with her God-informed role of wife, mother, and homeschool teacher. Mom's life, more than anything, has given me a sense of what my role as a woman should be.

After those years of intentional training in homemaking, I began to move into other areas of responsibility as the Lord opened new doors of opportunity. I still lived at home, but I found myself pulled in many different directions while still trying earnestly to seek the Lord and remain under my parents' authority. I became absorbed in my own responsibilities and projects and didn't have as much of a heart for my family or for being a part of the household operations. I found myself more and more in positions of leadership and enjoyed the sense of self-worth and fulfillment they brought me. But I continued to grow in my relationship with the Lord and spend time in His Word daily, seeking to apply it to my life. In the summer of 2005, the Lord began a deeper transformation of my heart.

Inspired by Crystal and Caleb, two friends who were avid bloggers, I joined the growing blogosphere and began to read a variety of blogs. I found my thinking challenged on numerous fronts. In December of that year, I read the book, *So Much More*, by Anna Sofia Botkin and Elizabeth Botkin, and was further challenged to view our modern culture through a biblical lens. I was compelled to think about societal conventions that I had previously taken for granted. Did God really intend for men and women to fill distinctly different roles in society—even in our day and age? Is it true that God's design is for men to primarily be the leaders and women the helpers? To even ask the questions caused my throat to constrict. This was hard to swallow.

The other thing that became evident to me was that in my determined efforts to suppress all my romantic inclinations and serve the Lord whole-heartedly, I had learned to reject my desire for marriage. It seemed to me that my desire for marriage was wrong and should be immediately recognized as such and disposed of as quickly as possible. Marriage was good for many of my friends who were getting married, but it was obviously wrong for me at this time in my life, so I must not even entertain thoughts of it. Clearly my emotional pendulum had swung extremely out of balance and now God was bringing me back to the center. During this time, I was reminded of the importance of family and was infused with a greater desire than ever to be a blessing to my own family and to take time to invest in the lives of my siblings. God had intentionally placed each of them in my life, and yet in my zeal to make a difference in the world, I was overlooking opportunities to make a difference in the lives of those closest to me.

The following summer, as I continued to ponder these new things I was learning, I found myself growing confused. Had I been heading the wrong direction all this time? If my desire to be a wife and a mother some day was of the Lord, should I be doing things differently to prepare for that role? With these questions in mind, and prompted by a request from my good friend Lydia to write a guest post for her blog on the topic of girls going to college, I began an in-depth search of the Scriptures to see what God had to say about these issues that face unmarried girls. While I valued both my own experiences and the experiences others shared with me pertaining to the questions at hand, I realized that I could not base my life and my decisions on such subjective criteria. Two people encountering the same situation could experience opposite results. I realized that this would result in a precarious foundation and I could not hope to maintain any semblance of stability or consistency if experience alone was my standard. So, I began my study with the presupposition that God's Word contained the answers to my questions about my role as an unmarried woman and would be my absolute standard. I committed to altering my lifestyle in whatever ways necessary to align myself with what God revealed in the course of my study.

As I prayed and sought the Lord, one night an analogy embedded itself in my mind...

The young woman carefully folded another shirt and placed it in the open suitcase. As she did so, the brightly-colored fabric of another shirt caught her eye. She eased it out from its sandwiched position and held it up for reconsideration. Did she really need it? She had to admit, it didn't seem quite as necessary now as when she had packed it a year ago. After a moment of intense internal debate, she folded it up and placed it back in the suitcase. After all, she might need it once she got there. There. She didn't know exactly where "there" was; nevertheless, there was no telling what she might need once she got... there. Might as well pack it all. She wanted everything to be just perfect when the time came.

She glanced at the four other suitcases surrounding her and carefully went back through each one, inspecting its contents and re-arranging it until it satisfied her. She had spent countless hours ac-quiring, packing and rearranging the items in each suitcase. As she closed the last suitcase, she emitted a hopeful sigh. She'd been at this packing business for many years and she was ready. The exciting possi-bilities raced through her mind again. She could hardly wait! Some-day—perhaps someday soon—she would finally get to go...there.

A look in the opposite direction illuminated another young woman as she hurried out the door. A moment later she reappeared—just to grab a handful of forgotten items before disappearing once again, leaving behind only the echo of the door as it slammed shut behind her. Later that night, her steps were considerably slower as she wearily reentered the room and collapsed in exhaustion onto her bed. Her room was in disarray and her thoughts were ten times more so as she drifted off to sleep. She didn't even notice as her dan-gling arm brushed across the thick layer of dust coating the top of her suitcase that had long ago been shoved out of sight under her bed. Perhaps she would need it someday, but there was no use worrying about it now. She was just too busy for that kind of thing.

One final gaze fixed itself upon a third young woman as she picked up a few odds and ends that had gotten out of place in her otherwise tidy area. As she returned them to their rightful spot, her eyes fell on the suitcase sitting inconspicuously toward the side of the room. A thought occurred to her and she quickly jotted it down on the travel checklist she kept handily stored in a drawer of her desk. As she looked over the growing list, she smiled contentedly and with a twinge of anticipation. She wanted to be ready for her trip—when-ever the day should happen to arrive. But until then, she had plenty of other things to occupy her time and energy. She must remain focused and faithful in what she had been called to do for the present time. With that thought on her mind, she replaced the list, gathered the necessary items and left the room, carefully closing the door behind her as she set about to carry on the duties of the day.

It was an imperfect analogy, to be sure, but it was a scenario that seemed to sum up the contrasting approaches to life embodied by most unmarried women today. The anticipated trip represented the probable future marriage and the suitcase and its contents represented the responsibilities of a married woman. Most of us who find ourselves in this position are bombarded with advice on all sides: "Make a difference in the world while you're single." "Pursue your dreams." "You must go to college if you want to be successful in life." "Focus on learning to be a keeper at home." "Find a ministry opportunity where you can serve others." "Get a good job so you can support yourself." "You always need something you can fall back on...just in case."

As I pondered the analogy and its implications, I found myself anxious to dig into Scripture and see what treasures I could uncover. I was more curious than ever to know what God had to say about unmarriage. For the purposes of my study, I couldn't settle on a "real" word to capture what I meant, so I coined my own—unmarriage—and defined it as "the state prior to entering a marriage covenant but beyond the time when a young woman is considered a child."

I pulled out my Bible and concordance and quickly set to work, looking up every passage, example or illustration that pertained specifically to women. I was actually quite taken aback by what I found. Almost every passage addressed to women is addressing *married* women. Profound, I know. Seriously, though, I was struck by the significance of this discovery. It reaffirmed an important truth that I was just beginning to grasp: marriage is normative. It is God's design for women to marry. God specifically created woman (Eve) to be married to man (Adam). This was God's design from the beginning. All the teachings about and examples of women throughout Scripture reinforce this truth.

I knew there were families and individuals who referenced this Scriptural pattern to advocate that every *unmarried* woman should devote her time and energy to preparing to be a *married* woman. While I understood the importance of daughters developing a submissive spirit, living under the authority of their fathers, and acquiring the skills necessary to run a household, I wasn't convinced that this specific application was truly a biblical pattern. I wasn't sure whether the probability of marriage deemed it necessary for a young woman to devote her years of unmarriage primarily, let alone exclusively, to developing those areas determined to be necessary for that future role.

In my analogy, this was akin to the young woman who spent years consumed by her preparations for a trip she assumed she would take, but didn't know when or to what locale. How could an unmarried woman possibly know how to prepare for marriage to a man yet unknown at a time yet undetermined? For while it is *normative* that a woman will marry, it is not *certain*. And for many, including me, many years would fill the gap between the time of childhood and entry into a marriage relationship. This led me to question the wisdom of setting forth marriage preparation as the primary motivation for the development of skills or the carrying out of daily responsibilities. On top of that, it is obvious that there is a great deal of uncertainty regarding the particular details of each marriage. How could an unmarried woman be sure that she was preparing appropriately for her future marriage?

Is it possible, I wondered, for an unmarried woman to be adequately prepared for marriage? Indeed! Not only is it possible, it is essential. But I came to see from my study of Scripture that the best preparation is not necessarily that which requires the *unmarried* woman to assume the responsibilities set forth for a *married* woman.

Astute observers will quickly agree that our society advocates a completely different approach to the question of the role of unmarried women. There is rampant disregard for God's unique design of the sexes, even in the church, and young women are encouraged to pursue the same course as their male counterparts. This could be neatly summarized as follows: complete twelve years of primary education, attend college and earn at least one degree, enter the workforce and climb the corporate ladder, make enough money so you can live comfortably and spend your latter days basking in the return from your gilded retirement nest egg. Somewhere along the way, meet the man or woman of your dreams, fall in love, and get married (if you so choose). Following the honeymoon, life will carry on "as it were," as you and your spouse continue pursuing your own ambitions, with household duties now equally divided between the two of you. Should children be deemed desirable at some point, the socially preferred one boy and one girl will be attempted for and, barring complications, will be added to the family picture for the duration of their first 18 years of life, excepting, of course, the 25,000+ hours they will spend in daycares and educational institutions outside the home. Meanwhile, the career-driven woman will spend her days running the proverbial "rat race," a continuation of all the goals and dreams she set out to reach as a young unmarried woman.

This is akin to the weary woman in my analogy who ran herself ragged in the busy activity of life, never giving thought to the future responsibilities of marriage, let alone preparing for such. Without any consideration for the teaching of Scripture, she merely set out to follow the course commonly practiced and encouraged by our present society. Independence is supreme. Though the woman gets married, it is little more than a social nicety. She continues to pursue her own goals and interests while her husband pursues his. Indeed, her total lack of thought and preparation prepared her perfectly for everything a marriage should not be.

I knew that this was far from the life I wanted to embrace, and essentially these two mentalities presented opposite extremes. Was there a balance between the two or would I learn that one of these, indeed, was God's design? I found that there is only one place where the Bible specifically addresses the situation of the unmarried woman in contrast to that of the married woman. I was challenged to carefully consider the words of Paul in 1 Corinthians 7:34-35, "There is a **difference** also between a wife and a virgin. The **unmarried** woman careth for the things of the Lord, that she may be holy both in body and in spirit: but she that is **married** careth for the things of the world, how she may please her husband. And this I speak for your own profit; not that I may cast a snare upon you, but for that which is comely, and that ye may attend upon the Lord without distraction."

Paul identifies a deliberate distinction between the focus and duty of the unmarried woman and that of the married woman. It was enlightening to discover that the words "difference" and "careth" come from the same Greek root. It is as though Paul was categorically separating the married from the unmarried by defining their unique roles. In other words, God has not equally bestowed the same roles and responsibilities upon all women, regardless of their matrimonial state. Married women have specific roles and responsibilities *because* they are married. Unmarried women have specific roles and responsibilities *because* they are unmarried.

This Biblical distinction is the premise upon which an unmarried woman should evaluate and base her decisions. Her primary focus must be on "the things of the Lord." This primary focus will lead her to live a life of holiness in body and in spirit because she is seeking to serve and please the Lord in whatever endeavor He may lead her. If her primary focus is on preparing for a husband, she will become discontent with being unmarried, which Paul proscribes—he wants the unmarried woman free from the expectations and duties of those who are married, so that she may "attend upon the Lord without distraction."

The crux of the issue for me was the acknowledgement that God is Sovereign and He alone knows what the future holds. Therefore, He alone is uniquely able to prepare me, or any unmarried woman, for what her future holds. Rather than dogmatically insisting that an unmarried woman should only be engaged in certain pursuits, young women should be encouraged to pursue "the things of the Lord." This will mean a different direction for different women—based not upon her own desires, or the changing philosophies of the world, but upon biblical principles and the personal leading of the Lord in her life as He molds her into the godly woman that He desires. I realized that this was, in fact, what the Lord had been doing and what Mom and Dad had been encouraging for years. Periodically I would approach them and ask if I was fulfilling their expectations for my involvement in the family and in the household duties. Without fail they expressed appreciation for my efforts and encouraged me to continue seeking the Lord and serving in various capacities as He led.

I realized the incredible blessing God had given me in Mom and Dad, and began to see more fully how their training had prepared me for a life of obedience and faithful service to the Lord. Although they have certainly made mistakes, I learned, just like Solomon expressed so many years ago, that the instruction I received from Mom and Dad served as a light to guide me in the way the Lord wanted me to go. ("My son, keep thy father's commandment, and forsake not the law of thy mother: Bind them continually upon thine heart, and tie them about thy neck. When thou goest, it shall lead thee; when thou sleepest, it shall keep thee; and when thou awakest, it shall talk with thee. For the commandment is a lamp; and the law is light; and reproofs of instruction are the way of life" Proverbs 6:20-23.)

The unmarried woman described by Paul can be related to the young woman who was mindful of the probability of a future trip and made notes in preparation for such. It would be wise for an unmarried woman to carefully observe the examples—both positive and negative—of those around her and learn from them. This principle is soberly portrayed in Proverbs 24:30-32. After observing the field of the slothful and its state of disrepair, the writer notes, "Then I saw, and considered it well: I looked upon it, and received instruction." Many little nuggets of wisdom can be gleaned by carefully observing the lives of others and viewing them in light of Scripture. Years ago I started keeping a small journal in which I record specific principles and ideas that I've gleaned from observing others in situations in which I anticipate that I might find myself at some point in the future—from courtship, to marriage, to parenting, etc. I have referenced it on numerous occasions and hope that it will continue to provide helpful reminders in the years ahead.

Now that I felt like I had a better understanding that my primary role as an unmarried woman is to care for "the things of the Lord," the next step was to find out what those "things" are. There are two examples given in Scripture that give special light to the meaning of this phrase. The first is found in a brief exchange between Jesus and Martha in her home.

"Now it came to pass, as they went, that he entered into a certain village: and a certain woman named Martha received him into her house. And she had a sister called Mary, which also sat at Jesus' feet, and heard his word. But Martha was cumbered about much serving, and came to him, and said, Lord, dost thou not care that my sister hath left me to serve alone? Bid her therefore that she help me. And Jesus answered and said unto her, Martha, Martha, thou art **careful** and troubled about many things: But only one thing is needful: and Mary hath chosen that good part, which shall not be taken away from her" (Luke 10:38-42).

It's not that it's wrong to be hospitable and to serve your guests. It's just that that was not what Jesus wanted Martha to be doing with her time right then. I was fascinated to discover that the Greek word for "cumbered" is the same one Paul used with the negative participle in 1 Corinthians 7 when he said he spoke these words so that the unmarried might "attend upon the Lord **without distraction**." Additionally, the word "careful" that Jesus used is rooted in the same Greek word as Paul used when he discussed what things the married and the unmarried "careth" for. Martha was distracted from attending to the Lord because she was caring for other responsibilities. Mary, on the other hand, had her focus right. She "sat at Jesus' feet and heard His word." Though we do not know for sure whether Mary was married or not, the example she provides perfectly complements the teaching of Paul in 1 Corinthians.

The proverbial light bulb went on in my mind as the perfection of God's plan became clear to me. He has intentionally provided the time of unmarriage for young people so that they can sit at Jesus' feet and hear His Word. He knows that there will come a time once they are married when they will not have the freedom to devote the same amount of time to such intense study and undivided focus. It will be their responsibility to care for the things of the world—how they may please their husband or wife, and eventually, their growing family. However, a foundation will have been laid during their unmarried years to adequately prepare them for this change in role and responsibility. It was a sobering thought as I concluded that we do ourselves and our future marriages a great disservice if we squander our time of unmarriage in ways that distract us from caring for "the things of the Lord."

The second example I turned to was Acts 18:24-25, the only other place in the Bible where the exact phrase, "the things of the Lord" is used.

"And a certain Jew named Apollos, born at Alexandria, an eloquent man, and mighty in the scriptures, came to Ephesus. This man was instructed in the way of the LORD; and being fervent in the spirit, he spake and taught diligently **the things of the LORD**, knowing only the baptism of John."

It was obviously the Scriptures that were the source of Apollos' teachings. The word "mighty," upon closer inspection, indicated that the Scriptures were rooted within him as a source of power. Apollos was not merely passing on second-hand information. He knew the Scriptures by heart. No doubt, this is why he was able to quickly transition to preaching Christ as the fulfillment of Scriptural prophecies when he was further instructed by Aquila and Priscilla. He was a humble student of the Scriptures and a very effective teacher of truth.

"The things of the Lord," then, are to be found in the Word of God, the written pages of Scripture, and the Person of Jesus Christ ("the Word made flesh"), as we sit at His feet and spend time with Him. I came to understand my primary responsibility as an unmarried woman as that of caring for "the things of the Lord." Thus, every decision with which I was faced should be considered in light of whether it would assist me in fulfilling this responsibility, or distract me from it.

Based upon what I had learned, a summary of my role and focus in life emerged: "Grow in my knowledge and understanding of Scripture and in my relationship with Jesus Christ." It almost seemed simplistic, but other Bible verses quickly came to mind, confirming that this understanding was consistent with the rest of Scripture. True success is found in delighting in, meditating upon, and obeying the Word of God.

"This book of the law shall not depart out of thy mouth; but thou shalt meditate therein day and night, that thou mayest observe to do according to all that is written therein: for then thou shalt make thy way prosperous, and then thou shalt have good success" (Joshua 1:8).

"Blessed is the man that walketh not in the counsel of the ungodly, nor standeth in the way of sinners, nor sitteth in the seat of the scornful. But his delight is in the law of the LORD; and in his law doth he meditate day and night. And he shall be like a tree planted by the rivers of water, that bringeth forth his fruit in his season; his leaf also shall not wither; and whatsoever he doeth shall prosper" (Psalm 1:1-3).

"Seek ye first the kingdom of God, and his righteousness; and all these things shall be added unto you" (Matthew 6:33).

This priority of the Word of God had to be effectively developed in my life because I knew that it would serve as a solid foundation for the years and responsibilities to come. I knew that the more I engrafted the Word of God into my heart, the more its transforming power would be reflected in my life. My decisions and choice of activities would be influenced not as much by my own desires, but more and more by the wisdom and ways of God as it enveloped my mind and became the expression of my heart's desire. It sounded like such a beautiful concept, but again a question propelled me to the pages of Scripture. How could this truly become a reality in my life?

As I read Proverbs 3:3 one day, I was struck by this thought—we have the capacity to write things upon our heart. "Let not mercy and truth forsake thee: bind them about thy neck; write them upon the table of thine heart."

As I pondered how this writing takes place, I thought of how we receive information through our senses, through what we see/read, hear, smell, etc. The phrase, "know it by heart" came to mind. When we know something "by heart" it is no longer necessary to receive the input from an outside source. It has been received and written upon the heart and can be recalled from the memory within. It dawned on me that this is why it is so critical to guard ourselves from input that is contrary to God's Word, and to fill our heart instead with what is true and pure. Of course, I couldn't just isolate myself from the world around me and all the unsolicited input that is contrary to God's Word. That is why we are exhorted to be "Casting down imaginations, and every high thing that exalteth itself against the knowledge of God, and bringing into captivity every thought to the obedience of Christ" (2 Corinthians 10:5). I realized that I had a very real responsibility to guard my mind and to be constantly aware of ideas, philosophies, and beliefs that might seep in unexpectedly and lead me astray.

I became even more convinced of the great danger that exists when we willfully subject ourselves to vast amounts of input that is contrary to God's Word. Whether it is done in the name of entertainment (such as watching movies), or attaining higher education (such as attending college), or out of some fabricated sense of deserving personal pleasure (such as reading romance novels); I was challenged to be much more selective about the input I allowed into my mind. There are many subtle philosophies that could easily slip past an overloaded or lazy mind and become lodged within my heart. The Bible makes it clear that I have to be sober and vigilant because "[my] adversary, the devil, as a roaring lion, walketh about, seeking whom he may devour" (1 Peter 5:8). The warning was clear—I could not afford to let my guard down even for a moment! Instead, I had to make a deliberate and conscientious choice to meditate on the Word of the Lord day and night—to read it, to study it, to memorize it, to ponder it—for this, above all, is what God desires from me.

I concluded my study with a sense of awe and excitement at the things

I had learned. I once again embraced my years of unmarriage as a unique time, a precious gift from the Lord. I committed myself anew to caring for "the things of the Lord"—understanding more fully that it was not only for my own well-being, but for the well-being of my future marriage and the generations of children that I pray will come after me. As I studied and learned, the Lord wooed me and drew my heart back to Himself.

The Lord renewed my love for His Word and instilled in me an excitement for His calling upon my life—both my present life of unmarried service to Him and the hope of a fruitful marriage in the future. He reminded me to trust Him and lean not on my own understanding, knowing that He will fully prepare me for marriage or any other future responsibilities by guiding me each day to invest my time and energy in those things He wants me to do. He affirmed the importance of honoring Mom and Dad, striving to be a blessing to them as their daughter and to seek their counsel and input before making decisions or pursuing new interests. I may be an adult, but I am still a daughter and a sister. I am part of a family, and it is in and through and because of my family that I can most effectively bless and serve others and advance the kingdom of God.

"Know therefore this day, and consider it in thine heart, that the LORD he is God in heaven above, and upon the earth beneath: there is none else. Thou shalt keep therefore his statutes, and his commandments, which I command thee this day, that it may go well with thee, and with thy children after thee, and that thou mayest prolong thy days upon the earth, which the LORD thy God giveth thee, for ever" (Deuteronomy 4:39-40).

As I look back over the course of my life thus far, I take great comfort in seeing that God is relentless in His pursuit of my heart and mind. He is constantly teaching me new things, reforming my thinking, and transforming my behavior. Perhaps that is one of the greatest things that I have learned—God's educational program for me will continue until my last breath. How blessed we are who call Him our Teacher and ourselves His students!

Chapter 13

"Some of my fondest memories involve serving beside my dear friend Natalie in various local homeschool ministry opportunities. Natalie truly captures the essence of the homeschooling experience through her humorous, yet touching recollections of the times we had as young homeschool graduates growing and learning countless lessons together."

Myklin Vinson

in which I serve tea and solve mysteries

By the time I turned sixteen I was involved in a variety of work experiences. The library had asked me to apply for a job there since I had been a reliable volunteer and was now old enough for a part-time position. Neither Mom and Dad nor I thought that it was something I should pursue at the time, though. Shortly thereafter I also gave up my volunteer hours since other opportunities were presenting themselves. I had occasionally filled in as secretary at our church when the full-time secretary was out of town or had other appointments. The church was growing and decided to hire a part-time secretary to help out with some of the increasing responsibilities. They asked if I would fill the position and, after discussing it with Mom and Dad, I accepted the offer. I worked three mornings a week answering the phones, proofreading and running copies of the mid-week paper and bulletins, greeting visitors to the church office, and a variety of other responsibilities as requested by the ministers. I thoroughly enjoyed my work and appreciated the friendships I developed and the things I was able to learn from the other adults.

Susan, the mother of a family I babysat for regularly, asked if I would serve as her personal assistant. She was a Director for Mary Kay Cosmetics and needed some help doing office work at her house. The hours varied from week to week and my responsibilities included publishing a newsletter and unpacking and checking orders as they arrived. This proved to be a great experience and I learned some valuable computer skills as a result. I also enjoyed developing a closer friendship with the family and have had fun trying to keep up with who's who now that they have adopted nine children in addition to the biological son that I used to babysit!

In the early months of 1997 some friends of our family, Ross and Linda and their daughters Jennifer and Wendy, began renovations on a building that they planned to turn into a Victorian Tea Room. Their daughter Jennifer was already using a portion of the building for her Grace-Works business and the Tea Room and gift shop would be an extension of that. That fall they invited Nicole and me, along with five other girls, to be part of their wait staff. We were thrilled! We had always loved pretending to be waitresses in our self-constructed basement restaurants. The thought of doing it for real seemed like a dream come true! Although we recognized some of the other girls and some of our paths had crossed briefly in the past, we didn't really know each other. I can still picture our small group gathered around one of the round floral-covered tables on the day we met for our server training. The group consisted of Myklin, Erica, Wendy, Rebekah, Brigette, Crystal, Nicole and me. Wendy had been a waitress before and conducted the training for us. We covered everything from the goals of the Tea Room, to our attitude and appearance, to the menu, floor plan, additional duties, and procedures for serving customers. There was a lot to learn, but I was giddy with excitement. I could hardly wait to be a waitress!

The following Tuesday was Server's Family Night and all of our families played the part of customers, or, in other words, our guinea pigs! It was an excellent way to begin learning "the ropes," since our families were very understanding and forgiving of our errors and any kinks in the system. Myklin was serving Mom and Dad and we learned later that when Dad had inquired as to what the soup du jour was, Myklin eagerly replied, "Oh, that means the soup of the day!" She had just learned the translation of the French term at the training the weekend before and jumped at the chance to pass on her newly acquired knowledge. Of course Dad already knew what it meant and just wanted to know what the soup of the day was. We all had a lot yet to learn...

Shortly after the Tea Room opened, Trisha was hired on as a waitress. She, Myklin, Nicole, and I became the Thursday crew. A dear lady, Brenda, served as the hostess and Myklin, Trisha, and I usually served as waitresses while Nicole filled the "extra person" position. She remained in the back, boiling hot water, dipping soup, organizing plates of food, scraping dirty dishes, and occasionally busing tables or filling water glasses for us. The arrangement worked perfectly since Nicole was not as much of a people-person and had an incredible gift for organization and efficiency. Within the first year of the business, Mom was hired on to do kitchen prep work on Thursdays. So for several years Mom, Nicole, and I made the weekly trek to the Tea Room and worked together. Mom put us all to shame with her tireless work—never stopping for a break, and consenting to sit and eat with us at the end of the day only when she was sure that every responsibility had been completed.

In the early days of the Tea Room, the kitchen was a small back room behind the dining room. The dishwasher consisted of three sinks, plus Ross, Don, Gerry, and even Dad on a couple of occasions! Yes, every dish was washed by hand—often multiple times each day. I remember waiting anxiously for used silverware to go through the rigorous cleaning process and be delivered back to our silverware tray so that I could reset tables that had just been cleared so that the next round of guests could be seated. Every inch of space was being used and while the close quarters resulted in some tense moments on our busiest days, the environment was warm and cozy. All the staff gathered for prayer each morning before we opened our doors. Prayer request cards were placed in the waiting area for customers who wanted to request prayer for particular situations or needs. Mrs. Lamp shared these with us and we faithfully prayed for each request we received.

We certainly had our fair share of high-maintenance customers—like the lady who complained about the late arrival of her muffin since she had already reapplied her expensive French lipstick and couldn't afford to reapply it again so soon—but our goal was to make the customers feel at home and refreshed by their time at the Tea Room. Tucked onto a little side street of the old Riverside neighborhood, one had to know about the Tea Room in order to consider it as a lunch spot. And even then, it was debatable whether the prospective patrons would actually be able to locate the building! Drive-by clientele would be almost nil, so we had to depend on other forms of advertising to attract lunch and tea-goers. We soon found that this would not be a problem. Our dining room only seated 50 and we regularly had a packed waiting area by the time we opened the restaurant doors at 11:00. There was a steady stream of diners until we finished serving lunch at 2:00 and then the afternoon tea guests would begin arriving. By the time we had finished serving the three-course tea and the last person had departed, we were exhausted!

I fondly recall our unlikely crew, squished around the back table at the end of the day, with extra seats borrowed from neighboring tables. Gerry and Wilta (Linda's parents and Tea Room handyman and cashier, respectively) entertained us with stories and witty remarks. Linda and Mom lovingly prepared for us the lunch items of our choice. And all of us waitresses spilled out our tip cans and eagerly counted our earnings. Logan (Myklin's brother) eventually came on board as the Thursday dishwasher and was a lively addition to our discussions. Brenda warmed us with her smile and always-encouraging words. Even to this day, those "Tea Room people" are some of the dearest in the world to me.

I began my years at the Tea Room just before my seventeenth birthday and continued until shortly after I turned twenty-one. In those four years I learned several valuable things, such as: how to treat people kindly even when I didn't think they deserved it, how to work hard even when I didn't feel like it, how to brew a proper pot of tea, how to carry a tray full of water glasses without spilling it, how to multi-task without going completely insane, how to arrange a plate of food attractively, how to set a beautiful table, how to handle stress in high-pressure situations, and how to demonstrate a servant's heart. What an education!

Toward the end of 2001 I got a call from a lady named Wendy. She was organizing a co-op for homeschoolers on the West side of Wichita—West Wichita Homeschool Ministries (WWHM)—and was looking for someone to teach some early level music classes. The co-op met on Thursdays, so it would mean giving up my job at the Tea Room. After praying about it and talking with Mom and Dad, I decided to accept her offer. I was teaching piano privately on Monday through Wednesday and I had occasionally held group classes for my students, but I didn't really know how to organize a semester-long music class. I began my search for just the right curriculum. The students would range in age from six through about ten. Some of the students had a musical background while others had none. The search proved to be in vain, so I finally settled into writing my own curriculum, which I dubbed, *Music Matters*. It included Scripture verses about music, listening and movement activities, introductory music reading, beginning keyboard skills, theory games, and choir selections. By the time I was finished designing all of the pages and printing and binding the student workbooks, I was excited!

Registration Day was held at the beginning of January. I arrived at the church building with my colorful poster and class description hand-out and eagerly waited at my section of the registration area to see who would sign up for my class. Several families signed up right away while others took flyers so that they could read more about what I was offering. By the end of the day, I had a handful of students signed up and the count-down to the first class began. The following week I arrived at the church building toting a huge collection of music supplies and workbooks for each student. I was directed to a small upstairs classroom and began making preparations for the arrival of the students. I could hardly wait! I felt like a real teacher—with a classroom and students and everything!

The semester flew by! Week after week our little class met and I developed good relationships with both the students in the class and their parents. Some elements of my curriculum worked really well. Others...well, not so well. But in the end we all had a fun time. The students completed the class with more of an appreciation for good music, and I with more of an appreciation for the challenge of developing and implementing effective lesson plans.

The following semester, at the request of several families, I offered additional levels of music classes. With these new classes on the schedule, I set to work again, writing curriculum appropriate for each group. I was also asked by one of the moms to coach a girls' choir for her daughter and a handful of other girls. Although I had been in several girls' choirs and had taken a smattering of voice lessons over the years, I felt wholly unqualified to attempt such an undertaking. But neither the girls in the choir, nor their parents, seemed to mind my inexperience. The hour we spent together on Thursday afternoons quickly became a highlight of my week.

The co-op was growing and more classes were being offered that semester, so the organizers decided to expand the hours and offer lunch for the participating families. They also wanted to provide a short character-building lesson during the lunch hour, so Myklin—who was teaching a class at the co-op called *What Every Girl Should Know*—and I were asked to spearhead this effort. We agreed, and *Character Quest* was birthed! After doing some praying and brainstorming together, Myklin and I developed an outline for a series of weekly skits centered on I Timothy 4:12, "Let no man despise thy youth; but be thou an example of the believers, in word, in conversation, in charity, in spirit, in faith, in purity." We titled our theme, *Looking for the X-Rep* and engaged the students in our search for this mysterious and elusive person. Myklin became "Detective Shirley U. Jest" and my persona was "Private I.C. Clearly."

We spent two weeks focusing on a character quality representative of one of the characteristics listed in our theme verse—truthfulness, discretion, generosity, enthusiasm, boldness, and self-control. The first week of each character quality focus, Myklin and I presented a skit to introduce and explain the character quality, all the while uncovering clues that would ultimately lead us to the *X-Rep*. Then, students would be enlisted to serve as investigators to help us track down the *X-Rep*. If they saw someone exhibiting the qualities we had described, they filled out an *X-Rep Recommendation Form* and place it in the designated locked box. The second week of our focus on each quality we selected names from the box and called those people to the front for further investigation. Anyone deemed "suspicious" following the investigation was placed on a list for further scrutiny throughout the remainder of the semester.

Other than a simple list of objectives and a brief outline for each character quality, we were flying by the seat of our pants each week! Every Wednesday night found me up late, usually sitting at the bottom of the stairs in our basement, talking on the phone to Myklin as we hashed out the details for the next day's *Character Quest*. During our lunch time sessions, we memorized verses, did object lessons, learned songs, conducted wacky investigations, and more. Every week was completely different and always a surprise to the children and parents—and sometimes even to us! Thankfully both Myklin and I thrived on improv and had a blast playing off of each other...except that I would always end up forsaking my New Jersey accent for her decidedly Southern accent part way through our dramatic presentations. I've never been any good at maintaining accents. I suppose it just added to the craziness of our little show each week. Regardless, the kids really seemed to get into it and we were never at a loss for submitted *X-Rep Recommendations* to call up for our investigations. A few bright ones in the bunch even caught on to our plan and submitted forms marked, "Jesus." But we weren't ready for those just yet...

The climax came during the big presentation at the end of the semester when each class had the opportunity to give a presentation highlighting what they had learned. Interspersed among the presentations, Myklin and I recapped the "clues" we had discovered about the *X-Rep* and followed a map that was supposed to lead us right to the *X-Rep*! The suspense grew with each subsequent appearance and Myklin and I tripped around cluelessly while the "X" marking the spot was clearly displayed behind us on the stage for everyone to see. Of course the kids couldn't help but yell to us to try to get us to turn around and see it for ourselves. But we were as good as deaf. The time had not yet come. Several appearances later, the tension was high and we were literally shaking with excitement because we felt like the moment of truth had arrived! Indeed it had. In perfect unison, we spotted the "X" and slowly turned it around to reveal an image of a cross on the reverse side. As we did so, the lights dimmed and a voice, pre-recorded by Myklin's Dad for the occasion, pierced the air:

The investigation into the identity of the missing X-Rep is hereby closed! To those of you who have taken part in this investigation and have persevered to the end, congratulations!

Throughout this semester, you have received clues, by which you have sought to identify and recommend those who you thought best fit the descriptions of the X-Rep. Perhaps you have striven to exemplify these character qualities in your own life, in hopes of being recommended. Yet, in the course of this investigation, no doubt the clues have led you to realize only One Person can fully meet the description of the X Rep...Jesus Christ.

Maybe you have already discovered that the elusive title of "X-Rep" stands for "Example Representative." Who alone is the perfect example in every area of life? That is none other than Jesus Christ Himself.

As you have seen, God's Word—the Bible—is our road map, our instruction manual for life. But it is impossible for any of us to meet the requirements found in the Bible, because we have all sinned against God. The penalty for failing to meet these requirements is death. But because of His great love for each of us, God sent His only Son, Jesus, to live a perfect sinless life here on earth. He was put to death by being crucified on the cross, paying the penalty for our sins.

However, Jesus did not remain dead! He rose back to life, conquering for each of us the power of death, so that we could live forever with Him in Heaven! Though you played the part of one searching for the X-Rep, you need not search for Jesus. He is here, right now. He is standing at the door of your heart, knocking, waiting for you to receive Him. His Word says that "As many as received Him, to them He gave power to become sons of God, even to them that believe on His Name." If you have never received Jesus, take this moment to do so now. "For whosoever shall call on the Name of the Lord, shall be saved."

For those of you who have received Jesus and made Him the Lord of your life, in the same way that Jesus is our X-Rep, we too are His representatives to the world! As we live our lives according to God's Word and grow closer to Jesus, those around us will see Jesus in our lives. So, to those of you who have begun this journey already and to those who are beginning it for the first time, press on! Don't give up! YOU are Jesus' X-Rep to the world!

It was an exciting conclusion to the semester, but the fun was just beginning!

The next semester, my little choir of four girls more than doubled in size and we moved on to more challenging choral arrangements. They had developed a higher level of confidence, having performed for both the WWHM closing program and as guest musicians at my annual Christmas piano recital, and were blending together much better. We continued to learn and grow together, whether we were singing warm-ups, working on breathing techniques, drilling tough harmonies, or laughing over silly mishaps. They were a precious group of girls and I loved spending time with them and watching them grow and mature over the course of the several months we worked together. That spring, they received two performance invitations. One was from me...to sing a couple of pieces at a big Patriotic-themed Musical Dinner that my piano students and I were planning. The other was from the Teaching Parents Association...to sing at the opening of the keynote address at the annual homeschool convention. We were delighted. And quite nervous. But we committed it to prayer, asking the Lord to help us be a blessing to all who were in attendance.

Myklin and I were asked to continue our lunch-time *Character Quest* presentations and we eagerly agreed to do so. We also decided to jointly offer another class—*Drama and Public Speaking*, or DAPS, as it quickly came to be known. Our aim was to compile the things we had each learned through years of Bible study and experience to help other young people become more effective communicators. We both realized how our varied acting experiences helped us develop the confidence and skills to become better public speakers and wanted to use drama as a vehicle to help others develop communication skills as well. The idea infused us with excitement and we carved out a day at the library to begin our curriculum development. We poured through various resources, studied page after page of Scripture, prayed, talked, shared ideas, and reflected on helpful personal experiences until by the end of the day we had a rough outline for our 12-week course.

We were excited to see our plans taking shape, but the work had just begun. We divided out the writing and teaching responsibilities. Each unit was split between us, with Myklin writing and teaching one week and me writing and teaching the other. That sounded doable.

The first day of class arrived and Myklin and I greeted our five students with enthusiasm. They were each given a personalized binder that contained the lesson for that day. That pattern continued for the duration of the semester; Myklin or I would write the lesson for the week and print the pages off for distribution the night before the class. We continued our Wednesday night "meetings"—conducted over the phone into the wee hours of the morning as we planned the details for not only our

Character Quest presentations, but now for our DAPS class as well. The students in our DAPS class were wonderful and we often recruited them to put their newly learned skills to practice by helping us out with various aspects of *Character Quest*. Our theme for *Character Quest* that semester was "Learning to Listen to the Voice of God" and once again we used a variety of skits to reinforce that concept each week. Lunch time immediately followed our DAPS class, so we often found ourselves scrambling at the last minute to gather props, review outlines, and coordinate entrances before the seven of us raced down the hallway to the lunch room. I'm pretty sure that at the top of the list of qualities for good acting it says, "Must be willing to look like an idiot in front of crowds." In that case, we were a group of highly qualified actors and actress!

Thus ended another semester of WWHM. And thus ended my involvement with WWHM. After careful consideration and time spent seeking the Lord, I decided not to return for another year at the co-op. I was sad to leave and would definitely miss all the crazy improv sketches with Myklin and our DAPS students, but the Lord was leading me in other directions.

Chapter 14

"Natalie's amazing ability to bring out the best in her students is reflected in the creative way she teaches and lives her life. Her students come to her to hone their musical gifts—and they learn to play beautiful pieces. But they walk away with life lessons—and they learn to live beautiful lives!"

Michele Chapman

from homeschool student to
full-time *teacher*

I was sitting on board an airliner, en route to Indianapolis for a three-week music course called Sound Foundations. I was 17 years old and this would be the longest I had ever been away from home. The course promised to be intensive, but other than that, I didn't really know what to expect. However, there was one question I hoped to have answered at some point while I was there—how could I tell what key a particular piece of music was written in? For anyone even remotely educated in music, no doubt the question is shocking. It is unthinkable to consider that I had been taking piano lessons for no less than ten years and still had no idea how to tell what key a piece was written in. I am sure that the absence of that knowledge is due in part to my own lack of interest in such theoretical concepts throughout most of my years of lessons. But a look now at the many theory books I completed only out of a sense of duty reveals a gross disconnect between the theory answers I was filling in week after week and my understanding of their relationship to the music I was playing.

For a girl who had been at the end of the line in the recital line-up for years (my teacher always had the students perform according to level, with the beginners first and the most advanced players at the end), those three weeks were a shocking revelation of my own lack of knowledge and skill as a pianist. There were students attending the course who were a hundred times better than me in every area! I was woefully unaware of the vastness of the music world and the extensiveness of the skills that could be acquired. Music history, theory, composition, orchestration—all were new to me. I had never composed a single note of music in my life, and yet by the end of the three weeks we were to write two original compositions and one piece orchestrated for a full orchestra! It was unreal. I'm sure my eyes were glossed over most of the time as I tried to absorb all the information, as well as study for final exams, apply new concepts, observe masterclasses, participate in electives, and more. Nevertheless, by the end of the week a passion had been ignited within me!

As soon as I returned home, I switched to another piano teacher so that I could focus on advancing my skills. Shortly after I returned, I also officially opened the doors of "Natalie's Piano Studio" for business. I had started teaching several boys from one family the preceding fall, but didn't have a clue what I was doing and eventually the lessons died off. A couple of evenings at Sound Foundations I had taken an elective session called Piano Pedagogy—the art of learning how to teach piano. As a result, I felt like I had a better idea of how to get started, and that April I sent out a letter to all the families that had asked me to teach their children. I included specific instructions and policies regarding fees and practicing. The ball was rolling, and as word spread that I was teaching, I gradually began to increase my student load. The only problem was that I still didn't really enjoy teaching. In fact, most days I dreaded it. Until I caught the vision for something more...

About a year later, I attended a weeklong piano pedagogy workshop that was offered through the International Academy of Music—the same Music Academy that offers Sound Foundations. The week was transforming. The workshop instructor was Andréa, a young woman who just oozed energy and excitement. It was contagious! She did far-out things like use colored pens to write her students' assignments. What?! Assignments were to be boring, written in pencil, preferably on a blank sheet of paper in a drab looking spiral notebook. Right? She made big, exaggerated motions when explaining concepts to her students. If I even tried that my students would look at me like I was crazy! Wouldn't they? Or, they might think I was actually having (dare I say it?)...f.u.n. while I was teaching. Horrors! Needless to say, I left that workshop with a whole different image in my mind of what it could look like to be a piano teacher. The only problem was that now I felt completely inadequate and incapable of being the kind of teacher I wanted to be. I had only a fragment of the knowledge and experience of this inspiring teacher. Only one thing kept me going when I was ready to throw in the towel.

During my quiet time one morning, I came across a sentence in a verse that seemed to be God's promise to me. It was in Ezekiel 36:36 and it read, "I the LORD have spoken it, and I will do it." In that moment I felt certain that my role as a piano teacher was no longer a self-imposed duty, but a Divine calling, at least for this time in my life. God had called me to teach and He would do it through me. I cannot tell you how often I have quoted those words to myself when I feel inadequate or burned-out or overwhelmed. With that promise in mind, I determined to become the best teacher I possibly could for the glory of God and the benefit of the families and students in my studio.

As soon as I arrived home, I joined several on-line music teachers' forums and became more active in our local music teachers associations—asking questions, attending workshops, participating in festivals, etc. My students bombed the first couple years of our state Music Progressions evaluations. But I had warned them of that possibility and we plodded on, learning and growing together. I gained valuable experience and received practical tips from other teachers so that we would be better prepared in the future. I started thinking creatively and pulling some of the ideas I'd used in other teaching experiences to enhance piano lessons for my students.

My friend, Joel, had gotten me hooked on the Print Shop graphic design software and I had been using it for personal design work for years. Now I put it to work in my fledgling business as I began designing materials for use in my studio. I had also attended an apprenticeship track at our annual ATI homeschool conference that included a session on graphic design led by a dynamic and enthusiastic young man who had started his own graphic design business. The colorful pages of notes I had received were well-worn and had suffered from at least one water spill, but they were an invaluable reference for me as I worked to learn good principles of design. I wanted to produce high-quality materials that were eye-catching and effective. With new project ideas in mind, I found myself "tuning in" to design work everywhere and picking up pieces that I especially liked so that I could imitate good designs in my own work.

One of my first projects was a personalized assignment book for each student where I could write their assignments and they could track their practicing each day. *Noteworthy News*—the official studio newsletter was launched, containing information about upcoming events, student achievements, inspirational quotes, and a Question of the Month contest. I had fun designing the newsletter each month and it proved to be an effective way to communicate with my studio families.

I started developing a theme each year with specific goals to work toward, and a variety of incentives to inspire each student to work hard and do his or her best. One year our theme was, *Practice Your Way to a Party*. Each of the students set their own goal for how much time they wanted to practice each week. At the end of the year, everyone who had reached their goal was invited to a party. For the boys, I threw a pizza party and we played lots of fun, active games. For the girls, I planned an elegant tea party and encouraged them all to come dressed in their best afternoon tea dresses. We had a lovely time donning our hats and sipping tea together!

The following year the theme was *Milestones to Musical Mastery*. The wall above the piano became a road map of sorts, with eight milestones placed along the way at regular intervals. I walked students through the steps of taking a piece from the very beginning stage of learning it to a polished performance-ready state. Once a piece reached that point, we recorded the title and date and they got to move ahead to the next milestone. On each milestone marker was the name of a famous composer. Throughout the year, I scheduled several historical tours where we would travel back in time to meet that composer. We enjoyed climbing into our attic and snacking on German hard rolls while learning about Johann Sebastian Bach. And George Frederic Handel seemed like more of a real person after we spent an afternoon in the royal throne room listening to some of his most famous compositions and looking at the portraits and period mementos on display around the room.

The next year, I introduced *The Box Club*. It's one of the simplest incentive themes I've done, but proved to be very motivating. I posted membership rosters on the wall above the piano and the first person to arrive at each level was listed as the Club President. The second was the Club Vice-President. Toward the end of the year, all the students who had been admitted to the club as officers were invited to a meeting at the studio where we planned and organized a special year-end event. We called the event *The Box Club Musical Dinner* and decided to give it a patriotic theme. The event included dinner and a musical show comprised of a variety of selections by all the students and a few guest artists. We recruited some of the moms to be in charge of preparing the food and employed the students as hosts or hostesses and table servers. We printed and sold tickets ahead of time so that we would know exactly how much food to prepare and how many tables to set up. As had become the tradition for my studio recitals, we commissioned one of the other students to draw the artwork for the programs and one of the Club Presidents agreed to be the emcee for the event. From the singing of the Star-Spangled Banner, to a simple piano solo of I'm a Yankee Doodle Dandee, to a hilarious musical sketch by two sisters, to an impromptu encore by an unsuspecting audience member, the whole evening was a tremendously fun and memorable experience.

The following year saw all of us *Traveling to Triumph!* I drew a huge map of the world and stuck it up on the wall above the piano. Thirteen capital cities around the world were marked as destination points on the map. The year saw students traveling thousands of "miles" and collecting spending money along the way. At the end of the year, I held an auction with items available from each of the representative countries. A former student of mine was working for an auction company, so I recruited him to come in and serve as the auctioneer for the event. With the assistance of our neighbor, who had a son living overseas, I was even able to secure one of the items I really wanted—kinder surprise chocolate eggs from Germany! Some of the students had racked up hundreds of dollars in spending money and went away with a huge stash of goods! But by the end, every student had won the bidding on several items and left pleased with the outcome.

After spending a year traveling the world (on the studio wall, that is!), I decided to stay a little closer to home and dubbed the next year, *An American Adventure*. The adventure was centered on the idea of setting specific goals at the lesson each week and then practicing with the aim of achieving those goals. Throughout the year, I organized a tour of six of the most famous American landmarks. Students could earn tickets to attend the tours and we had a great time writing new lyrics to the tune of "Yankee Doodle" while visiting the Statue of Liberty, engaging in fierce rhythmic battles between the North and the South at Gettysburg, reenacting the story of Lewis and Clark at the St. Louis Gateway Arch, blasting away balloons that contained pertinent historical information at Mount Rushmore, racing against the clock to beat Santa Anna to the mission at The Alamo, and constructing our own suspension bridge at the Golden Gate Bridge.

The weeks prior to each tour found me buried in books, articles, pictures, and website links as I studied and outlined lesson plans. Half of the fun of putting together these events for my students is always the process of learning new things in preparation for them. That's one thing Mom and Dad instilled in all of us kids—a love for learning. Every situation in life was turned into a learning experience and we were always being told to go look things up for ourselves, or study it more in-depth if we were interested in it. Especially as I got older, the detailed school assignments from Mom and Dad became sparser. I had my required school subjects and knew what I had to get done each day, but other than that I was free to explore other areas of interest on my own. I went through all sorts of phases. For a while I was really interested in creation science. I read numerous books on the subject, gathered statistics and facts, and wrote a paper outlining my findings. At one point, the Great Awakening was of particular interest to me. So, I learned about the great men like George Whitefield that were so influential in the movement and the profound effect it had on our young nation. My interest in government was sparked and I spent time studying the structure of our nation's government and the purposes of the three branches. One thing led to another and there was never any want of new things to be studied and learned. That same excitement for learning new things carried over into my teaching and now I found myself immersed in one thing after the next as we toured our way across America.

Instead of traveling around the world or even just the country, the following year found us traveling up. Well, climbing, actually. We were *Climbing the Ladder to Success*. I wanted to encourage my students to become very fluent music readers. And the best way to do that is to play through a *lot* of music. After years of researching the process, I had also finally learned how to produce CD recordings using a piano, microphone and laptop computer. I was thrilled and wanted a way to incorporate this into the theme for the year. With those objectives in mind, I set the stakes high. I placed a big ladder on the studio wall, above the piano. For every ten pieces the student learned, they got to advance to the next rung of the ladder. If they reached the top rung, they would have learned 100 pieces! Once they reached each rung, I let them select two of the ten pieces to record during their lesson and told them that at the end of the year I would compile them all and burn them onto a CD for them. But the biggest reward would be reserved for only the very diligent students.

With Proverbs 22:29 ("Seest thou a man diligent in his business? He shall stand before kings; he shall not stand before obscure men.") serving as a key source of inspiration, I developed a list of ways that students could demonstrate diligence. In return for their diligence they would receive Diligence Dollars (DD). At the end of the year, there would be an opportunity to join me on a trip to a professional recording studio. The owner of the studio agreed to give us a tour and explain the different pieces of equipment to us and then each student would be allowed to record a piece of their choosing. Each student would then receive a CD commemorating the occasion. The cost to each student would be $250 DD, so they would have to work consistently all year long to earn this privilege. The challenge proved to be more difficult than some expected, but twelve dedicated students reaped the rewards of their diligent efforts and joined me for their first professional recording experience the following spring.

One of the things I noticed as a result of doing the recording project that year was that many of my students lacked the performance experience necessary to play at the level I knew they were capable of. They were unprepared for the pressure of such an intense situation. So for the following year I brainstormed to come up with a way to incorporate more frequent performance experiences. The outworking of that thought process became the theme, *Let's Have a Ball!* Throughout the course of the year I scheduled six musical balls. Each one had a specific theme— A Fall Ball: Autumn Inspirations, A Thanksgiving Ball: Sacred Music, A Christmas Ball, A Mid-Winter Ball: An Evening of Serious Music, A Spring Ball: Fresh and Original Music, A Grand Finale Ball: The Best of the Best. It was incredible to see the improvement in the students as they developed confidence and poise and learned how to handle their nerves. I certainly don't have a studio of concert-level performers, but we are learning to perform to a standard of excellence and to work toward this end with all of our hearts as unto the Lord.

Inspired by a Music Olympics festival that our Wichita music teachers association was planning for the following summer, I decided to build the next year's theme around the Olympics—*Go for the Gold!* In the spirit of the Olympics, I established five teams and placed each of the students on one of the teams. Throughout the year, they could earn points for completing assignments and meeting other requirements. Approximately every six weeks, we held an Olympic Event where the students met together to compete for more points, play games, and perform for each other. At the conclusion of the event, the team with the most points was awarded the gold—each student on the team received three gold dollar coins. It was fun to watch the students develop a sense of team spirit and work together to earn more points and attain a higher level of musical skill.

Part of what I love so much about teaching is the challenge of identifying each student's strengths and weaknesses and looking for creative ways to help them progress in their abilities. Planning yearly themes for my studio gives me a chance to evaluate what areas need work across the board and think of ways to address those needs in a way that will motivate the students to work hard and strive for excellence. While there is always an element of competition included, I have found that it's important to design the incentive program in a way that gives students of all ages and levels an equal opportunity to reach the highest goals and experience personal success and achievement in their own endeavors. The yearly theme is an element that has become a trademark of my studio and now by the end of spring, students start begging me to tell them what the theme is for the next year. But I take great pleasure in telling them that they'll have to come back for lessons in the fall to find out!

Chapter 15

"Natalie is a model learner and a respected professional piano teacher. She pursues her varied interests and excels at each one. As her piano teacher/mentor, I often refer my college piano pedagogy students to her exemplary work, even though she did not attend college herself."

Sylvia Coats

to graduation and beyond!

Slowly I pushed the door open and peered inside. The room was empty. Just what I was hoping for. I slipped in, slid quietly onto the back row and gazed around the room at row after row of vacant pews. In a few short hours these pews would be overflowing—with family, friends, and other well-wishers cheering on the graduating class of 1999. But for now, all was quiet. Things had been busy around our house that week as preparations were made for the graduation ceremony and the party we were hosting at our house following the ceremony. I felt the need to steal a few moments away to just be still and commune with God.

I pulled out the small pocket Bible I had carried into the room and opened it. I don't even remember anymore what I read, but the sweet words washed over me and refreshed my soul. Even though I would be giving a speech in front of a bigger crowd than ever before, I felt surprisingly calm. In fact, I was eagerly anticipating the moment. It had been a long journey to arrive at this point and now I was ready. Ready to inspire the world and share a glimpse of God's work in my life to this point! I had thought and prayed long and hard as I prepared and was confident that I would be sharing what the Lord wanted me to share...

Well, it's been a real joy and privilege to be homeschooled these past nine years. I've had a lot of opportunities and I wouldn't trade it for anything. I knew as I came up here today that anything I would say would soon pass away and would soon be forgotten, so I chose instead to share with you a verse because it says the Word of the Lord will never pass away. That verse is Proverbs 4:26 and it's one that's really encouraged me during these past few years of high school. It says, "Ponder the path of thy feet, and let all thy ways be established." I know that it could be applied in many different ways, but specifically in this area of graduation it came to mean to me that rather than following along some specific way that someone else has set out, to take the time to ponder, and to think about, to consider that path and to determine if it was the way that God would have me go and if it would lead to the place where I should end up. And Jesus said that the path to eternal life is hard and that the gate is narrow and that only a few find it. Many of you well know, I'm sure, that often the right path is the one much less traveled.

And the second part of that verse says, "let all thy ways be established." And they should be established or confirmed by God for my life because He's the One who has placed me here, who has placed each of us here for an important purpose and if we are truly willing to follow Him, then He will show us the way as it says in Psalm 16:11, "Thou wilt shew me the path of life; in thy presence is fullness of joy." It won't be something obscure or hard to find. However, often following Him requires following just one step at a time, not knowing the whole path or not having the whole path illuminated, but just a small light so that I know where to take the next step. It has to be the path that's right, right from the start, because each of our times on earth is so short that we don't have time to take the wrong path and get to the end and turn around and realize that it was wrong from the start. If I do stay on the path, it's exciting to know that that path will lead to eternal life and that nothing that we do will be in vain because all God's ways are eternal. In the words of a missionary—Adoniram Judson—he said, "Let us then each morning resolve to send each day into eternity in such a garb as we shall wish it to wear forever."

Looking to the future, I've also had some time to reflect on the past, on many memories that seem to be from a time so long ago and I know I've only lived 18 years. There are many people who have invested in my life in many different ways that I couldn't even begin to name them all, but I'd like to thank a special few.

First of all, my Dad—our principal with the iron rod. He's the one that forced us out of bed three mornings a week to do our exercising and running that we all love so much. He's the one whose voice could strike terror into the hearts of his children with just four simple words, "Come to my room." He's the one who's so good to remind us all the time that we do not live in a democracy, but a dictatorship. A benevolent dictatorship, of course. He's the one who faithfully edited everything I wrote, returning it always with more red ink than black. He's the one who taught me to do everything with excellence. He's the one who set the example in spending time with the Lord every morning.

Mom, our devoted teacher in word and in deed. She's the one who has every book on every subject and saves them all for reference. She's the one who taught us the necessity of a daily trip to Wal-Mart or McDonald's. She's the one who traded in a quiet house and her own career for a house full of noisy kids, a never-ending pile of laundry and a desk you can never see the top of. She's the one who has given up hours of sleep to listen to all of my woes and all of my dreams.

Nicole, my best friend since childhood and partner in crime. She's the one who worked by my side in setting up every store you could possibly think of in our basement and building a tent out of every blanket, sheet or scrap of material we could find. We were continually reprimanded, though, for the many holes we punctured in our wall while we in vain tried to keep our tents from caving in on us with thumb tacks. She's the one who worked with me in making every babysitter wish that they had declined the job offer. Though now we both agree that we've been repaid in full! She's the one with whom I talk long into the night, solving all the world's problems. She's the one who has stood faithfully by my side through the thick and the thin.

Nadine. She's the one who has never hesitated to tell me the truth about anything, whether I wanted to hear it or not. She's the fashion expert of the family—always sure to inform us if something is not in style. She's the one who could speak for several hours straight, reciting only movie lines. She's the devoted little sister, who was always a step behind in our mischievous little schemes. Just far enough to take the blame in each case. Beneath her sometimes tough façade, she's the one with a heart of gold, always willing to add the extra special touch to make someone feel special.

Noelle, our surprise little package bundled up in sweetness and smiles. Our little El Destructo, as we often referred to her. She's the one that reminded us of the temporariness of everything we called our own. She's the one who loves to call us all together to be the devoted audience of her many performances and singing debuts. She's my diligent little piano student who so graciously puts up with her demanding teacher, the one who shares my love for music. She's my special little friend and buddy.

Naomi, our sensitive little sweetie who breaks into tears at the slightest reprimand. She's the one who can innocently rearrange any sentence and repeat it in such a comical style as to have her audience rolling on the floor, gasping for breath. She's our little organizer who always plays with her toys in a straight line so as not to get them out of order. She's the one who's always there to give someone a hug when they're feeling sad.

Joey. He's the one who's teaching us all what it's really like to have a brother. He's the one who helped us understand why someone invented a door that locks. He's the one who walked down an aisle full of elderly ladies, smiling and saying, "hi" and then at the end turned around and stuck his tongue out at them all. He's the one who can be giving a hug with one arm while pulling things off of the table with the other. He's the one who, in the midst of being disciplined, can flash that irresistible little smile that melts us all to pieces.

My Lord and Savior Jesus Christ. My Father, Big Brother and Best Friend. He's the One who has reminded me that without Him I am nothing and that His grace is sufficient for me. He is the strength of my life. He's the One that has taught me that true joy is found only in Him. He's the One who has always been faithful to direct me in the way I should go and to guide my every step. He's the One who reminds me of the importance of living each day in light of eternity. He's the One who is with me yesterday, today and forever. To Him be all the praise and glory.

There were 29 students in my graduating class. I only knew about half of them. And yet, there was camaraderie. Though the specifics were different for each of us, we held in common that our parents had accomplished what few would even think of attempting in those days. They had taken personal responsibility for our education and successfully navigated through the requirements to bestow upon us a high school diploma. To be honest, the requirements in Kansas were pretty vague. Mom and Dad weren't quite sure what sort of documentation would be necessary, so they asked me to take the GED tests at a local testing center. I complied and found myself for several weeks in a row sitting in a room full of mostly grown men who had dropped out of high school in their younger years. Among the bunch was one other homeschooler—I found this out later when he turned out to be one of the other graduates participating in the same graduation ceremony as me. The tests seemed incredibly easy right off the bat and by the time I completed the math portion of the test, I couldn't believe how low the expectations were for a high school level education. The night after I took the math test, I got a call from the Testing Center director who called because he was sure I would want to know that I had gotten a perfect score on the test. I thanked him for his thoughtfulness, hung up the phone and laughed! Why? Brace yourself.

This is my royal confession.

I never finished Algebra 2. Or any higher math. (I'm sure some are horrified at the confession, but other homeschool Moms reading this can take a deep breath and say, "I am not a failure if some of my children haven't finished Algebra 2.") I took a college accounting class during high school that was offered by Jim, a homeschool Dad who was a CPA, and got an A in the class. And I tried to keep up with my math lessons through high school. But, truth be told, they took so much time and I had so many other responsibilities and interests that it just kind of slipped by the wayside. Looking back, I wonder if it was our family road trips that saved me and got me through the math portion of the GED.

Some families like to sing while they travel; others like to play license plate games or word games. But not our family. Our family solved math-ematical word problems. Thanks to Dad. Whenever Dad was the one driving, he would entertain himself by mentally presenting various problems and then solving them. Things like, "We're racing to beat a train to a railroad crossing, but just as we get to the crossing, the gates come down. How long will we have to wait, to the nearest second, if the train's speed is about 50 mph, and there are 6 locomotives, each about 40' long, pulling 80 cars, each about 30' long?" or "We're on vacation in our Suburban, which is about 20' long, driving along an interstate at about 72 mph. We pass a truck, which is about 68' long. The time it takes to pass the truck, from when the front of our car is abeam the back of the truck until the back of our car is abeam the front of the truck, is about 5 seconds. How fast is the truck going, to the nearest mph?"

Once he had solved his clever problem, he would present it to the rest of us and offer to reward the first one to figure it out correctly with a free treat at our next stop. If Dad was offering to pay for something, it was serious business, so we all scrambled to get our pencils and notebooks and spent the next half hour littering our papers with all sorts of formulas and markings and trying desperately to figure out what Dad had easily calculated in his head. Eventually an answer was forthcoming, although when Dad would ask us to explain how we arrived at the answer, we would try to weasel our way out of it by claiming that he hadn't stipulated that requirement when he presented the problem. Either way, Dad would follow up by explaining to his captive audience the various formulas and equations used to decipher the word problem and arrive at a solution. His mathematical acumen fascinated me, but I was never particularly driven to pursue higher math studies.

There were many areas I was interested in by the time I graduated from high school. Since I had decided not to pursue a college degree, I began looking for other ways to develop skills and advance my education. I was running my own piano studio, so I was interested in both the philosophical side of teaching and the practical side of running a business. There were several professional organizations for music teachers in our area and after attending a couple of meetings as a guest, I decided to become a member. The South Central Kansas Music Teachers Association (SCKMTA) was a smaller, close-knit group comprised primarily of teachers from the suburbs and rural areas. The Wichita Metropolitan Music Teachers Association (WMMTA) had a significantly larger number of teachers and was more formal. The teachers of both organizations welcomed me warmly and gave me a great deal of advice and encouragement in my early years of teaching and running a studio.

Once I had been a member for about a year, the SCKMTA members elected me to serve as Secretary and by the third year of my involvement with the group, they asked me to take on the responsibility of chairing their year-end music evaluation program—Music Progressions. I still didn't know any better at the time, and in my blissful ignorance agreed to do the job. It was a huge responsibility that involved numerous tasks. Nevertheless, I enjoyed the challenge and looked for ways to streamline the process and reorganize the Chairperson files. And thankfully, they didn't leave me to fend for myself! Other members pitched in to help me learn the ropes and get the work done. Since that time, we've employed this same tactic on other unsuspecting newbies and I joke now that it is the official initiation into our association—once you've been the Music Progressions Chairperson, you're a full-fledged member! Looking back, though, this was a very effective way to help me assimilate into the group.

The following year I was asked to serve as the President-Elect, a two-year term that would be followed by another two-year term as President. The thought was quite overwhelming and I spent a considerable amount of time thinking, praying and getting counsel before I finally agreed. It was an enjoyable role and I had fun coming up with creative themes each year to help direct our activities.

By the end of my term as president, I was nearing the completion of my process toward becoming a Nationally Certified Teacher of Music— an accreditation offered through the Music Teachers National Association (MTNA). I had started a couple of years earlier under the mentorship of my teacher Dr. Sylvia Coats. She outlined what she would require me to do in order to meet the performance requirements. Her plan included "mini-performances" wherein I would work on specific pieces of repertoire and then play them at the SCKMTA meetings for the other teachers. The thought terrified me! I was a terrible performer and there was not an ounce of pleasure in the thought of performing difficult pieces of Classical repertoire for my music teaching colleagues. But under the guidance of Dr. Coats, one by one I learned my pieces and one by one I performed them at the meetings. I knew that my performances were a far cry from being virtuosic, but the other teachers did everything they could to relieve my nerves and encourage me in my efforts. Finally the performance requirements were met and I had Dr. Coats' letter of verification, along with the two required reference forms to officially start the certification process. The only problem was that I didn't have the money required to send in the application.

The application fee was $200 and although I could have set aside that amount from my teaching income by the end of December, I knew it would be best to send everything in right away so that I could move on to the next phase of the process before the end of the year. I was operating on a strict budget and had a policy of not dipping into my savings unless it was an item I had specifically been saving for or there was an emergency need for cash. I began praying that somehow the Lord would provide the amount that I needed in order to send in my application before the end of September. My first week of teaching began and I could hardly believe what happened when Caleb Davis arrived for his piano lesson. He handed me a check, not for the monthly fee—which at that time was $50—but for the combined total of the months of September through December: $200! He said that his Mom decided to just pay for the whole semester at once so that she wouldn't have to remember to write the check each month. I was ecstatic! As soon as I had a chance I called Staci, Caleb's Mom, to tell her how I had been praying for the money to send in my application and she was the answer to that prayer. She rejoiced with me to see God's hand at work. The next day I dropped my application and all the required documentation in the mail. The certification process had officially begun!

As soon as I received word that my application had been approved, I could move on to the next step—demonstration of proficiency in Music Theory, Music History/Literature and Pedagogy/Teacher Education. In lieu of a college transcript documenting coursework in these areas, I filed a request to take the three proficiency exams. The materials from my Sound Foundations course eight years prior proved to be a helpful resource and I was so grateful for the excellent foundation it had given me in these areas of music study (guess that's why they named it Sound Foundations!). The Kansas Certification Chairperson at the time lived only about thirty minutes away, so we arranged an afternoon for me to go to her house and take the exams. I had no idea what to expect, so I was relieved to discover that between the materials I had studied and the years of teaching experience I could draw upon, I was well-prepared for each of the exams. Within a few weeks I received word that I had passed. I was elated and delved into the final step of the process with vigor!

As I explored the details of each option for the final requirement of the certification process, I determined that the certification portfolio would be the most beneficial to me personally. With the decision made, I downloaded the guidelines and began penciling notes in the margins. I would be required to document evidence to substantiate my competency as a music teacher and adherence to Professional Teaching Practices, Professional Business Management, and Professionalism and Partnerships. Although the project was overwhelming, I knew that going through the process would help me become a better teacher. Plus, a number of incredible resources had helped prepare me for the standards I now had to demonstrate.

Within my first year of teaching I joined an on-line community of piano teachers. It was an e-mail based forum comprised of piano teachers from around the world. I quickly became enthralled by the discussions that took place among the teachers and was amazed at the dedication and creativity that they invested in their teaching. It was there that I first heard the term, Studio Policy and learned about the importance of developing one for my studio. It was there that I first began to understand the ins and outs of the business side of running a studio. It was there that I first felt like I was part of a bigger community of music teachers, all of us striving to impart to the next generation the skills and joys of playing the piano. I grew to love this group of virtual colleagues whom I had never met in per-

son, but from whom I learned so much!

Several years into teaching, at the encouragement of Dr. Coats, I enrolled in the Piano Pedagogy class offered through Wichita State University (WSU). Dr. Coats was the instructor and the semester-long class provided me with a more thorough understanding of piano pedagogy history, teaching methods and philosophies, and learning styles. I learned how to write good lesson plans and had the chance to put them into practice with the group of students we taught through the WSU piano lab. The weekly homework assignments forced me to think more critically about my teaching and to develop a personal philosophy of teaching. That semester served to fill in many of the gaps in my own understanding of effective teaching and provided me with lots of tools and resources that I could draw from in my teaching. Plus, now I can say that my official college GPA is 4.0 (impressive, I know...).

In the process of implementing a more professional approach and because of a desire to communicate more effectively with the families in my studio, I became interested in building a website for my studio. The only problem was that I didn't have a clue how to do it! I tried searching around on-line for tutorials that would walk me through the process, but couldn't find anything that really fit the bill. I talked with several of my friends that were skilled in web design and tried to pick their brains, but the terminology seemed confusing and I still couldn't gather exactly how to go about designing my own website. After hearing several people recommend Dream-weaver as the top-of-the-line, industry-standard, software, I finally decided to plunk down the large chunk of money to purchase the web design software. As soon as it arrived, I installed it onto my computer and prepared to explore and experiment with it. Haha. The interface was foreign to me and completely non-intuitive. I could hardly figure out how to type text into the program, let alone do any sort of page layout. My "learn-it-by-myself" M.O. struck out on this one.

Shortly thereafter Mom saw an ad in the paper for a web design workshop. It was being offered by the web developer for the local school district. I immediately signed up, paid my $20, and eagerly waited for the day of the workshop to arrive. Perhaps I would finally be enlightened and could enter into the elusive world of web design. But it was not to be. The instructor was using another software program and the class was so specific to it that there was hardly anything that I could apply to my own learning efforts. I left disappointed, but still determined to navigate my way into this uncharted territory. I began my search on-line again in earnest and this time I struck gold! A company called ExecuTrain offered a multitude of computer courses, including several in web design. A little more digging revealed that they had a training facility right in Wichita!

I called their local office and found out that their primary focus is on training executives and employees of the major corporations in the area, however, once I explained my situation and interest to them, they were willing to let me enroll in the classes and even agreed to charge me a discounted rate as a small business. I was ecstatic! I finally felt like I was getting somewhere in my quest to enter the world of web design. And this time, the classes were everything I hoped for and more! The trainers were extremely knowledgeable and were excellent communicators. Each student (myself and the two other corporate employees who spent most of the time surfing the Internet) were seated at our own computer workstations and the instructor walked us through the process of coding an entire website in HTML. After completing two HTML classes, the ExecuTrain instructors offered to reschedule the Dreamweaver classes since the current schedule conflicted with my teaching schedule. I readily agreed and spent the first two days of my Thanksgiving break that fall absorbing all that I could about web design and the Dreamweaver software. By the time I had finished the four day-long classes,

I could get around easily in the software, had a working knowledge of the terminology, and knew enough HTML to troubleshoot basic problems. I had finally broken in and now a whole new world was opening up before me!

Once I had my studio website up and running I delved deeper into the field of web design, attempting to learn as much as possible by researching various aspects on-line and checking out programming books from the library (does this make me a geek?!). Eventually I took on the task of developing websites for both of the local music teachers associations and I enjoyed the challenge of trying to create a unique, but attractive look for each site. I earned a reputation of sorts for being the computer guru (they are nice enough not to call me a geek!) of the group and was called upon to give workshops to help train other teachers to use technology more effectively in their studios. I found that many teachers wanted to be able to produce professional-quality materials for their studios, but didn't even understand the basics of how to operate their computer programs. I made every effort to ascertain their needs and interests and then conduct the workshops in a way that they would understand and leave them feeling like they were capable of developing the skills necessary to reach their goals. I gave a similar workshop at our state music teachers conference one year. And Dr. Coats even asked me to fill in for her one week when she would be out of town and give a workshop on how to establish a successful independent studio to her graduate pedagogy class.

These workshops proved to be a ton of fun and it was exciting to watch the other teachers' eyes light up as they learned how to do things that they'd always wanted to be able to do. It's not unlike teaching a student to play the piano. In fact, in one workshop I drew that analogy—many times, as teachers, we get frustrated when a student comes back to a lesson and plays a piece the same way they played it the week before in spite of the fact that we gave them all sorts of suggestions for ways to improve it. Why is this? Simply put, it's because the student wasn't willing to invest the time or energy to change the way they were playing the piece. Similarly, teachers find themselves operating their studios the same way year after year, regardless of the fact that they have been given ideas of ways to improve and run their studios more creatively or efficiently. Why is this? Simply put, it's because they are not willing to invest the time or energy to change the way they do things. Of course, this is not limited to the area of music teaching. The principle holds true in many facets of life. And so, both my studio teaching and the workshops I've given have centered on the idea of inviting change—always looking for ways to do things more creatively, more efficiently, more effectively. This is the impetus that led to the next development.

With my involvement in both the on-line community of music teachers and our local music teachers associations growing, I began receiving numerous e-mails from music teachers asking questions about ideas I had shared or requesting assistance with computer-related issues. Invariably, after attending a workshop, teachers had questions about something I had said or needed a reminder of how to do something. I found myself e-mailing the same directions and files repeatedly. So in the summer of 2005 an idea was conceived. After reading the book Blog by Hugh Hewitt, I was inspired with the possibility of creating a blog geared toward independent music teachers. This would enable me to provide valuable resources for other teachers and help them navigate the often overwhelming plethora of material available on the Internet. It would also allow me to direct people to specific files or links on the site without having to e-mail them. The idea grew and developed and in September of that year I officially launched MusicMattersBlog.com. Although it hasn't cut down on my e-mail load (I receive at least ten times as many e-mails now as I did before!), Music Matters Blog has proved to be an additional way to connect with music teachers, share *the Lord with them, and explain how the principles of His Word guide the daily operations of my studio.*

On numerous occasions I have received e-mails from other music teachers asking how I can be so open about my faith and incorporate such obviously biblical material in my teaching. They go on to say that they would probably lose students if they did that, so they prefer to be more private with their faith. My response is always that I am grateful for the free society in which we live that allows us to operate our businesses in accordance with our beliefs and philosophies. My studio families are free to leave at any time if they are unhappy with my teaching style or methods. However, that has seldom been the case because they know before they ever sign up for lessons what my teaching philosophy and policies are. In fact, that's often exactly what they are looking for in a teacher. So it's a perfect arrangement—we are all on the same "page," working toward the same goals and objectives, and communicating openly along the way. In many instances, teachers are stifling their own religious freedom. And I dare say, we have little right to complain about the freedoms being taken away in the public sector when we in the private sector abdicate our own freedoms.

All of these diverse experiences prepared me for the task that was now at hand—the compilation of my certification portfolio. At long last, the final page was signed, copied, and placed in the binders. I packaged them up according to the guidelines and sent them off with a sigh of relief and a prayer that they would be accepted. All that remained was to wait for the decision of the certification committee.

The call came after I'd already arrived in Austin for the MTNA Conference that spring. The timing couldn't have been better, because it was official—I was a Nationally Certified Teacher of Music! Or, as Nicole's message declared, I was now qualified to put initials after my name.

Before the expected eight weeks had elapsed, my letter of acceptance arrived in the mail, along with a beautiful certificate that is now displayed in my studio. Of course the initials after my name don't automatically make me a better teacher, but I have no doubt that I am a better teacher today because of the process I went through to get those long-anticipated initials (NCTM) after my name!

That spring I was approached by a member of the WMMTA nominating committee. They wondered if I would consider serving as the next President of the organization. This would involve serving one year as the President-Elect, followed by a two-year term as President. I was just finishing my term as the President of SCKMTA and wasn't sure if I was ready to move into that position on an even larger scale.

I had already served in a couple of other board positions since my second year of membership in the organization. Now I was being asked to step into a position of greater responsibility and I didn't know what to do. I prayed about it and got counsel from Mom and Dad and the former President. Honestly, whenever I am asked to make a long-term commitment of some nature, the thought crosses my mind that perhaps I shouldn't because I would really like to be married instead. However, I have learned that decisions must be made based on the present and not on future probabilities. I would have said no to a hundred different opportunities by now if I was intent on just waiting for some young man to come along and ask me to marry him! If the Lord does allow me to marry at some point, then my role and responsibilities will change at that time. But I must patiently wait upon the Lord to bring it about in His time.

There have also been numerous times when I have been called upon to make a decision and have wished that Mom and Dad would just tell me what to do. But they rarely take that approach. They eagerly offer me counsel and help me analyze the implications of a decision, but always encourage me to seek the Lord and depend on the principles of His Word and the leading of the Holy Spirit. It certainly makes things harder for me! But I am so grateful for ways the Lord has grown my faith as I wrestle with such situations and seek to make decisions that are honoring to Him and a blessing to those around me.

The way ahead seemed clear to accept the office of President-Elect. I would definitely be stepping outside my "comfort zone." Part of my hesitation was the fact that the former president had done such an amazing job that I couldn't imagine following in her footsteps. I didn't want to lose the enthusiasm and momentum she had helped create in the organization. Before the changeover the following year, Wendy graciously agreed to meet with me, so I drafted a list of questions and sent them her way. We met together a couple of weeks later and she gave me helpful advice and encouragement that made me feel better equipped to assume my responsibilities as President.

About a month before our first board meeting, I was at a get-together and got to talking with a friend who was handling a high level of responsibilities and training in a corporation. As I shared with him some of my uncertainties, he helped me talk through why I was feeling that way and how to overcome my apprehensive attitude. He also gave me some great advice and helped me think through effective ways of casting a vision and implementing it. That was the impetus I needed to really jump in and take on my responsibilities with enthusiasm instead of succumbing to my fears and taking a passive leadership role.

Every day leading up to the first board meeting found me praying fervently for wisdom. As I made the 20-minute drive that July morning, I prayed the whole way and combated the knot I felt in my stomach. Once I arrived at the downtown library and made my way up to the board room I had reserved for our meeting, I plugged in my laptop and took my seat at the head of the table. Soon the other board members arrived and I called the meeting to order. From that moment on, I was filled with a peace that "passes understanding." I felt acutely that the Lord was in control of the meeting and that He would give me the wisdom I needed to respond appropriately and wisely in each situation. The other board members were extremely supportive and encouraging and it is with gratitude and amazement that I reflect on all the people whom God has placed in my life to give me the education, training and encouragement that I need to be successful.

Homeschooling has prepared me for a life of learning, because one of the most valuable things I've learned is that true education is not limited to the walls of a classroom. True education takes place every day as I learn from the expertise and experience of those whom God has placed in my life. This understanding is what has helped me learn and grow, even through the difficult life lessons that God has allowed me to experience.

Chapter 16

"Natalie's initiative and desire to serve others shows the tremendous impact one life can have on others. Good intentions are good; good results are even better. I've witnessed this throughout her entire life. She helps to show us what's possible."

Bruce Jeffrey

a road of adventure

Julia and I sat at the table with pens and notebooks, enthusiastically discussing ideas and jotting down notes. The two of us had first met through our Wichita homeschool support group. She and her younger brother Ian were being homeschooled, and when we first met her Dad was awaiting a liver transplant. He had been called shortly thereafter for the transplant and although the initial operation was successful, he died right afterward due to complications that were never fully determined. Julia's Mom, Bev, even in the face of this tragedy, remained committed to doing whatever it took to provide for her family and continue homeschooling Julia and Ian. Over the years, Julia and I became close friends. We made a point to read the same series of books, adopting for ourselves special friendship phrases. We wrote letters back and forth to each other, even though we only lived about 15 minutes apart. We traveled with each others' families for vacation. We participated in the same activities and enjoyed many of the same life experiences. But our deepest bond was one of the heart. We loved sharing our latest ideas and planning ways that we could accomplish great things for God's Kingdom. Our deepest desire was to leave a lasting mark on this world and to use our time here to influence as many people as we could for eternity.

Now we sat, working on our next grand scheme. We had talked about it before, but we were finally putting pen to paper and making our plans. We were in the preliminary stages of organizing our first Bible Club. Our plan was to use her church building since it was located in a part of town where we had a better chance of reaching the urban children that we were hoping to target. But we had a lot of work to do before everything would be ready to go. First on our list was to write the curriculum. We had stacks of children's idea books and curricula spread out on the table around us. We decided that the best approach for a group of mostly unchurched children was to start at the beginning. We would start in Genesis and go through the 7 days of the creation week—telling stories, doing object lessons, putting together crafts, and playing games. We would also focus on one character quality each day, giving the children concrete teaching that they could apply in their daily lives. By the end of that first meeting we had a good start on our curriculum. Now we needed a name for our club. A name that would capture the heart of what we were doing. A name that we could use in years to come as we developed new themes and continued to conduct Bible clubs (we were sure this would be an overwhelming success and that this would be the key to bringing revival to all of Wichita...what can I say, Julia and I are both visionaries and we like to dream big!). Finally, the name had to capture the spirit of an...adventure. That was it! *Adventures in Character*.

With those important elements decided, it was time to move on to the next step. We recruited our siblings and a handful of friends to help us teach and organize the games and crafts. The Horns, an older couple from Julia's church, agreed to handle the refreshments and lunch arrangements in our *Character Café*. Various other friends filled the roles of official storyteller, activities director, and piano player. The plan was to meet from 8:00–4:00 each Tuesday for three weeks in July and to conclude the final week with a special presentation for the parents.

Julia and I designed flyers and a group of us got together to pray and pass them out in the neighborhood. Everyone we invited was receptive and we could hardly wait until the children started pouring through the doors later that month. We finished writing the curriculum and held a training day for all of our friends that had agreed to be teachers. Julia and I continued meeting together to pray and complete the final preparations. We were praying that God would bring exactly the children that He wanted to be a part of the Bible club and we excitedly anticipated what He was going to do.

Finally, the morning of the first day arrived and a few of the children from Julia's church were the first to sign up. We waited expectantly. A little while later a handful of children from a family in the neighborhood arrived. We were thrilled! But where were the others? We had passed out many more flyers and thought that parents and children would jump at the chance to be a part of this adventure. But it soon became apparent that no one else was coming. Although struggling with disappointment, Julia and I reminded each other that we had prayed that God would bring the children that He wanted and it was our duty to trust Him. We conducted the activities of the first day with enthusiasm and there was a great spirit of unity amongst all the children and various helpers. In a short time we all got to know each other very well and we had a blast together! Our small group of children genuinely enjoyed the personal interaction and was fully engaged in the stories and songs and other projects. As planned, we concluded the month with a presentation for the several parents and were satisfied that we had done what God called us to do. The results of our endeavor were in His hands. Only later would we look back and realize that this was the first step on the road to an even bigger adventure!

That fall Nicole and I, along with Julia and her brother Ian, and Stephen and Daniel—two other brothers who had been involved in the Bible Club—met together with our parents to discuss an idea we had begun to entertain. We had started contemplating it about a year before, but had sensed that it wasn't the Lord's timing so had put it on hold. Now we were ready to discuss it again and this time we believed that the Lord was directing us to move forward with it. All of our families were actively involved in the Teaching Parents Association and had been working in various capacities with the convention each year. It had occurred to us that if there was a special program offered for children, many families would love coming to the convention together. This would relieve the pressure of families having to find a babysitter for their younger children. So we began to devise a program for children aged six to twelve where they could be in an environment with teams of other homeschooled children, under the supervision of homeschooled teenagers whom we would train to be teachers. We would fill the days with stories, games, crafts, and more, centered on a biblical theme and designed to support parents by giving their children an appreciation and vision for homeschooling.

We presented our idea to the TPA Board (which included two of our three families) and they eagerly offered their support and encouragement. We would work closely with them to secure the necessary facilities and handle the registration process. Plans were beginning to take shape and we could hardly wait to see what God would do through this children's program that we soon dubbed...*Adventures In Character*.

Our small team of siblings and parents met together regularly to pray, write curriculum, plan activities, and develop our theme. All of us had been involved for several years now in Children's Institutes, so we had some excellent resources and experience from which we were able to draw as we commenced this daunting task. With Rich and Susan Neu overseeing our small group, we got to work. We poured through all of our resources, brainstormed, and talked through lots of ideas as we compiled our curriculum. We were learning not only the skills involved in such a process, but also how to handle the frustrations that come when dealing with people that have different perspectives and ideas as to what should be done or how it should be done. We saw our own shortcomings exposed as God stretched us and used these experiences to develop character in us.

As we continued our preparations, I was asked to be the song-leader during the weekend of Adventures In Character (AIC). At long last, the Lord was fulfilling my dream! Or so I thought. As much as I wanted to jump at the opportunity, I committed the matter to prayer before giving a final answer. In the following few weeks as I spent time praying and reading the Bible, the Lord made it clear to me that it was not His will for me to accept this opportunity. I was especially convinced of this as I read the account in Luke 5 where several of the disciples have been fishing all night. When morning dawns, Jesus approaches and commands them to cast their net on the other side of the boat. As ridiculous as Jesus' command may have seemed, Peter responds, "Master, we have toiled all the night, and have taken nothing: nevertheless at thy word I will let down the net." *At thy word.* The driving force of my decision needed to be the Word of the Lord. Not my own desires and dreams. Not the hopes or requests of other people. But the Word of the Lord. The Lord knew that I wasn't ready yet. I still needed to learn to trust Him and wait for Him to give me the go-ahead.

Although I was greatly disappointed, the memory of how God had worked the last time He had asked me to trust Him and lay my dreams at His feet made it easier to decline the offer to be the song-leader. I continued to help with the writing and other preparations for the weekend, but when the convention arrived, I found myself once again helping with the workshop taping and watching the exciting world of AIC from the "outside." It was certainly a lesson in humility for me, no doubt one that the Lord knew I needed. My heart was pulled toward AIC and I longed to be a part of it, but my responsibilities were elsewhere, at least for the time being. I was reminded of the words of missionary Jim Elliot, "Wherever you are, be all there." I had to learn to invest myself 100% in the things God had given me to do right then and not miss out on those opportunities because I was waiting for the next opportunity that promised to be bigger and better. God was training me to be faithful in the little things. And it started with obedience. My heart had to be sensitive to God's direction and willing to obey whatever He called me to do...or not do, as it seemed was more frequently the case with me.

God's blessing on our efforts was evident. Over 150 children enrolled in AIC that first year and it was an overwhelming success! Everything ran smoothly. The teachers put a great deal of time and energy into their preparations and did a wonderful job working with the children on their teams. The children had a blast and the parents overflowed with gratitude for providing a way for them to attend the convention as a family. We were in awe of how God brought all the details together and were soon making plans for the next year.

The first year had been an eclectic collection of skits, activities and lessons, but as we began our preparations for the second year, a theme began to develop. It was based on Proverbs 18:10, "The name of the LORD is a strong tower: the righteous runneth into it, and is safe." In addition to the skits and stories based on various character qualities, we thought it would be exciting to portray more dramatically the story of Dietrich Bonhoeffer, a courageous man who personified the truth of that verse. Nicole took charge of that aspect of the planning and found a script that she was able to use as a starting point. She spent hours writing, editing, revising, and praying until finally she had a finished product that she thought would work. Then came the next big hurdle—recruiting actors and actresses. Up until now, much of our stage time was ad-libbed and the stories we told had been learned by observation. A frequent technique used was that of the story-teller describing the story as it happened with the actors and actresses merely taking their cues from the story-teller. Using a real script was a bit outside our league. But Nicole pressed forward. We all brainstormed to come up with a list of people whom we knew had acting experience, an interest in acting, or at least had dramatic personalities! After many phone calls and explanations of what we were doing, the job was almost done. Only one part remained to be filled: Dietrich Bonhoeffer.

As we sifted through lists of names and flipped through mental files of everyone we could think of in the area, we came up blank. Then, all of a sudden the possibility of Ben playing the part came to mind. Ben would be perfect! Their family had been friends of ours since before I was born and we had kept in touch over the years. To say they were into acting would be an understatement. For years his Mom, Bobbie, had been overseeing the homeschool theater group in their area and we would often make the trip to watch their excellent, professionally-performed productions. The only problem was that they lived in Kansas City, a good three hour drive from Wichita. Logistically, it seemed impossible. But we decided to give it a try. Nicole called Ben, explained our idea to him and asked if he would consider filling the role of Dietrich Bonhoeffer. Ben was already familiar with Bonhoeffer's life and after discussing some of the details, he agreed on the spot (we have always held that it was the fact that he was offered free lodging and meals at the Hyatt for the weekend that sealed the deal!). Not only that, but Ben also had a contact in the theater lighting business and was able to get us a great deal on lighting. One of his friends who had been involved in theater work in Kansas City volunteered to come with Ben to be our lighting technician. Another friend volunteered to come and help with the directing. We were amazed to see God turning our small dream into a big reality!

As the weekend of AIC approached we grew more and more excited. Nicole mailed the scripts to all the actors and actresses so they could memorize their lines and she spent time blocking, designing sets, collecting props, searching for sound effects, and organizing all the other little details that had to come together to make the production a success. On top of that we were busy writing curriculum, memorizing Scripture verses and putting hand motions to them, and planning the rest of the assemblies (according to our calculations, we determined that the drama would comprise the length of about three of our assemblies).

One afternoon, as I was working on AIC planning, the Lord laid on my heart the words for a song. I jotted them down and pulled out a manuscript book and spent several hours notating the melody and arranging a piano accompaniment. I had had very little experience writing music and no experience writing piano arrangements, but somehow the Lord used my years of playing and the few theory and song-writing courses I had at Sound Foundations to develop a song. I tentatively announced at our next staff meeting that I had written a song that I thought we might be able to use. I felt very vulnerable sharing something I had written with the others. What would they think? What if they didn't like it? What if it sounded dumb? Even as I played and attempted to sing it for them, these thoughts flitted through my sub-consciousness. Everyone had gathered at the piano to look over my shoulder at the handwritten manuscript in front of me and as I finished, the declaration was unanimous. They liked it! I breathed a sigh of relief. *Run to the Lord* had passed the test and it was added to our plans for the weekend.

Once again Mrs. Neu asked me to be the song-leader and once again I sought the Lord for direction. I knew He had brought about a change in my heart because I was able to pray in submission, longing to truly know His will and without a determination to have things my own way. My heart was even more wrapped up in AIC this year, but more than anything I wanted to be in the center of God's will. And so it was with overwhelming joy and excitement that the Lord gave me assurance that this year I could accept the position! My affections had been tested and purified. The Lord knew that I needed to be drawn first to Himself—that I needed to find my joy and fulfillment in Him alone and not in anything that I was doing. It was a lesson I would be reminded of over and over again in the following years and I have thanked God many times that He was gracious and patient enough to help me learn it while I was still young.

The much-anticipated week finally arrived. Thursday was our designated set-up day. We hauled all of our supplies, sets and props into the huge Exhibition Hall of the Century II Convention Center. Booths made of pipe and drape were arranged in an L-shape and served as the team booths. A huge open area housed the stage at the opposite end, with rows of chairs flanking it in the front and facing away from the team booths. Adjacent to our AIC area was the Exhibitor Hall where vendors from across the country would soon be setting up their displays of homeschool curricula and merchandise. The noise and lack of lighting control would be a major hindrance to the Dietrich Bonhoeffer drama. Nicole had foreseen this dilemma and had presciently secured a large room in another part of the building that would better suit our needs. While the rest of us rolled up our sleeves and got to work organizing all of our craft supplies and setting up the stage, Nicole gathered together with her group of actors and actresses in the afore-mentioned drama room. It would be their first time to rehearse the drama. It would also be their only time to rehearse the drama. A long day awaited them and they eagerly began running through each of the scenes. Questions abounded. Would things go smoothly? Would everyone remember their lines? Would all the sound effects work properly? Would all the children be able to see the stage? Would they even like it?

The teachers and assistant teachers who had applied and been accepted to teach the teams of children arrived at 6:00 that evening for training. After some preliminary ice-breaker games and introductions, we began the training with a challenge from Mr. and Mrs. Neu, exhorting us to invest wholeheartedly in the children throughout the weekend and to be committed to a life of holiness before the Lord. From there, we walked through the curriculum, one session at a time, giving more detailed explanations and examples of the activities, and trying to assuage any overwhelming feelings they might be experiencing in the face of such a daunting task. Above all, we committed our task to the Lord and to the best of our ability left the results of our efforts in His hands.

Friday morning dawned bright and early and found our staff team traversing the hallways from our rooms at the adjacent hotel to the convention center. The morning training time passed all too quickly and the arrival of the children was upon us. We scattered to our assigned posts, opened our doors and began to greet the line of parents and children that were waiting with anticipation for this moment. Each family was assigned to a team and each team consisted of 15-20 children, led by one teacher and one assistant teacher. Rather than segregate the teams by age, we followed the biblical model learned from the Children's Institutes of placing all the children from each family on the same team and integrating the various ages into one team. Although some teaching challenges presented themselves, the benefits were obvious. Older students were challenged and given the opportunity to be Student Assistants on their team, receiving additional responsibilities and encouragement to be an example and help to the younger children. Younger children, in turn, could look up to and learn from the older children.

Once most of the children had arrived, the schedule was set in motion! We began with a short time in small groups so that the students and teachers could get to know each other and become comfortable working together. Then it was off to the first assembly! My friend Trisha and I took the stage and began teaching the students our Bible memory verses for the weekend and several songs, accompanied by hand motions to make the words easier to remember. We soon gave up our spots and welcomed one of the other staff members who had prepared a short skit to introduce our first principle for the day. Twenty minutes later the teams of students were on their way back to their team booths so they could spend the next session completing crafts, playing games or participating in various activities to help reinforce the principle they had learned.

Like a well-oiled wheel, the day ran smoothly. At dinner time, parents trickled back into the AIC area where they were met by excited little voices describing in great detail what they had experienced. All of us AIC staff and the teachers enjoyed a tasty pizza dinner and a wonderful hour of fellowship before it was time to resume our posts and prepare for the final session. The children returned with full stomachs, eager to see what was on the agenda for the evening. The final session saw us again splitting the time between the team sessions and the assemblies until eventually the adult keynote session concluded and parents ventured back into the AIC area to pick up their children and take them home for the night.

After we finished cleaning the area up, all the teachers and staff members gathered to discuss our thoughts and feelings about the day and spent some time praying for specific requests. Then we called it a night and headed for our respective abodes to catch a few hours of sleep before repeating the same routine the following day...except for the special surprise that we had promised would be awaiting the students' return the next morning.

Reports from parents the next morning indicated that their children had been pestering them to hurry up so that they wouldn't miss any part of the day's events. We were thrilled to hear it and kept hoping and praying that our "special surprise" would live up to the expectation we had created. Eventually the moment arrived. We gave detailed instructions to each team, lining them up in a single-file line to make the journey to the other side of the building where the drama room awaited us. We had to travel through one end of the Exhibit Hall and didn't want to be a distraction to the shoppers...or lose any children along the way! Almost 200 children made barely a peep as we wove our way through the crowds and filed into the smaller meeting room. The curiosity level reached a high point as we instructed them to be seated row after row on the carpeted floor in front of a small stage. We had captured their attention. But could we hold it? As soon as the last child was seated, the lights were lowered and the sound of multiple "radio" broadcasts split the silence, intermingled with bursts of light flashing from alternating sides of the room. The children sat transfixed as the story of Dietrich Bonhoeffer unfolded before them. They were not alone. I looked on in awe as this group of mostly untrained actors, with only a day and half of rehearsals under their belt, put forth a remarkable performance.

My appearance before the group at the end of Act I was marked with an audible groan as I announced that it was time to go back to the AIC area for the next team session, but I reassured them that we would be back to continue the story. A buzz of excitement filled the air as the children recapped the story once back in their booths. They could hardly wait for the signal that it was time for the next assembly. After reviewing our songs and verses, we were off again to our drama room, where Act II was about to take place. Again the students were mesmerized by the lights, the sounds, but mostly by the story of this courageous man as they were transported to an earlier time, and shared with him in his struggles and triumphs. And again, the students could not contain their disappointment when I announced that the story would be continued at a later time.

The suspense was ripe as a short time later the children followed our well-traveled path and found their places one final time in our drama room. Act III was full of emotion as Dietrich Bonhoeffer wrestled with questions of what was right and wrong and ultimately faced death as a consequence for his actions. The somber ending concluded with his lone voice, joined eventually by every other member of the cast, singing *A Mighty Fortress Is Our God* as they took their places on the stage and lifted a hymn of praise to God. I let the moment linger and infuse itself in our hearts and minds before assuming my place at the front to lead the children in a hearty applause for such an outstanding production. It was obvious that the huge undertaking had been well worth it. It was even more obvious that God had been present among us, working His wonders on our behalf. And Adventures In Character would never be the same!

Chapter 17

"One of the beauties of homeschooling is the freedom it gives students to pursue their individual interests and hone their personal strengths. Natalie made the most of those opportunities as a student. Now she has an amazing skill set that she uses to invest in others and motivate them on to higher achievement."

Julia Camenisch

the plot thickens

G od had accomplished through Adventures In Character something far bigger than we ever dreamed was possible. Now the standard had been raised, our sights had been set higher, and we were inspired to dream even bigger! The following year, as our core staff met together to begin planning, the idea was birthed of developing our whole program from scratch. We could write an original drama, curriculum, and songs, all centered on a specific theme. The response from the previous year had revealed that a continuing drama had the potential to make a more lasting impact on the children than isolated skits and stories. We found that it also captured their attention and left them eagerly anticipating what would happen next. If we were to write our own drama, founded upon the philosophies and lessons we wanted to impart to the children, the possibilities would be extensive and the impact even greater. It was an exciting proposition, but we had no idea where to start. The task of writing the drama was delegated to our "master story-teller," Daniel.

Our theme would be one of forgiveness and our adventure would lead us into the high seas aboard the deck of the H.M.S. Nevigrof (forgiveN spelled backwards). Plans took shape, curriculum was written, sets were constructed, and we were ready to set sail. Or so we thought. As time ticked away, we discovered that the scene outlines Daniel had written had remained just that—outlines. Nicole and I, and we assumed the others, had envisioned a fully scripted drama and were shocked when Daniel presented us with the outlines. He had recruited some friends to be his crew members and he planned to assume the role of captain in his story-telling adventure. We couldn't imagine how a full length drama—eight scenes worth!—could be adequately performed from merely paragraph-length outlines for each scene. But there was nothing we could do. It was Daniel's responsibility and it would succeed or fail miserably on his head. That was my attitude and I convinced myself that I was perfectly justified in it.

In the process of planning, we had come up with the seemingly brilliant idea of distributing a passport to each child when they arrived. In order to make it official, it would need to include their picture. The computer gurus (I'm being nice by not calling them geeks) in the group devised a plan for quickly taking a snapshot of each child as they arrived, storing it in a file, merging it with our passport template, and printing them out in batches to distribute to the children shortly after they were escorted to their team booths. Now, if you are personally acquainted with any computer gurus you should know that there is a word that didn't belong in that sentence. Quickly. The fact that we even envisioned this being a quick, seamless process is now laughable. But we were idealistic. The reality was soon evident. From the moment the first child stepped on the "X" to have her picture taken until the last child was escorted to his team, I have no idea how long it took. But we experienced more glitches than we could have imagined. The process was anything but seamless and we were retaking pictures and distributing replacement passports the rest of the weekend. I was incredibly stressed out and found my attention diverted almost constantly by the computer problems. That stress, compounded by my frustration with Daniel, left my heart far from where it should have been safely resting and trusting in the Lord.

The weekend was a blur. I hardly remember the details. All that sticks out in my mind is the inner turmoil that plagued me. And yet, the Lord's work on our behalf again was evident as comments from parents and children, and even observing bystanders, indicated that they had been blessed and touched by every aspect of the program. And I admit, I almost choked when one of the teachers innocently asked if she could get a copy of the drama script because she had loved it so much she wanted to use it for another program. She thought I was kidding when I told her that it was just an outline and all the dialogue had been adlibbed. I'm sure God thought that was a funny way of telling me that things didn't have to be done my way or meet my expectations in order for them to be successful. Unfortunately, it took me longer than I care to admit for the humor to sink in. What I didn't realize is that God was patiently chipping away at my prideful, self-centered heart. And He was using AIC as His carefully selected tool. Time would reveal that He still had a long way to go.

The following year a number of our charter staff members moved on to other opportunities, so we added six new staff members. Rich and Susan Neu continued to oversee our planning and preparations, but left the majority of the responsibilities up to us. The idea for our theme that year was confirmed in an amazing way. I was sitting at the kitchen table, thinking and praying about it one morning and began jotting down ideas. I was reading in Colossians 1 and was struck by verses 26-27 that declare, "...the mystery which has been hidden from ages and from generations, but now has been revealed to His saints. To them God willed to make known what are the riches of the glory of this mystery among the Gentiles: which is Christ in you, the hope of glory." The concept of doing a mystery, with a theme that would ultimately point to Jesus as the answer, seemed really exciting! As soon as Nicole came into the room, I started excitedly sharing my idea with her. She got a funny-looking smile on her face and ran back downstairs. She was back a moment later with a little notebook in her hand. She opened it up and held it up for me to see. Across the top of the page, in big bold letters she had written and underlined the words, "A MYSTERY!" In our own thinking and praying about a theme for the year, we had come up with the same idea. It was thrilling to consider that God was the one directing our plans and laying the ideas on our hearts so that we could proceed in accordance with His will for AIC!

When we met with the other staff members to discuss our ideas, the vote was unanimously in favor of a mystery theme. The adventure would take us to the far-off land of Skitzofrania where we would follow the path of three quirky detectives trying to crack the case of a missing person. Thus was born *DISAPPEARANCE! An unknown identity. A far off place. Face to face with danger. Detectives needed.*

The planning began in earnest, but Nicole and I soon grew frustrated because of the lack of follow-through among some of the staff members. We divided the writing responsibilities amongst us, with each of us responsible for writing a drama scene and a curriculum session. But some of the staff members would show up at meetings with unfinished work, accompanied by excuses for why it wasn't done. There didn't seem to be the level of wholehearted commitment that we expected, and several of us had to pick up the slack for the others. My attitude was such that I didn't really care why it wasn't done or what the excuse was. If someone had committed to fill a role or take on a responsibility, they had better make sure they got it done. Nicole felt the same way and eventually we decided that something needed to be done. My preferred M.O. in such situations is to let it go unresolved and assume that things will get better. I have been accused on more than one occasion of being an "eternal optimist." Nicole, ever the pessimist, saw things quite differently. If we didn't deal with the problems, they would only get worse. We solicited counsel from Dad, who agreed that we needed to address the problems we were observing.

We e-mailed some of our concerns to Mrs. Neu, since she was more closely involved in the meetings and working with the staff than Mr. Neu, and arranged to meet in person to discuss what steps needed to be taken. Our sentiment was that several people needed to be removed from their staff positions and she agreed that that was a reasonable approach. We spent some time in prayer and then wrote out a list of the general responsibilities and expectations for each staff member. After about an hour and half, we left with a plan in place. At the meeting the following night, Mrs. Neu would read the list of responsibilities and ask each person how they felt they measured up. Then she would ask a couple of people to step down from their positions and would move one person to a different position.

Later that same afternoon, I called Myklin to make her aware of what was going on. She and her brother Logan had put in a considerable amount of time and work and I didn't want either of them to think that this was being directed toward them. We wanted them to be prepared for what was to take place at the meeting. We talked for a few minutes and prayed together before hanging up. We wanted to seek God's direction and be sure we were doing things His way. At least that's what I said. But inwardly, I really wanted to do things my way. If people weren't living up to my expectations for them, in my mind they were "dead weight," burdening the rest of us and impeding our efforts. There was no real peace or resolution in the path we were taking, but this was the course we had charted and I figured there was no turning back.

Shortly after the phone conversation I got a call from another staff member. One of those we were planning to ask to step down. He was calling to say he wouldn't be at the meeting the following night. We talked for a while and the discussion turned to AIC and where he was at personally. He was very honest and very humble in acknowledging his shortcomings and some things he was struggling with. The conversation was enlightening as I heard him express these things and realized what a rough time he was having. Instead of being critical and unforgiving and thinking only of my own frustrations, I found myself encouraging him and trying to understand how he was hurting. I hung up with him and prayed that he would find in the Lord the one who could bring healing.

Only a few moments later, the phone was ringing again. It was Myklin. She and her family had been discussing some things since our earlier conversation and were not convinced that our plan was the best way to handle the situation. Her Dad and Logan pointed out that often failure on the part of those under authority is a reflection of the leadership—or lack of good leadership. We discussed her thoughts at length and prayed together again before hanging up. The Lord had gotten my attention. And it didn't feel good. For some time a quote had continued to surface in my thoughts and I had done my best to dismiss it, "Attitude reflects leadership." Rather than being quick to point my finger at the faults of the others, I needed to examine my own life. This required honesty and humility—both of which I was sorely lacking.

After a night of soul-searching, I awoke the next morning and spent some time reading my Bible. I came across a couple of verses that grabbed my attention, "And John answered and said, Master, we saw one casting out devils in thy name; and we forbad him, because he followeth not with us. And Jesus said unto him, Forbid him not: for he that is not against us is for us (Luke 9:49-50). My attitude had been like John's. I was treating my brothers and sisters in Christ like they were on the enemy's side. But we were in this together. We were working toward a common goal and God had placed us together to work as a team. My attitude was a self-righteous one of superiority instead of brotherly love. Instead of me exposing the failings of the others, God was revealing the true nature of my own heart. And it wasn't pretty.

I called Mrs. Neu a little while later and told her that I thought the Lord had shown me that the way we were headed was not the way He wanted us to resolve the situation. We still needed to address the issues we had observed—lack of commitment and irresponsibility, but instead of cutting off those people who were not performing up to our standards we needed to help them refocus and encourage them. Our goal needed to be to strengthen our team, not tear it apart. She was receptive to the new direction and said she would think and pray about it to determine the best way to handle the meeting.

When I checked my e-mail that afternoon there was a message from Chandler saying that she would be really late to the meeting if she was able to make it at all. I was so discouraged because I felt like it was important for everyone to be at the meeting. I began praying that somehow God would intervene and work out her schedule so that she could be at the meeting on time. I had a hard time remaining focused on my students as I taught that afternoon, since so many things were heavy on my heart. But the Lord helped me get through the day.

Shortly after 6:30 Mrs. Neu arrived so that she and Nicole and I could pray together before the meeting. The others began arriving around 7:00. Tiffany called to say that she had come across Myklin and Logan on the side of the road with a broken down car. She had picked them up and they were all on their way. Shortly after they arrived I was shocked to see Chandler walking up the driveway. I was so excited! God had answered my prayer!

The meeting got underway with Mrs. Neu opening in prayer and then discussing the list of responsibilities we had developed. Then she opened it up for each of us to share what was on our heart and how we felt about our commitment to AIC. It became a wonderful time of refocusing and recommitting to the vision God had given us for the year. The atmosphere was one of support, and our friendships were forged more deeply as we spent time praying together for the ministry of AIC and for each other. I went to bed that night after the meeting, confident that God was our capable Leader and that if we remained firmly rooted in Him He would hold us together and strengthen us. There were still struggles, but we were committed to working through them. We experienced the strength of God being made perfect in our weaknesses.

Finally the weekend arrived. Again we attempted the picture-taking process as the students arrived and again we experienced numerous glitches and frustrations. I found my focus constantly divided between the computer issues associated with the registration process and being available to help the teachers or work with the students. My role was to lead the songs and memory verses during the assemblies and I was able to play the part well when I was on stage, but off stage, I struggled to remain focused and not succumb to frustration and irritation over petty issues. But it turned out that was the least of my problems! Friday night, a girls choir I was directing sang for the opening of the keynote addresses. After we were done and I was back in the AIC area, I discovered that my purse was gone. It appeared that it had been stolen. While this would have been enough in and of itself, the situation was compounded by the fact that I was leaving from the convention center Saturday night to drive to California where I would be spending the rest of the summer working at a camp. I had numerous important papers in my purse, along with approximately $70 in cash—more than I ever carried! A search effort at the end of the day Friday by a crew of AIC helpers turned up empty. The purse was definitely gone. We reported the theft to the convention center staff and they assured us that they would let us know if they found anything. We all began praying for the return of my purse, but we knew it would take a miracle.

Before I went to bed that night I read Psalm 30. The last sentence of verse 5 practically leaped off the page at me, "weeping may endure for a night, but joy cometh in the morning." Immediately my heart was awash with peace and trust in the Lord. Somehow I knew that I would get my purse back the next morning. I was free from anxiety and slept soundly that night. The next morning I awoke eager to see how the Lord would work this out. As soon as I got down to the convention center I contacted one of the employees and asked if they had had a purse turned in. He said he wasn't sure, but walked with me over to the office to find out. We walked through the glass exterior doors and into a back room. And there, sitting on an old metal desk, was the most beautiful sight—my purse! I was ecstatic and immediately offered up my thanks to the Lord. A quick examination of its contents revealed that everything was still there. Everything, that is, except for the cash. I was sick to lose so much money, but incredibly relieved to have everything else back.

Once I was back in the AIC area, I shared the story with the other staff members. They sympathized with me over the loss of the money, but were also encouraged to know that God had allowed my purse to be returned. By the time the children arrived that morning, things were running smoothly and I was in good spirits. Just before dismissing the teams to go back to their booths at the end of the first assembly, though, I was surprised when Bev came up on stage and commandeered my microphone. She briefly shared with all the children what had happened regarding my purse and then explained that some people had taken up a collection on my behalf and wanted to present me with a gift of cash. I was in shock. This was completely unexpected and I hardly knew what to say. After offering a heartfelt thank you, we dismissed the teams and I counted the money I had received. $80. Unbelievable. God had provided above and beyond what I ever could have hoped and I felt incredibly blessed to be surrounded by such a loving, generous group of friends and co-laborers.

Nicole had taken on the task of compiling the drama scripts, editing them, and directing the drama again that year. She did a marvelous job and again it was an overwhelming success! The children loved following the mystery and got to be part of the action by submitting their suspicions of who was guilty into the "Tip Box" we had placed on display for that purpose. With one twist after another and several dead ends, the students were left hanging at the end of every scene, wondering what would happen next. The actors and actresses did a superb job memorizing their lines and capturing our imaginations with their convincing portrayal of the characters. We began to see more and more how effective the dramatic element was at presenting concepts that could be explained and reinforced during the time on their teams. And even though we had included numerous subtleties and complexities beneath the surface of the script, we were shocked at how much the students picked up and the depth of their comprehension of the story. These six to twelve year olds were capable of more than we were giving them credit for!

By the time the next year rolled around we were already thinking of and discussing new theme ideas. Eventually the idea of a courtroom drama surfaced and we ran with it. We outlined three primary qualities that we wanted to write into the story—honoring parents, telling the truth, and standing alone. Since there would be very little scene changing throughout the eight scenes, we knew it had to be a strong story and that we would have to recruit effective actors and actresses. The brainstorming, planning and writing began in earnest. Again there was a great deal of enthusiasm as we discussed our ideas and outlined our individual responsibilities. But again, problems with lack of follow-through quickly surfaced. With Mr. and Mrs. Neu stepping back somewhat from their responsibilities with AIC, I assumed the role of Staff Leader and found myself growing frustrated with the lack of dependability we were experiencing with some of the other staff members. In particular, several of the guys found themselves overwhelmed with added school assignments, family responsibilities, and now challenging writing projects for AIC as well. I would love to say that I was gracious and understanding and encouraged the rest of the staff team to come alongside them to support and help them. But unfortunately, this was not the case. The lessons I had learned the previous year had apparently been short-lived.

Due to her work responsibilities, Nicole was unable to be a part of AIC that year. In her absence, I drew several of the other staff girls into my frustrations as we openly discussed how the guys were failing to live up to their responsibilities. Several times we found ourselves forced to pick up the slack and take on the work they were supposed to do just so that it would be finished by our deadlines. I discussed these issues at length with Dad and finally expressed that I felt it would be best to remove one of them from his position as a staff member. Based on the perspective I shared, Dad agreed that it seemed appropriate, but advised that I arrange to meet with his parents to let them know what was going on and receive their counsel before proceeding. I also called Mrs. Neu to update her on the situation and she said that she would defer to my judgment and that she trusted me to make the right decision. I agonized for several days and nights over the situation and prayed for wisdom in dealing with it. But in many ways, I think I had already made up my mind about what I was going to do.

It was Wednesday morning when I made the call. There was a pit in my stomach as I explained to David's* Mom that I would like to meet with her to discuss some concerns I had regarding her son's involvement with AIC. She was available that morning and offered to come over to meet at our house before I started teaching lessons for the day. A half hour later we were sitting at our dining room table and I was sharing some of the problems I had observed regarding her son. She was very understanding and, amid tears, agreed that I was justified in asking him to step down from his staff position. We discussed the issue some more and she gave me some counsel on the best way to approach my discussion with David. After a parting hug, she returned home, and I moved on to the next unpleasant task of the day—making phone calls. I called one of the other staff guys to apprise him of the situation and see if he would be willing to meet the following night to help me convey the decision to David. He agreed to be there. Another call to David finalized the meeting time and location.

The following night, the three of us pulled up metal folding chairs beside a table in the basement of Trinity Baptist Church. The guys would be holding a weekly Bible Study there later that night, so it was a convenient place for the meeting to take place. After opening in prayer, we got right to the issue at hand. I laid out the areas where I felt like David had not fulfilled his responsibilities and explained that because of where things stood at this point I was asking him to step down from his position as an AIC staff member. We still wanted him to be a part of the weekend event and continue in his position as one of the area leaders, but that he would do so in a non-staff capacity. He listened respectfully until I was done and then said that he understood my decision and would abide by it. I was floored by his humble and gracious attitude. He didn't offer excuses or attempt to defend himself in any way. He understood that the decision had been made and he willingly submitted to it. My respect and admiration for him multiplied and I have often reflected on how much I learned

(*not his real name)

from his example. The three of us chatted casually for a little longer until we finally parted ways. I drove home considerably more at peace than I had been on my way there, but I couldn't help but wonder if I had done the right thing.

Truthfully, although I had followed all the right principles for dealing with the situation and had acted fully under the authorities involved in the situation, I later understood that it was the attitude of my heart that needed an adjustment. I was guided by a prideful self-righteousness that set myself up as the standard to which I held others. I saw my way as the right way and, in many cases, the only way. I was motivated not by love and compassion, but by a desire to exert control and run things my way. I was a control freak. But I didn't even know it. And if anyone had asserted that I was, I would have adamantly disagreed. I was blinded by my pride and it continued to rear its ugly head in the following weeks.

Soon another one of the staff guys was slacking in his responsibilities and again I became irritated. My good friend and fellow staff member Tiffany and I found ourselves with an extra workload as we assumed the responsibilities that were not being completed. We commiserated together and became more and more disgruntled over the whole situation. It all came to a head one Sunday evening after a church service where the three of us were present. Toward the end of the previous week we had all been at the church for various reasons and a situation arose that called this staff member's honesty into question. That Sunday night, after being apprised of the situation, Craig, the Pastor of the church (also Tiffany's dad), called the three of us into his office to discuss the situation. Tiffany and I brought forward our complaints and waited for a response.

After offering a brief explanation of his actions to clarify that he was not acting dishonestly, he proceeded to humbly acknowledge his shortcomings in other areas that had been of concern to us. He also shared about some of the personal and spiritual struggles he was experiencing. As he shared, my heart was pierced. Once again I was guilty of judging and acting harshly toward a brother in Christ when what he needed was love and support. I was thoroughly convicted and once he finished sharing I was compelled to confess my own sin of slandering him to my family and other staff members. On more than one occasion I had shared negative and hurtful information with others for the sole purpose of making him look bad and myself look better. Now I was ashamed and asked him to forgive me. He did so immediately and then confessed that he had done the same. I responded likewise in forgiveness, but wouldn't you know it, in the back of my mind I was wondering what on earth he could have had to say about me that was negative! It seemed that I was doomed to the bondage of a prideful, self-righteous heart! But God was using these situations to expose the ugly impurities in my heart so that He could purge them from me and continue refining me.

Tremendous restoration came about as a result of our confrontation and confessions that night and we experienced a much greater sense of unity in the final weeks leading up to AIC. We would need it, too, because less than a month before AIC that year, tragedy struck my family and the AIC team.

Chapter 18

"Natalie has an ability to creatively communicate, and her talent as an author is clearly seen within the pages of *Pajama School*. Unique life experiences have allowed her to provide an insightful and entertaining read. Her heart is to glorify God and to bless others, and through this book she has done just that."

Joel Strain

tragedy strikes *close* to home

It was Sunday afternoon, a little after 3:00. I had just awakened from a nap and was sitting in the living room talking with Mom, Noelle, Naomi, and Joey when the phone rang. Mom answered and after a very brief conversation we learned that it was Andrew Strain, informing us that his parents and two youngest brothers had been in a car accident. He had just received a call from the chaplain at a hospital in Joplin, Missouri, informing him that his Dad and two brothers had been admitted. His Mom was in the car as well, but her status was unknown.

As soon as Mom got off the phone, we called Dad up from his office so she could relay the information to him. We gathered around and began praying fervently for these friends who for years had been like family to us. For as long as I could remember, since moving to Kansas, we had spent almost every Thanksgiving and Christmas with the Strains. It was an unlikely match—them with five boys; us with five girls and eventually a boy. But our families became very close and some of my best memories are of our times together. Now it was with great concern that we pleaded with God for their safety and protection.

As we finished our time of prayer, Nicole called from work. She had heard about the accident and wondered if we had any additional details.

We didn't yet, but Mom was preparing to go to the Strain's house as soon as we got more information about the hospital and the condition of those in the accident. Before we had a chance to get the information, though, Nicole called back, this time as the bearer of the words that would replay themselves over and over in my mind for weeks to come. "Mrs. Strain is dead." Surely she was wrong. Nicole's sober words gave way to silence. This was for real. And I was in shock. I hung up the phone and slowly made my way upstairs where I was obliged to repeat those heart-numbing words to the rest of the family. Almost before I was done Mom was sobbing and crying out, "No! No! No!" Dad wrapped his arms around her and she buried her head in his chest. I was numb. Too numb to cry. But there was work to do.

We quickly determined that all of us would go to the Strain's house to be there and do whatever needed to be done at this point. We had no idea what. We had never experienced anything like this before. But we knew we had to go. I called Nicole to see if she wanted to come with us. She would request permission to leave and come right home. Dad asked me to call the Strain's to see what their plans were and make sure that it was okay for us to come over. I called and spoke with Nicole Strain, the wife of Jacob, the oldest Strain boy. She relayed some additional details to me. Mr. Strain and Joel were being life-watched to the KU Med Center in Kansas City. And then...another blow—Jed had been pronounced dead. Dead. More shock. More numbness. What else, Lord? My mind was racing, trying to process, but Nicole was still talking. She said to please come—they needed it. It was all I could do to climb the stairs again and face my family with the news that Jed, too, was dead. The response was a stunned silence. Was this really happening? Perhaps it was all a mistake. Perhaps the next phone call would be to tell us that everything was fine and everyone would be okay after all. But that phone call never came.

Nicole was on her way home and we were preparing to load into the suburban when Mom mentioned that someone needed to call Nadine, who had moved into her own apartment several months before, and let her know what was going on. The unpleasant task fell to me. I had barely relayed the news about Mrs. Strain when Nadine became hysterical and would not let me finish explaining the situation. In between her hysterics I managed to arrange to pick her up at her apartment to drive her to the Strain's where we would meet up with the rest of the family. Noelle, five days Jed's junior and deeply affected by word of his death, rode with me to Nadine's apartment. The ride was somber, each of us lost in our thoughts and trying to comprehend the reality of the situation. My heart cried out to God for help—for me, for the remaining Strains, for the many others who would be affected by this tragedy. We picked up a visibly emotionally wrecked Nadine and filled her in on what we knew so far. Then silence again. Each of us lost in our thoughts. My thoughts turned to the weekend before.

I had received a call from Don, asking me if I knew of someone who could use a free piano. A friend of theirs owned a rental house and had a piano he wanted to get rid of so he could clean the place up and prepare it for the next tenants. I had been considering how helpful it would be to have a second piano so that Noelle, Naomi, and Joey, who were all taking piano lessons from me, could practice during the day while I was teaching. I told him as much and asked about the quality of the piano. It was an old upright, but appeared to be in good condition. The only catch was that it had to be moved before the following Monday. I decided to go take a look.

Saturday evening I met Don at the location and we looked over the piano. Even though it hadn't been tuned in almost 20 years, it had held its tune surprisingly well and had a good touch. It was definitely worth the price—free! As I left the place, I had to figure out how I would get it moved, especially in such a short period of time. I decided to give the Strains a call and see if they would be willing to help me out. I spoke with Mrs. Strain and after explaining the situation, she volunteered that they could help me move it that night. They had been planning to go shopping for a fan, but would be happy to postpone the excursion to help me get the piano moved first. I arrived at their house a short while later. She had called Jacob to see if he would help as well. He was on his way and while we waited for him to arrive, she and I walked around her garden, looking at how the vegetables were doing, and admiring the flowers she had planted. Of all the women I knew, she was perhaps the closest to what I envisioned the Proverbs 31 virtuous woman being. She loved being at home and caring for her household, and it showed.

I had come from a wedding, so she gave me some of her clothes and shoes to wear so that my dress wouldn't get messed up in the move. I had to squeeze my way into the pants and shoes, but they would work. Jacob arrived and we all loaded up into several vehicles—me leading the way in my car, a couple of the boys following behind in the pickup truck and the rest riding in their white minivan. Once we arrived at the place where the piano was located, I pretended to help as they got the piano moved and loaded into the pickup in no time at all. They got it covered and secured and we began the slow drive back to our house. It normally would have taken about 30 minutes, but it took closer to an hour since special care had to be taken with the piano perched in the back of the truck. Jed rode with me and we enjoyed a variety of conversation topics—from what he was working on in piano (he was one of my piano students) to how he was doing on his lines for one of the lead roles in the upcoming Adventures In Character drama.

Once we arrived back at our house, the Strains were joined by Dad and they carefully maneuvered their way through the front door, down the hallway, and into the back bedroom. How they actually got the piano in that room, I have no idea. All of the ladies and girls stood outside and visited while they accomplished that feat! We were now the grateful and excited owners of two pianos. It had taken longer than expected and was late now, but the adventure had been fun and well worth it. The Strains prepared to leave, but their pickup refused to start. It was backed up to our front porch for the unloading of the piano and had been overworked! Apparently this was not the first time this had happened and the solution was for it to sit and cool off a while longer and then it would run fine again. Mr. and Mrs. Strain and Joel and Jed decided to head home while the others stayed. Nicole and I joined Jacob and his wife Nicole, Andrew, and Jonathan for a late night dinner at a local Mexican restaurant where we enjoyed a good time of discussion and fellowship. By the time we got back to the house, the truck had fully recovered and everyone left for home.

Now we had arrived at the Strain's house—abuzz with people and activity. The memories quickly faded and gave way to the stark reality of the day's events. As I walked into the house I saw everything from a new perspective. Every way I turned I saw Mrs. Strain. She had made their house a beautiful home and her touch was on every detail. I remembered back to that Easter when Mom and Dad and the three younger ones were in Colorado on vacation and Nicole, Nadine, and I had spent the afternoon at the Strain's. We were eating snacks in the living room while playing a game and Mrs. Strain had gotten a few crumbs on her pants. She carefully cupped that part of the fabric and half-walked-half hobbled across the room to the front door where she opened it and released the crumbs onto the front porch. (Little did she know that while she so meticulously avoided making a mess, Andrew remained in the living room, swiping crumbs from the table onto the floor...) But that was how Mrs. Strain was—neat and conscientious, yet always welcoming and hospitable. Now she was gone. Gone from this world forever.

The kitchen was the hub of activity and many friends were already gathered, manning the phones, gathering information and taking care of details. The oldest three Strain boys had just left for the KU Med Center in Kansas City so they could see their Dad and Joel. I was given an address book and asked to make phone calls to people who needed to be told of what had happened. The task was unpleasant, but I was glad to have something to do; anything to help. Eventually there was nothing left to do at the house. Almost everyone had left, including the rest of our family, except Noelle. Finally we left too. I wanted so much to do something more. To fix everything and make it all better. But instead I had to go home. There was nothing more I could do. Our home became a gathering place that evening for several families as we grieved together, prayed, and tried to talk through what had happened and what to do next. It was late by the time everyone was gone, and I found myself tucked away in the corner of my room on my bed. And then the tears began to flow.

I had held up fine throughout the day when there were things that needed to be done, when I was surrounded by people, and didn't have time to ponder all that had transpired. But now, in the quietness of my room, when I sat alone, helpless and pitiful before God, my heart was wrenched from within me and I sobbed uncontrollably. I could try to appear strong on the outside, but the reality of my weakness was not hidden from God. He knew. He knew the agony of my soul. He knew the pain of the loss I felt. He knew. And He alone could comfort my shattered heart. At some point that night, as I cried out to God, I believe He prompted me to write a letter to the rest of the families in my studio, sharing with them what had happened. I was hopeful that somehow God would use this tragedy to bring glory to Himself. This is the letter I penned the following morning, before my students arrived:

Dear students and families,

It is with great sadness that I write this newsletter update. Yesterday (Sunday), the Strain family (many of you know Joel and Jed from piano lessons and recitals, etc.) was in a car accident. Mrs.

Strain and Jed were killed. Mr. Strain and Joel were taken to the KU Medical Center in Kansas City and have undergone surgeries. Mr. Strain is recovering from a broken hand and punctured lung. Joel is recovering from intestinal bleeding and still has a severe back injury. As of now, his lower body is paralyzed. Please pray for Joel and Mr. Strain and their other family members—Jacob and his wife, Nicole, Andrew, and Jonathan.

Though this has hit many people very hard, including myself, I know that God has a purpose for all things. He has allowed this for a reason. Mrs. Strain and Jed both knew Jesus Christ as their Lord and Savior and so I know that I will one day see them again in Heaven. Their lives have impacted many people and I know that their death was not in vain. I pray that each of you will examine your own life and if you have not already, that you may come to know Jesus as your Lord and Savior—the Son of God who lived a perfect life and died, taking upon Himself the penalty for our sins and conquering death through His resurrection. Because of this, we have the promise that if we believe in Him, we too may live eternally with Him in Heaven.

Jesus said, "Verily, verily, I say unto you, He that heareth my word, and believeth on him that sent me, hath everlasting life, and shall not come into condemnation; but is passed from death into life." John 5:24

Love,

Natalie

I continued with my regular teaching schedule that week. It was the only thing I knew to do. All day I taught and conducted lessons as normally as I could. And every night I cried myself to sleep. I thought often of Jed and what an incredible young man he was—one of my most teachable, disciplined, and respectful students. He had flown through his books, asking questions at the end of each lesson to make sure he understood his assignments, and faithfully practicing every day.

He had performed excellently for a festival at one of our universities earlier that year and received the highest rating given. He always brightened my day with his ready smile and sincere "thank you" offered at the end of every lesson. Never again would I look up to see him walk through my studio door. Never again would his fingers touch the keys of my piano. Jed was gone.

I had never experienced death so closely before and it shook my world. The funeral for Mrs. Strain and Jed was held a week later. Hundreds of people came to mourn the loss of two amazing people. But we also came to celebrate—celebrate two lives lived for the glory of God and now transported to heaven to live for all eternity with their Lord.

As time passed I began to see God's hand at work in various ways. After months of rehab, Joel was functioning well and adjusted to life in a wheelchair with an amazing attitude and a quick sense of humor. He decided to continue taking piano lessons, and we saw God's perfect provision in that the week before the accident Joel had helped move into our house the piano that he would now be using since it would be impractical for him to take his lessons in my downstairs studio.

In the summer of that year I was teaching at a music camp and had a particularly difficult group of students for one of my theory classes. It was hard to keep their attention, and certain students in the group were constantly distracting the others. I prayed for wisdom and creativity, and asked the Lord to show me what I could do to make a difference in their lives. As I sat in the car one morning before the last day of camp the idea was clearly implanted in my mind, "tell them about Jed." The Lord wanted me to tell them about Jed and use it as a springboard to share the Gospel with them. I argued with Him for a few minutes. After all, it was not a Christian camp. Would it be appropriate for me to share something like that? His answer came back clearly, "Do it for My glory." Why did I even hesitate? Christians in other countries are dying for their faith every day and I was worried about sharing Jesus with a group of Jr. High students at a camp. I was thoroughly convicted.

That afternoon, as the time with this class drew to a close, I told them that I wanted to share a story with them. They sat transfixed as I told them about my student Jed. I told them about all of his fine qualities. I told them of his untimely death in a car accident. I told them that I knew I would see Jed again some day because Jed had a personal relationship with Jesus Christ. I told them that they can never know for sure when their day will come, but they can have hope for eternity if they give their life to Jesus Christ like Jed did.

It was a somber way to end the week and I don't know what effect it had on each of the students in the class. But I know that God was glorified. And I know that neither Mrs. Strain nor Jed died in vain. Their testimony lives on in their family and in the many people whose lives were touched by them—both in life and also in death.

Chapter 19

"Natalie is a beacon on a hill for Christ. Every child and teacher who comes through the doors of AIC is blessed by her fervent study of God's Word, and her ability to use it to encourage those around her. She is an inspiration to me of how mightily the Lord can use an individual who is completely devoted to Him!"

Laura Bergen

the adventure *continues*

The unexpected accident had left us without three of our actors for the AIC drama that year—Jed, who was cast in one of the lead roles, and Andrew and Joel, who had supporting roles. Another pair of brothers had indicated an interest in being in the drama on their teaching applications, so I called them and explained the situation. I knew it was short notice and they would have to memorize their lines very quickly, but they were willing to jump in and play the parts. I was overwhelmed with gratefulness. We were desperately needy and God was meeting our needs. We went into the AIC weekend that year feeling our dependence on God more than ever. Not just to orchestrate the details and keep things running smoothly, but to provide emotional stamina for many of us who still felt raw with the events of the preceding three weeks.

Thanks to the ingenious work of Josh, a new staff member and our computer operations manager for the year, the registration and picture-taking process was completed without a hitch. Moments after the children arrived at their team booths, name badges with their pictures were delivered. I am quite sure it was a miracle! I didn't have to spend another moment all weekend long thinking about name badges or computers. Instead I could focus on building relationships with the teachers and being available to help them.

One of the funniest incidents happened Friday morning during the teacher training. We had passed out polo shirts for all the teachers Thursday evening for them to wear throughout the weekend. The sizes ended up being incredibly large and looked very unkempt if they were left untucked. So Friday morning we told all the teachers that they were required to wear their polo shirts tucked in. Several girls, who had traveled with a group from Illinois to teach at AIC, came up to me after the training was over. Their faces were stricken and finally one of them blurted out, "We can't tuck our shirts in!" I looked down at their shirts and discovered that they had all cut off their shirts just below the waistline of their skirts. There was no way they could tuck them in. I looked up to see them waiting anxiously for my response. I'm not sure what they were expecting, but I burst out in laughter! There was nothing we could do about it at that point. They were all visibly relieved and soon joined in.

The rest of the weekend had various challenges, but in the end the program was another huge hit and parent after parent expressed what a blessing it was for their children to be a part of AIC. On numerous occasions parents shared that they were not planning to come back after a meal break, but their children were so excited about what they were learning and so eager to find out what was going to happen in the next drama scene that they were persuaded to come back after all. I now maintain that we are in cahoots with the TPA Convention Committee, devising creative ways of keeping parents at the convention longer!

The remainder of the year quickly came and went, and as January of 2005 approached, Mr. and Mrs. Neu stepped completely down from their responsibilities with AIC. Also, Jim Farthing, TPA's President, resigned and Dad assumed the role of the TPA Convention Director. After discussing it with Mom and Dad, it seemed natural for me to officially assume the role of the AIC Director. I sent out a letter to our previous staff members and a few others, inviting them to a meeting at our house so that we could begin working toward another year of AIC. Prior to the meeting, I spent some time outlining job descriptions for each of the various staff positions. In addition to these specific responsibilities, I came up with a list of responsibilities associated with the writing of the curriculum, drama and songs. On top of that, there were many other details that had to be coordinated with TPA. I had been attending the Convention Committee meetings throughout the previous year, but now I would need to work more closely with the TPA members responsible for different areas to ensure that all the details were taken care of. It was going to be an increased workload, but I was excited!

As I prepared for our first staff meeting, I spent time seeking the Lord for direction on what our theme should be. One morning, as I read through Zechariah, I was especially impressed with these verses, "And they shall be as mighty men, which tread down their enemies in the mire of the streets in the battle: and they shall fight, because the LORD is with them, and the riders on horses shall be confounded. And I will strengthen the house of Judah, and I will save the house of Joseph, and I will bring them again to place them; for I have mercy upon them: and they shall be as though I had not cast them off: for I am the LORD their God, and will hear them" (Zechariah 10:5-6). I wasn't sure exactly what direction to take with them, but I jotted them down in my notebook. The night of the meeting arrived and as we began our brainstorming session I shared those verses. Seth, one of our new staff members, immediately jumped in with his own ideas, expanding on the verses and expressing the idea of doing a war theme. We all quickly latched on to the idea and soon the storyline for *Enemy Encounter* was taking shape. The story would follow three boys from their time growing up together pretending to be soldiers in their backyards to the harsh realities of an actual war. Plans progressed smoothly and we found it easy to incorporate valuable life lessons into the drama and the team activities that would follow each scene.

Compared to the problems of the previous years, preparation for this year seemed like a breeze. Everyone got along well and did a good job of fulfilling their responsibilities. Josh took on the task of compiling and editing the curriculum, a task for which I had always been responsible in the past. But the Lord was slowly helping me relinquish my tight control of AIC. I was learning that He could work through any of us and success was not dependent upon me. In fact, based on all the previous years' experience, it seemed that the more I tried to control everything myself, the more difficulties we experienced. In addition to the curriculum and the registration responsibilities, Josh also volunteered to develop a website for AIC. We wanted to provide a way for parents to learn about the program staff and theme each year so that they would feel more comfortable sending their children. The bigger "order," though, was that we wanted potential teachers to be able to apply to teach through the website.

Laura, our registration supervisor, and Josh and I spent some time discussing what information we needed to collect and how we wanted to be able to handle the information. In the end, Josh developed an incredible system that was even better than what I had envisioned. I was impressed with the quality and capabilities of the site and it was a huge help in streamlining the teacher registration process.

The weekend of AIC arrived and it was incredible! The story captured the children's imaginations even more than any of the previous years. They identified with our three main characters and soon looked up to them—at least the good ones!—as celebrities. The little twists and turns in the storyline kept them on the edge of their seats, and during the assemblies they enjoyed marching while singing their own soldier song, and learning how to salute from a real Air Force officer. At the end of the weekend, they all went home with real metal dog tags engraved with our theme title and verse to remind them of the lessons they learned.

Prior to the conference that year, I was contacted by Emily, a young lady who was organizing a children's program to take place during the homeschool convention in Nebraska. She had been a Child Evangelism Fellowship (CEF) leader for years and they were planning to use those materials for their program that year. I shared with her about our organizational structure and the things we'd learned in our years of doing AIC.

We corresponded several times before their conference that April, and I was thrilled to hear back from Emily afterward that it was very well received. While the CEF materials had worked, Emily was interested in purchasing our *Enemy Encounter* program since it was designed specifically for a children's convention format. We agreed to sell it to them for a nominal amount with the understanding that they could adapt it to their needs and would provide feedback and ideas for improvement. Since we had had people request that we publish our program materials and we had seriously entertained the possibility of doing so, we thought this would be an excellent way to test-run it in another state and tweak the materials for future publication.

Josh agreed to film the drama that year, and he produced a DVD that we sent to the Nebraska staff, along with all of the Director files, to help them visualize all the aspects of the program. I sent everything to them in late summer and they were soon adapting them and preparing for their own *Enemy Encounter*, Nebraska style.

A few months later, our staff was back together again, brainstorming for the next year. We had a number of key staff people who weren't coming back due to other responsibilities, so I was praying that God would raise up others to take their places. God faithfully answered that prayer. At our first meeting, Kendra and Kayla, long-time friends of mine, attended and contributed lots of great suggestions and ideas. Kendra took on the task of compiling and editing the drama script and with her wealth of writing skills and experience produced a finished product that we still consider one of our best scripts. Kayla jumped into many aspects of the planning and worked on the drama, the curriculum, and lots of other details.

In October of the previous year, I had met Tiffany Hiebert at a family gathering. After finding out that she was pursuing a minor in graphic design at a local university, I asked her if she would assume the position of Student Workbook Designer. It was a brand new position. Always before, at the last minute, we hurriedly compiled simple activities and stapled them into a workbook for the students. Since it was one of the few things that the students actually took home with them from AIC and often continued using long after the event was over, it seemed short-sighted to be so haphazard in putting it together. Tiffany agreed to fill the position and was soon developing creative activities and new ideas that corresponded perfectly to the lessons we were planning.

Cori, after faithfully serving for many years as a team teacher, also came on board. She took over the huge responsibility of determining all the materials and supplies for the weekend and purchasing, organizing, and preparing them.

One major concern was that at our initial staff meeting that year, Seth was our only male staff member. By this point, the Lord had done enough work on my heart and given me a greater understanding of the roles of men and women to the point that I was even open to the possibility of AIC being directed by a young man with a vision for its ministry. However, no one had stepped up to fill that role and after discussing the matter with Dad, who remained the TPA Convention Director, I continued to serve as the Director. I began to pray that God would at least bring another male staff leader to our team. Just a few days later I received a call from Phil, the father of Caleb, one of our lead characters in the *Enemy Encounter* drama. Caleb had been hoping to be asked to be on the AIC staff this year and was disappointed when he found out that we had begun our preparations and hadn't contacted him. Phil asked if I would consider allowing Caleb to serve on staff. I was thrilled and told him that his call was an answer to prayer!

These, along with five returning staff members, including myself, comprised the team for what became the year of *The Quest: A boy's journey...for the glory of the King*. The theme was inspired by Psalm 145:4 and 7, "One generation shall praise Your works to another, And shall declare Your mighty acts. They shall utter the memory of Your great goodness, And shall sing of Your righteousness." We wanted the children attending AIC to catch a vision for passing on their faith to the next generation, to see beyond their own lives and dream about how they could prepare now to pass on the truths of God's Word to their children.

As we wrote the script for the story of Andrake, a young page on his journey to become a knight, it became a striking allegory of the life of a young boy today, on his journey toward manhood. We wove throughout the story some of the philosophies of our modern culture—materialism, domineering feminism, and rebellion—and attempted to portray a compelling picture of their biblical counterparts—stewardship, masculinity/femininity, and obedience to authority—in such a way that the children would be drawn to live their lives according to God's standards rather than the world's.

Aaron played the part of Andrake masterfully and earned the admiration of boys and girls alike. Aaron had made his acting debut as one of the soldiers in *Enemy Encounter* the previous year and the diligence and excellence he had demonstrated in his responsibilities had easily earned him a "callback." This was the first time we had written a script starring only one main character, but an outstanding effort by Aaron, a cast of wonderful supporting actors and extras, many committed teachers, and God's hand of blessing produced another fruitful and successful AIC.

Each year I receive many encouraging and grateful comments from families who participate in AIC, but the year of *The Quest* seemed to generate even more that were specific:

"We have not done this in the past, and I cannot begin to tell you how impressed I am. Every time I looked in on the children during the conference, it seemed all was going well, the children were kept busy and everybody was happy! [My boys] were already asking us when they can go back to AIC! I foresee my boys talking about it all year long until the next conference!"

"I want to tell you that AIC was excellent this year. When my 6 year old explained sin to me the other day and said that even taking a 'little piece of candy' was sin, I knew you all had her attention and had actually taught her something. Thank you!!"

"I heard so many comments from moms that they were surprised to see a place for the children and that most conventions don't welcome children. Thank you for your long hours of work to make our convention what it should be—a support for FAMILIES."

"My nine-year old son commented on how nice it was to be in a place where there were lots of girls, but he didn't have to worry about looking at them because they were all dressed modestly."

"Our family used to not be committed to homeschooling through high school, but after my children attended AIC for the first time last year and saw all the high school aged homeschoolers helping and realized what it would 'look' like to homeschool through high school, we've never thought again about the possibility of not homeschooling all the way through."

It was with full hearts that we wrapped up another year of AIC, overwhelmed at the never-failing love and mercy of God and eager to see what He would continue to do in the years ahead. But I never imagined what the following year would bring.

Chapter 20

"Who would have thought that among her many responsibilities, volunteer work, and the countless number of lives she makes a point to invest in, Natalie would also have the time to write a book? With her sincere personality, good sense of humor, and creative mind, *Pajama School* is a guaranteed great read for everybody!"

Kyle and Jynae Wilson

caught in the middle

Planning for the next year of AIC began just like any other, but I was completely unprepared for the "bump" looming ahead that threatened to knock me off the road altogether.

With very little changeover in our staff, we began discussing possibilities for our theme even earlier than usual. We planned an official brainstorming session in December and began praying that the Lord would give us clear direction. The weekend before the meeting, I spent some special time in prayer and Bible reading, seeking guidance from the Lord. I had begun a habit of reading the "Proverb for the day" (the chapter that corresponds to the particular day of the month) and was reading chapter 2 that morning. As I read the first six verses, an idea sprang to mind. I pulled out my notebook that I use for all sorts of random thoughts and plans and jotted down the words, *Treasure Hunt!* Our drama story could revolve around a treasure hunt of sorts and simultaneously the AIC students could be on their own search for wisdom, gathering clues throughout the weekend to lead them to a final treasure. I had no idea how the details would come together or if the rest of the staff members would be in favor of the idea, so I just outlined a few other ideas and then committed it to the Lord, asking Him to guide accordingly.

The following Monday night, the staff members gathered at our home. After a time of prayer and sharing what the Lord had been teaching us, I opened up the meeting for a discussion of ideas for the theme. Seth started off the discussion by saying that he had been thinking it would be neat to build our theme around the idea of hunting for treasure. Tiffany shared several different ideas and finished off with the possibility of doing a treasure hunt. Other staff members had thought of some other theme ideas, but soon the consensus revolved around a treasure hunt theme. After sitting in quiet amazement and listening to the discussion, I started my turn by asking if everyone wanted to see the idea I had written down. I turned my notebook around and held it up so that everyone could see the large words I had scribbled at the top of the page a few days before. *Treasure Hunt!* Everyone was equally amazed and we took it to be confirmation of the Lord's leading. Thus began our planning for the year!

Our AIC staff has always believed that the best way we can make a lasting impact on the lives of the children who attend AIC is not through the drama, or the curriculum, or the songs, or the funny mishaps, but through the overflow of our own hearts and lives as we walk with the Lord Jesus Christ. With that in mind, and because our theme revolved around the idea of searching for wisdom, each staff member committed to reading the "Proverb of the day" each day between that first meeting and the weekend of AIC. So by the time AIC arrived, we would have read through the book of Proverbs six times. If we were going to be writing and teaching about wisdom, we wanted to make sure that we were actively pursuing it in our own lives! Since some of the stated purposes of Proverbs are "to know wisdom and instruction; to perceive the words of understanding; to receive the instruction of wisdom, justice, and judgment, and equity" (1:2-3), we figured that reading it regularly was a great way to go about achieving our objective of growing in wisdom.

Once the general concept of the theme was decided, we began the more detailed scripting and curriculum writing. We used the eight characteristics of "wisdom that is from above" listed in James 3:17 as the outline for each scene of our drama and the corresponding curriculum sessions. We wanted to emphasize the importance of honoring and learning from our parents, and leaving a godly legacy for future generations. Thus was borne *LEGACY—Looking for the Truth. Chasing a Treasure. Finding Wisdom.* The drama followed the story of the five Wissen children who embark on a search for the treasure that their parents left them before they died. Along the way, they learn more about their parents through the stories of the people they meet whose lives were impacted by Mama and Papa Wissen. They are guided by the entries in a journal kept by their parents and the watchful eye and timely counsel of the Conductor who seems to have more than just a passing interest in the children's journey.

We divided out scenes among the drama scriptwriters and met several weeks later to assess our progress and make sure that we were all on the same track. Unfortunately, the evening of the meeting rolled around and we hadn't gotten much farther than we were at the first meeting. The concepts we had discussed were still too vague and it seemed like an impossible task to reconstruct the events of the past in the Wissen parents' lives in a cohesive manner so that the Wissen children would have a trail of clues to follow. I have always maintained that it is essential that we put far more thought into the underlying foundation of the script than what will ever come through in the dialogue. In order for the story to be effective, the plot and philosophies we aim to convey must be skillfully woven beneath the surface of what will be readily visible to the audience member. In other words, there must be depth. This time, though, I was afraid that we had dug our plot too deep and now we were drowning in a sea of murky ideas that couldn't be fleshed out on paper, let alone on a stage. So we scrapped it and started over. In order for this story to work we couldn't start at the beginning, we had to start long before the beginning.

A couple days later we were back on track again. This time we had written out the whole history of the people and events that transpired before the opening scene of the drama. Now as we worked on our scripts, there would be cohesiveness and clarity. The story began to take shape and we were excited to see all of our ideas mesh together into an exciting script! It never ceases to amaze me how God can take the individual scenes, written by various people with different writing styles and perspectives, and weave them into a cohesive whole. But year after year, that's exactly what He does. Once we have our basic outline and character descriptions, we work either on our own or in pairs for a couple of weeks, scripting each scene. Then we meet back together to read through the whole script. There are always plenty of little changes that need to be made, but for the most part the characters are consistent and the storyline flows well. Although come to think of it, considering what God did with the Bible, I guess this is a piece of cake for Him!

As things progressed on the AIC side of convention planning, on the TPA side, things were unraveling. There had been some friction on the board for several months due to some decisions that were being made and the tension continued to build. It all came to a head at a board meeting one night. I wasn't there, but when Mom and Dad got home that night, they were distraught. The board had voted in favor of a decision that was convention-related and Dad was the only one present who cast a dissenting vote (Mom abstained). He disagreed strongly with both the decision and the way in which the decision had been reached, but didn't know what to do about it. The following days were spent in many late night discussions as Mom and Dad and I tried to hash out the issues and come up with solutions. Dad spent many hours thinking, praying, writing and making phone calls, trying to resolve the situation, but a consensus could not be reached.

I was sitting at the kitchen table, working on some AIC responsibilities, when Dad emerged from the basement and relayed the news. He had just received an e-mail from the TPA Board president relieving him of all of his TPA duties. Mom and Dad were removed from the board, Dad was removed from his position as the Convention Director and

Database Manager, and our family was removed from being the organizers of the Used Book Sale. I was in shock. Always the "eternal optimist," I had been sure that everything would get resolved and the TPA Board members would pull together and be stronger and more effective than before. But I was wrong.

The following month leading up to the convention was filled with more conversations, more e-mails, more phone calls, and many more tears. Our family was in pain, reeling from this unexpected blow and yet groping for the strength to thank and praise God in the midst of it. I clung to the promise that "all things work together for good to them that love God, to them who are the called according to his purpose" (Romans 8:28) and to the understanding that God uses even the most difficult and painful circumstances to accomplish His purposes. As much as my heart was breaking within me at the ramifications of this decision, my spirit was overwhelmed with peace. God was sustaining me and giving me the strength to continue on.

The TPA Board asked me to continue to serve as the AIC Director even though Dad was no longer the Convention Director. I agreed to do so for that year, but the future was much less certain. I couldn't imagine continuing to serve on the Convention Committee without the rest of my family. Always before, our family prepared and planned for the convention together. Always before, we attended the committee meetings together. Always before, we brainstormed, and planned, and discussed ideas together. Perhaps, I surmised, this was God's direction for our family and it would also be the end of my involvement with TPA. I was full of questions and no answers as the weekend of AIC approached. I mentally and emotionally tried to prepare myself for what was probably my last year of AIC.

In the midst of my weakness, the Lord showed Himself strong. The weekend of AIC was the most stress-free of any I'd ever experienced. Each of the staff members fulfilled their responsibilities with competence and excellence. For the first time ever, I found myself sitting and enjoying the assemblies, or visiting with friends who stopped by to say "hi" without feeling pressure to tend to other needs. It was an awesome weekend in every respect!

In the weeks and months following AIC, I began praying in earnest about my future involvement with TPA and whether I should continue as the AIC Director. Mom and Dad both encouraged me to seek the Lord's direction and assured me that they would be supportive of whatever decision I felt the Lord wanted me to make. Pray as I might, though, I could not arrive at a decision that I really believed was from the Lord. I continued to wrestle with this decision until one day when Dad sat down to talk with me and find out how I was doing. I began weeping and shared with him how difficult this decision was proving to be. After learning that the primary reason for my uncertainty was due to the situation that had transpired on the board, he determined that he needed to try once again to take some steps to bring about resolution. He felt that it was his responsibility, as my Dad, to step in and try to work some things out on my behalf, even though he realized that doing so would open wounds that were still raw.

When Dad told me that he had resolved to take some specific steps to resolve this situation, my heart was flooded with relief and I told him how grateful I was to know that he was willing to "fight" for me, in a sense. I was no longer left on my own, fending for myself, trying to figure out what I should do. Now, Dad had entered the "ring" and would be on my side. Numerous e-mails and conversations followed as we sought counsel from long-time friends, and tried to determine the best course of action to take to initiate resolution. Finally, we arranged a meeting between the TPA Board and Mom, Dad, and me for the primary purpose of helping me see the situation from both sides in the hope that it would enable me to make a decision about whether to continue to serve as the AIC Director. The TPA Board had continued to express their desire that I remain in this position and I knew they needed a final answer soon. The meeting could have gone better, but it also could have gone worse. It wasn't fully what I had anticipated or hoped, but the Lord did use it to move me closer to a decision.

A few nights later, I sat up late into the night reading my Bible and journaling when all of a sudden the Lord's direction became crystal clear. I was reading in 1 Corinthians and stopped short when I read chapter 8, verse 13, "Wherefore, if meat make my brother to offend, I will eat no flesh while the world standeth, lest I make my brother to offend." I had read this passage before, but now I saw it in a new light and was struck by Paul's attitude toward his fellow believers. Instead of focusing on what was right for himself regardless of how it affected others, he was willing to relinquish even those things which were no big deal to him if they would cause offense to his brothers. Paul understood the second greatest commandment, "Thou shalt love thy neighbour as thyself" (Mark 12:31). My conscience was pierced as I realized that my decision had been hinging primarily on what I determined to be best for myself and what I thought I could handle. Now God was refocusing my thoughts.

I began to consider what would be the most loving way to treat my brothers and sisters in Christ who were on the TPA Board and convention committee. What would be the effect of stepping down as AIC Director? Or of continuing to serve? Although it has always been my hope that God would raise up another person to serve in the position of AIC Director in my place if He leads me in a different direction, I knew that there wasn't yet anybody to take on that responsibility. It would take time and some deliberate mentoring to make the transition smoothly. If I stepped down, effective immediately, there would be numerous ramifications of that decision that would negatively affect AIC and, by extension, TPA and the homeschool community. And so it was that the Lord, with absolute clarity, answered my prayer and showed me what to do. The next morning I shared the things the Lord had shown me with Mom and Dad and told them that unless they had any objections my decision was to agree to continue serving as the AIC Director the following year. They reiterated their desire that I follow the Lord's leading and that they were fully supportive of my decision.

In late December, after months of intense emotional wrestling and wondering if I would ever be confident of the Lord's direction, I sent an e-mail to both the TPA Board and the AIC staff, letting them know that I had decided to come back as the 2008 AIC Director. And on that same day, I felt a heavy burden lifted from my heart and my enthusiasm and vision for AIC returned full force.

Just one month later, I found myself sitting in our living room with a group of nine other young people. The Lord had faithfully raised up a team comprised of mostly returning staff members and three new ones—Aaron, Emma, and Joel—on board to fill the roles of those we "lost" to marriage and subsequent new family responsibilities. In praying and preparing for the meeting, I had been impressed with a theme idea of building our lives according to God's design. The inspiration for the theme came from 1 Corinthians 3:11-15, "For other foundation can no man lay than that is laid, which is Jesus Christ. Now if any man build upon this foundation gold, silver, precious stones, wood, hay, stubble; Every man's work shall be made manifest: for the day shall declare it, because it shall be revealed by fire; and the fire shall try every man's work of what sort it is. If any man's work abide which he hath built thereupon, he shall receive a reward. If any man's work shall be burned, he shall suffer loss: but he himself shall be saved; yet so as by fire."

As we sat around that night, praying and discussing ideas together, the prospect of a Western theme about a group of settlers heading west to build new lives for themselves quickly materialized and gained support, despite my adamant declaration that I would never do a Western theme. I warmed to the idea and consented, under the condition that it absolutely could not be corny! Everyone concurred and the drama brainstorming ensued. At Seth's suggestion, I dragged a huge white board up from my studio and grabbed a marker and began taking notes as ideas were presented. By the end of the night, we had a good outline for the drama scenes, Seth volunteered to oversee the planning and writing of the curriculum sessions, Cori offered to do the final editing and printing of the curriculum again, Tiffany agreed to design the student workbooks, and every staff member volunteered to be in either the drama-writing group or the curriculum-writing group. As the meeting wrapped up, we all expressed amazement at how much had been accomplished so quickly. If this was any indication of how the rest of the year would go, we would have the smoothest year ever!

We were not disappointed. At the next meeting, I showed everyone the theme and logo idea I had come up with for the year. *WESTWARD! Building a new life...by God's design.* Almost immediately everyone gave their approval and the decision was made to use both the theme and the logo I presented. The casual reader will not understand how shocking this was without further explanation, so let me enlighten you. This same decision in previous years often required up to three meetings. Various staff members would draw or download images and present them as logo possibilities. This was always followed by extensive critique and counter-ideas, and our informal votes would be split evenly between all the staff members. Likewise, theme ideas would be suggested and immediately received with exclamations of, "I don't like that at all" or "That doesn't really capture the story line of the drama" or "That sounds too much like a bank slogan," etc. Hours would be spent wracking our brains, dreaming up new ideas, searching foreign dictionaries on-line to find interesting translations of key words, pouring over the thesaurus to learn other ways of saying the same thing that nobody liked the first time, and eventually deciding to table the discussion and revisit it at the following meeting. Amazingly, a consensus would finally be reached. Not a unanimous decision, mind you! With our mostly opinionated group, we were content with a majority vote. And even then, the final result was usually a combination of a font from one person, a key image from another person, and contributing logo elements from one or more others. But the end result was always the perfect fit for that year and no one would have guessed the great lengths we went to to get there!

There were minor glitches and miscommunications that are to be expected when working on a project the size of AIC, but these were all resolved quickly and peaceably and the preparations continued to progress ahead of schedule. The drama script was written and edited with several days to spare. The only problem was that we still didn't have an actor in place for our lead role. The first person we had discussed for the role didn't work out and the second person had to back out at the last minute due to other responsibilities. So Aaron, our Drama Director, was left scrambling, trying to come up with other possibilities. But our list was essentially exhausted, and the large cast required for the drama was already employing many of our favorites in other key roles. God had always provided before and we were counting on Him to do so again, but His timescale was obviously not the same as ours.

The night of the first rehearsal, I had just arrived at the church when my friend Jynae called. Jynae had been a part of AIC since its beginning, but had just gotten married the previous August. Her husband Kyle was a basketball player at Wichita State University and within a month of their marriage they were living overseas where he was playing basketball for a professional European team. They were back for the summer with hardly anything to do, so Jynae eagerly agreed to help out on stage and together we were able to persuade Kyle to be one of the cronies in the drama. Kyle had done very little acting, but his was a small goofy part that would be impossible to mess up. After I gave Jynae directions to the church, I informed her that we no longer had a lead character. I overheard her relaying the news to Kyle and then him in the background jokingly suggesting that he could play the part. We all laughed and then I hung up. But by the time they arrived at the church, I had talked with Aaron about the possibility of having Kyle fill the lead role. We both thought perhaps it was the Lord's direction, so when Kyle arrived I sprang the question on him. Thankfully he didn't dismiss it immediately, but agreed to read the part that night and then read over the script and pray about it before making a final decision.

Two days later I arrived at the church for the next rehearsal, eager to find out what Kyle had decided. I was overjoyed when he said that he had decided to fill the role and would rearrange some of his scheduling conflicts to allow him to be at the rehearsals. Once again, God answered our prayers and met our needs. We felt like God was running late, but in retrospect I see that God was way ahead of us, orchestrating all the details to bring about His plan in His perfect time.

Within moments of opening our on-line teacher registration, we received the first application. Many more followed until we had 50 young men and women—homeschoolers who were still in high school or had already graduated—signed up to be teachers and assistant teachers for AIC. This marked our ninth year of AIC and it was thrilling to see that many of those signing up to teach were former students. Seth eagerly agreed to take on the responsibility of Teacher Training, something that I had been responsible for since almost the beginning of AIC. And yet, as I was praying one morning before our first staff meeting, the Lord impressed on my mind the idea of relinquishing this task and asking Seth to do it. I knew that he was passionate about studying the Word of God and teaching it to young people, so I knew he would be well prepared and do an excellent job. When I called and shared my thoughts with him, he was quite surprised and replied that he had just been talking to his Mom a few days before and told her that he would be interested in doing something like that rather than working in his previous role of coordinating the one-on-one counseling booth area for students in AIC who needed extra attention. It appeared that God was already way ahead of us on this one too!

Every aspect of our preparation was coming together so smoothly that I, in my lack of faith, wondered what we were overlooking or what disaster awaited us. Less than a week before the AIC registration deadline, I found out. I was working with Lisa, our Registration Supervisor, and Josh to coordinate student registrations with Tom and Birgit, the ones handling the adult convention registration. Tom e-mailed me the database with student information, and when I opened it my heart sunk. I quickly scrolled to the bottom of the list and was dismayed to see that only 150 students had registered. Like the previous several years, we were planning for 300 children. That was the number we used to determine how many teachers to recruit, how many supplies to purchase, etc. Everything was based on that number. We had never actually hit the 300 mark, but we were always over 250, so 300 was a good, safe estimate. I had no idea how to handle this unexpected dilemma and didn't think there was much I could do to improve the situation. But God could.

I immediately sent out an e-mail to a list of people who had been recruited as "prayer warriors" for AIC. Periodically I sent out e-mail updates with a list of specific prayer requests and praise reports. I let everyone know that we were running low on registrations and asked them to pray that God would bring 300 children. It seemed like an unrealistic request, but I took comfort in knowing that with God nothing is impossible. The prayers went up all week long and the Saturday deadline came and went... almost. It was 10:00 that night when I got the e-mail from Birgit with the t-shirt count. As I scanned the e-mail, my eyes fixated on the number that jumped out at me from the center of my screen. It was followed by five exclamation points, like this: 290!!!!! I almost choked! If I was a screamer, I probably would have screamed, but instead my heart poured forth praise to the Lord for showing His great power on our behalf. By the time the last of the registrations trickled in, we had over 300 children registered—more than we'd ever had before—and we expected a handful of families to register at-the-door. I jokingly told everyone to stop praying for more children and to start praying for the miracle of the widow's oil—that our supplies would miraculously multiply so that we wouldn't run out. God saw fit to answer that prayer as well. We finished the weekend with a grand total of 329 children and didn't run out of anything!

With many of the major responsibilities in the capable hands of various staff members, leading up to and throughout AIC, I was more stress-free and peaceful than I had ever been. There was still much work to be done, but I didn't experience the added burden of assuming tight control over every detail. At last I experienced the blessing of letting go and trusting God to work through each one of us to accomplish His purposes. I had always said that AIC was the Lord's program, not mine, but after years of going through God's customized education plan (a.k.a. AIC), I finally understood what that meant and what it looked like in practice. I found myself continually giving thanks to the Lord for the dedicated efforts of every member on the staff team, each of whom was pouring his or her whole heart into their responsibilities. There was incredible unity of spirit as we worked together to impact the next generation for Christ. To be honest, it's impossible to put into words the depth of love and admiration I have for these fellow homeschoolers who are my dear friends and co-laborers. And it was through their vision that the Western theme became a reality and resulted in one of the best years ever!

Chapter 21

"God very often uses a change of scenery and circumstances to display His sovereignty and strength to us. Natalie relates this truth in *Pajama School*, and it was a blessing for us to share part of her journey with her."

Jared and Kim Meidal

far away from home

My friend Sarah and I were sitting on the floor in the basement talking when the idea popped into our conversation. Wouldn't it be an incredible experience to work together at a summer camp? For years I had felt a draw to inner city mission work, but had no idea how to break out of my middle-class suburban lifestyle to pursue that desire. However, as we grew excited about the possibility, I vaguely recalled the name of an organization that I thought was involved in inner city mission work: World Impact. Perhaps they had a summer camp where we could work. I pulled up the World Impact website on my computer and, sure enough, there on the home page was a link to their camp ministries. As it turned out, they had several camps, but the one called THE OAKS captured my attention.

After Sarah left, I spent the rest of the night exploring the website, learning everything I could about the World Impact organization and dreaming about the possibility of working at THE OAKS—their Southern California camp. They had positions open for summer camp staff the following summer and I had plenty of time to apply. The next day, I could hardly contain my excitement as I shared my idea with Mom and Dad. I told them everything I had learned from the website and what it would entail to work there for a summer. They knew I had a passion for this type of children's work and as we discussed it and prayed about it, they encouraged me to apply. As it turned out, Sarah decided not to pursue the idea, but at Mom and Dad's encouragement, I applied and prayed that the Lord would direct me according to His will. It was the beginning of 2003 and it would be several months before I knew for sure if I had been accepted.

In early spring, I received a phone call from one of the staff members at THE OAKS, asking me if I had time to do a phone interview. I did and the questioning and interviewing began in earnest. I was taken aback by the personal nature of some of the questions, but answered as transparently as I could, knowing that it was important for the summer campers to be in a safe environment. After the interview questions were over, it was time for the role play. I was completely unprepared for what happened next. The staff member on the other end assumed the role of one of the campers and presented situations that I was expected to provide counsel for over the phone. It was the most awkward thing I have ever done and I fumbled my way through the hypothetical scenarios. By the time we were done, I felt ridiculous and knew that my interviewer was less than impressed. That concluded the interview. I hung up, certain that I would not be accepted to work at the camp.

Nicole and I had been praying about some other opportunities in our area, but progressing with those was contingent upon whether or not I was accepted to work at THE OAKS that summer. After my interview flop, we began praying more earnestly, anticipating that the Lord would close that door and lead us into these other opportunities. For that reason, I was totally surprised when I received a call from Sean, the camp program director, offering me the position of Camp Registrar. It was a position they had never had before for a summer staff member, since a wife of one of the full-time staff members at the camp usually handled all the registration needs. But they wanted to increase the efficiency of the registration operations and relieve this lady of those responsibilities. It was not what I expected, since I had applied to be a counselor, but based on how we had been praying, I determined that this was the Lord's will. I accepted the position and began making preparations for a summer away from home. This would be the longest, by far, that I had ever been away from home, so it would be an adventure, not only for me, but also for my whole family.

Since I was hired for one of the leadership positions, my reporting date at the camp was earlier than I expected. I was to be at the camp by the Monday following the weekend of AIC! By the time AIC rolled around, I was packed and ready to go. I loaded my car not only with the supplies for the weekend, but also with all of my luggage and supplies for the summer. As soon as we were finished cleaning up from AIC, Nicole and I said our tearful goodbyes to the rest of the family and began the long drive westward. We had decided that Nicole would drive with me out to camp and then fly home, returning at the end of the summer to pick me up, at which point we would take about a week to drive home and do some sight-seeing along the way. This would give me the flexibility of having a vehicle to use throughout the summer.

We drove to a friends' house in the southwestern corner of the Oklahoma panhandle the first night, visited for several hours before retiring for the night and then arose early the next morning for a full day of driving. We made it all the way to the eastern part of California and found a nice motel where we stayed that night. Monday morning we were back on the rode and we crested the final hill into the picturesque camp site in the late afternoon. The camp appeared mostly deserted, but we finally navigated our way to the program office and received instructions about where I would be staying. That night we had a barbecue by the pool and Nicole and I met several of the other staff families and individuals. The next morning, Nicole and I said our farewell before she departed on the camp airport shuttle. I knew it would be hard to spend a whole summer separated from the sister who had become my best friend.

My first week at camp was spent getting oriented to my new surroundings and receiving training in my responsibilities from the lady who had previously handled registration. That weekend, I traveled to Van Nuys, since I had made arrangements to visit the parents of a good friend of mine. They welcomed me into their home and took me under their wing, along with their Hungarian granddaughter who was visiting America for the first time, and took us all over Los Angeles. We enjoyed exploring the booths of goods set up all around the perimeter of the Rose Bowl in Pasadena, visiting the Getty Museum, walking and eating lunch on the pier, and picking fresh fruit from their back yard for our fruit salad that night. It was the perfect introduction to Southern California and I drove back Sunday evening, invigorated and ready to embrace my summer responsibilities with renewed energy. But that enthusiasm was soon replaced by a growing fear.

As I charted my way back up the highway and across the back roads into the camp, I became aware that something didn't seem quite right...

Journal Entry—June 8, 2003

I headed up Highway 5 and was lost in thought, so accidentally missed the Lake Hughes Road exit. I checked the map real quickly, though, and saw that I could pick up Highway 138 and just come into the camp that way. I got off at the Highway 138 exit and watched closely, veering to the right on N2, the country road that would turn into Pine Canyon Road and take me to the camp. The road became very windy and narrow, working its way up and through the hills. It was absolutely beautiful! There was no other traffic on the road and eventually I came to a sign that indicated that it was the end of the county maintained road. Sure enough, at that point it went from bad to worse! But I pressed on, sure that this was the right way according to the map.

There was still no other traffic and I started to get a little scared. A verse immediately came to mind, "What time I am afraid,

*I will put my trust in thee." And another one followed right after,
"A certain man traveled from Judea to Jerusalem and was overtaken
by thieves along the way." Ahh! Bad verse! As I drove, it occurred
to me that my tire was not in the best of shape to handle this un-
maintained road [it had been flat that morning and I filled it with
air right before leaving to return to the camp] and that my cell
phone had no reception out here. Reality hit. It was just me and the
Lord. I know God's been trying to teach me to rely upon Him and
not be so self-sufficient. I didn't think this was such a good way to
reinforce that, though, so I encouraged Him to wait and try it some
other way. But it was as though the Lord was asking, "When I
remove every means of security, will you still trust Me?" "When you
are faced with uncertainty—an unfamiliar situation and potential for problems, will you still find strength and courage in Me?"
"When you are brought to the end of your rope, will you let go and
let Me hold you in My hand?"*

*Wow! It is so much harder to trust God when I realize how
little control I have. But at the same time, it gives me a new
capacity to trust God—it broadens my perspective and gives me an
incredible appreciation for God's sovereignty. He is in control and
He is watching over me and taking care of me. In Him I am always
secure. I must trust Him—I want to trust Him in every situation.*

*I did eventually make it back to civilization (and did end up
seeing three other vehicles along the road), but God taught me an
important lesson—one that I'm sure was preparation for what
He knows I needed to learn for the upcoming weeks.*

The summer began with an intense time of training and team-build-
ing and I soon found myself experiencing some unexpected challenges. It
was evident that my background was strikingly different from almost
every other staff member at the camp. I was confronted repeatedly

with the realization that the way I was raised was in sharp contrast to the way many of the others were raised. I grew up in the conservative Midwest in a homeschool family, surrounded by fellow homeschoolers, while most of my fellow staffers were raised in more liberal parts of the country, in public or private schools, surrounded by peers. We had vastly different perspectives on life and Christianity, and I found it hard to reconcile the differences.

For years I had been learning and teaching the importance of standing alone, but now I just felt like I was standing out. I wanted to fit in with those around me, but I wrestled with the question of whether I was compromising in areas that I shouldn't be. Standards that had seemed clear before now approached nearer a shade of gray as those around me questioned my decisions and bold statements. I spent several weekends alone in the hills on the camp property communing with God before an answer finally resonated with my soul. The answer came, not in an earthquake or a burning bush, but in the still small voice conveyed through the counsel of another dear girl at camp. Ellen was the Performing Arts Director that summer and struck me immediately as one who was a deep thinker and good communicator. She had come from an incredibly rough background and had dealt with more difficult challenges as a child than I will probably ever have to deal with in my whole life. As we talked one afternoon, I shared with her some of my struggles and expressed how difficult it was for me to understand Christians who didn't abide by certain standards or engaged in wrong behaviors. She looked me in the eye and asked a question I will never forget, "How do *you* know it's wrong and *I* don't?" In other words, did I have access to some source of information to which she was not privy?

It was a rhetorical question, of sorts, but as I pondered it, I was struck by the implications of it. In essence, Ellen was saying, "Don't tell me what the standard is. Tell me what the source of your standard is." I had been so hung up on my idea of what was right and wrong that I had loosened my grip on the true foundation—the eternal, immutable Word of God.

I wasn't privy to some innate understanding of what was right or wrong in God's eyes. But I did have the benefit of years of biblical training by Godly parents and many hours spent in personal Bible study. Any honest discussion or debate could only take place if the Bible was our common starting point. Each person's understanding of life was influenced by his or her own upbringing and presuppositions, but if we were willing to approach such differences from a truly biblical foundation, we could learn to "Prove all things; hold fast that which is good" (I Thessalonians 5:21).

I know these were things that I had heard numerous times, but until I was put to the test, it didn't become a reality. With this understanding, I had the freedom and security to say, "Maybe the way I've been doing this particular thing is not right. Let's look at what the Bible says to find out." I had the boldness to say, "This is what I believe is right and here are the biblical commands and principles that lead me to that conclusion." My objective became not one to win people over to my way of thinking or doing things, but to challenge people to study the Bible, to give wise biblical counsel, and to trust that God would grow each of us to new levels of understanding and maturity in His time.

The weeks following this important lesson the Lord taught me were marked by numerous conversations and discussions. I remember talking with one of the other girls about dating. When I told her that I had never dated anyone, she looked at me like I had just revealed that I was raised by a pack of wolves. She went on to say that she had heard of some book called *I Kissed Dating Goodbye*, but didn't know that there were actually any people who did that. I laughed and then was able to share with her some of the things the Lord had taught me about keeping myself pure—both physically and emotionally—for the one I would marry. We had a good discussion and she shared about some of the regrets she had from her own dating relationships.

Discussions with other staff members followed as well—from theological issues, to the morality of family planning, to acceptable styles of music, and more. I was stretched and challenged and humbled in ways I had never experienced before. I was challenged to proclaim the truth of God's Word with more fervor, while at the same time to be less dogmatic about the areas where my understanding of Scripture did not point conclusively to one particular viewpoint. I learned to accept the fact that I could be wrong, and that in areas where the biblical teaching seemed clear I could present the truth in love and let God change minds and hearts in His time—whether mine or others.

While I continued to grow in wisdom and mature inwardly all summer long, I also developed many lasting friendships and enjoyed some wonderful new experiences—camping out under the stars, hiking to the top of Half Dome at Yosemite National Park, cliff-jumping, walking the Santa Monica Boardwalk, sitting in the bleachers of an LA Dodgers game, sipping smoothies in the small smoothie place down the mountain from the camp, playing in the sand on Venice Beach, and more. The weekends were full of such varied excursions, while the days at camp were busy with a never-ending list of things to do. Week after week flew by as one group of campers arrived and another departed. While campers and counselors enjoyed the beauty and activities outdoors, I was busy preparing for the next week of camp—contacting group coordinators, updating spreadsheets, printing team rosters, and any number of other little tasks to help the program run smoothly.

I relished any time I got to spend with the campers, and several of the counselors eagerly welcomed me as a guest at their meal tables or invited me to join their group on excursions when I was available. I was also recruited to be one of the Bible teachers and loved spending the mornings with campers and other teachers, enacting familiar Bible stories and teaching important truths about God. In the evenings, I played the keyboard as part of the worship team and spent time praying with the others on the Leadership Team before going back to our rooms for the night. The work was exhausting, but rewarding as we saw smiles of delight on the faces of children who came from neighborhoods where they experienced drive-by-shootings almost daily. I heard some of them exclaim surprise over getting to sleep in their own bed for the first time ever. Others were grateful to receive three full meals a day. Inspired by their time at THE OAKS, many campers would return home and share Christ with their families and become the first fruits of church plants in their neighborhoods.

When I sent in my forms to THE OAKS at the beginning of the year, I had thought that I was applying to be a counselor and make a difference in the lives of inner city children. But by the end of the summer, I found out that God had enrolled me in yet another real life educational program that left THE OAKS of Southern California forever etched on my heart as the place where God taught me what it really means to dwell together in unity with my brothers and sisters in Christ.

Chapter 22

"*Pajama School* is a must read for any discouraged homeschool parent or frustrated homeschool student. Natalie captures the essence of what home education is all about by letting the reader get up-close and experience the joys and struggles of life in a homeschool family."

Trisha Thomison

marrying off my sister

It was a sunny Saturday afternoon and I was in the kitchen doing some baking when Dad came up from his basement office and stood on the other side of the kitchen island. "Just got an interesting phone call," he stated matter-of-factly with a funny-looking smile escaping from his lips. I looked up at him, waiting for the details. "Want to guess who it was from?" I immediately guessed the name of a couple we had been waiting to hear from. "Nope. Andy Bloyer." Again, Dad couldn't hold back the grin. "Want to guess what he was calling about?" I had my suspicions, but let Dad convey the news. "He was asking permission to court Nicole." "Really?!" I exclaimed, matching Dad's excitement. Dad went on to relay more of the details of the conversation. Then he grabbed his keys and was off to make the short drive over to the Davis family's furniture store where Nicole was working. He wanted to pass on the word to Nicole in person right away. That was as close to giddy as I had ever seen Dad!

Nicole was mostly surprised when Dad told her about Andy's call and asked her to think and pray about it. Andy had called a few times in the preceding weeks, ostensibly just to chat. We all found this highly curious because although they had lots of mutual friends and had been at a lot of the same gatherings over the years, Nicole and Andy didn't know each other very well. He had been attending flight school in Arizona and had not been in the habit of calling her regularly for friendly chats. We learned that he would be graduating and returning home at the end of the year. Now he was wondering if when he returned home he could spend more time getting to know Nicole with the intent of marrying her.

Nicole didn't say much about it when she got home from work, but she spent that night and the next day thinking and praying about Andy's request and formulating several questions that she wanted him to answer before making her decision. Interestingly, several weeks before, Nicole shared with me that she had been considering officially committing another year of work to her boss at the furniture store, but had felt a caution from the Lord about making the commitment. As we discussed this, we wondered aloud at what the Lord might have in store for her in the near future. Now we knew. After receiving Andy's responses to her questions and spending considerable time in prayer and seeking the Lord's will, Nicole was convinced that she should consent to Andy's request to court her. Dad passed Nicole's answer on to Andy and the next day a gorgeous bouquet of flowers arrived at the door for Nicole—the first of many to follow!

Upon returning home after his graduation, Andy became a frequent guest at our house and our whole family quickly grew to love him as a son and a brother. He obviously had a heart for the Lord and treated Nicole with tender love and affection. Although we had known the Bloyer family as acquaintances for many years, through Nicole and Andy's growing relationship we developed a much closer friendship and soon became like family. Andy has one older brother, two younger sisters and six younger brothers. Joey was thrilled to acquire so many new brothers all at once, and Andy's sister, Melodie, became one of Naomi's closest friends. Our families had much in common and found it easy to spend hours at each other's homes engaging in discussions, eating scrumptious meals, playing games, and just enjoying times of fellowship together.

The months flew by quickly and we eagerly awaited the day Nicole and Andy would announce their engagement. I had banked my prediction on a special Valentine's Day outing Andy planned for Nicole, using a bit of reverse psychology to surmise that he would think that no one would expect him to propose on Valentine's Day because a Valentine's Day proposal is so conventional. It seemed like the perfect occasion. He rented a small plane and flew Nicole up to Hutchinson to a small restaurant for a romantic dinner with just the two of them. They would be returning right around sunset. But the evening came and went with no proposal.

Several weeks later I was sitting on the couch late in the evening, reading the current issue of WORLD magazine. Nicole and Andy were together (as they were every night!) and had gone over to a local park for a walk. When they returned several hours later, Nicole practically threw her body across my lap and tried to grab the magazine. (It is actually not uncommon for various members of the family to fight over who gets to read the current issue of WORLD magazine first when it arrives in the mail, but this seemed a little over the top!) In surprise, I pulled it away, telling her to stop. Instead, she again grabbed for the magazine. This time, even more perturbed, I tried to push her off and asked her what her problem was. She stood up in frustration and commented on my lack of observation skills. It was then that I noticed the sparkle coming from her left hand. She was engaged! And it had caught me completely by surprise! I was thrilled and went on to extract details about the proposal from them, which they agreed to share after calling the rest of our family from their bedrooms to come and hear the news.

Nicole wanted a small wedding ceremony with just their families, so after she and Andy discussed various options, they decided to hold the ceremony at his Grandpa's lake home in Wisconsin. It could be an outdoor wedding and reception, and then they could hold a larger reception back home once they returned from their honeymoon. Both Mom and Dad and Andy's parents liked the idea, especially because it would mean less work and less money! Nicole and Andy handled most of the arrangements themselves and I helped design the wedding announcements and put together the music for the ceremony. Prior to their engagement, I was inspired to write a song for the two of them and now that they were officially engaged, I made plans to do a recording of the song, since they wouldn't be using vocalists during the ceremony. Chad and Michele Chapman, some friends from church, agreed to sing the vocal parts while I played the piano, and they made arrangements with a friend of theirs who owns a recording studio to professionally record the song. It was my first experience in a recording studio and we had a blast working on the project! Four hours after arriving, all the parts were recorded, mixed, and mastered, and I held a beautiful CD in my hand with the single song, *One Heart*, based on Jeremiah 32:38-41.

As soon as Chad and Michele dropped me back off at home, I jumped in my car and raced over to the furniture store to share my excitement with Nicole and let her listen to the CD. She was able to take a short break from her work, so she put the CD in her player and listened to it. At the end, she said it was nice, then pulled the CD out and returned it to me. I was crushed. I had spent hours composing, arranging, and recording the song especially for her and now she hardly seemed to like it. I made my way back out to the car and drove home in tears. I had tried so hard to be supportive and encouraging of Nicole and Andy's relationship and do whatever I could to help them out, but this was more than I could handle. When I got home, I told Mom and Dad what had happened and then collapsed on the couch, emotionally exhausted.

Several hours later, Nicole arrived home and I was awakened from my nap to discuss the situation with her and Mom and Dad. She had no idea that I had been hurt by her response and was indeed excited about the song, but demonstrated her excitement in a much more subdued manner than I would have. We were able to talk through the issue and resolve what was ultimately a miscommunication. Both of us were experiencing a range of emotions as she prepared to marry Andy, and neither of us was accustomed to openly expressing our feelings.

Because of Andy's personality and influence, she was learning to be more emotionally vulnerable, but I was determined to keep my innermost feelings to myself. I had to remain strong and unaffected. Or so I thought.

I was pretty good at keeping my emotions under control. But one day, as I sat in my studio by myself, playing the piano, I broke down. Thoughts of insecurity and doubt flooded my heart and mind as I questioned why nobody wanted to marry me. Three of my other close friends—Myklin, Trisha, and Rachel—had all announced their engagements and were getting married within a month of Nicole. Until now I had felt only happiness and excitement for my sister and friends, and was fully confident that the Lord was in control and would allow me to marry in His time if it was His will. But in a moment, my faith and confidence were shattered. I felt worthless and alone. As tears streamed down my face, I poured out my heart to the Lord and told Him of my doubts and fears, of my desires and dreams. As soon as the words were formed in my mind, the Lord was whispering words of peace and hope into my weeping heart. Verses long ago memorized flooded my mind:

"Set your affection on things above, not on things on the earth. For ye are dead, and your life is hid with Christ in God" (Colossians 3:2-3).

"Thou wilt keep him in perfect peace, whose mind is stayed on thee: because he trusteth in thee. Trust ye in the LORD for ever: for in the LORD JEHOVAH is everlasting strength" (Isaiah 26:3-4).

"Thou wilt shew me the path of life: in thy presence is fulness of joy; at thy right hand there are pleasures for evermore" (Psalm 16:11).

"Let your conversation be without covetousness; and be content with such things as ye have: for he hath said, I will never leave thee, nor forsake thee" (Hebrews 13:5).

The tears dried up as I meditated on the beautiful and special promises that God impressed on my heart. For years, Jesus had proved Himself my faithful and steadfast Friend and He was not about to leave me now. I clung to Him and left the room that day depending on His strength and rejoicing in His presence. Far more than consigning to tolerate my years of unmarriage, God again enabled me to embrace them and eagerly anticipate how I could make the most of them for His glory.

With my heart and mind back on track, we were nearing the final days before the wedding. A few days before the wedding, Nicole, Andy, Nadine, and I drove to Wisconsin together to make last minute preparations. The rest of our family loaded into the suburban to make the 12-hour drive. We pulled into the small town of Webster and quickly found the old motel where we would be staying. Once we were checked-in and settled into our rooms, our family met the Bloyer's at the town burger joint for a meal of greasy hamburgers and french fries. Apparently this is a traditional outing for the Bloyer's when they visit their family in Webster, so we were happy to join them for the experience.

The next morning we traveled to the nearby town of Siren for a round of miniature golf and shopping in the small country store. That afternoon, we gathered at Andy's Grandpa's home for lunch and relaxation and were later joined by my Grandpa and Grandma and Aunt and Uncle, who drove up from Chicago for this special celebration. In addition, our good friends Doug and Jennifer graciously consented to make the trip to Wisconsin to be the photographers for the wedding.

Once everyone arrived and was ready, the rehearsal commenced. We ran through the ceremony, making sure that everyone knew where to be and what to do. Everything was fairly simple, so our biggest concern was the weather. Forecasters were calling for rain showers, but we were hoping and praying that the Lord would bless us with a clear day—at least until after the ceremony was over! Once Nicole and Andy were satisfied that everything had been adequately discussed, it was time for the rehearsal dinner. And by rehearsal dinner I mean that everyone grabbed their hotdog, stabbed a skewer through it, and made their way to the fire pit where we roasted hot dogs and marshmallows the rest of the night! A few hours later, we all parted ways in hopes of getting a good night of sleep before the next day.

August 20, 2005 dawned bright and sunny, and our family walked the short couple of blocks to the local diner where we enjoyed a hearty breakfast. It was a bittersweet time as we anticipated the impending marriage while also confronting the reality that in a few hours our family dynamics would be forever changed. It was hard to imagine what it would be like without Nicole living at home. For twenty-three years of my life, she had been my roommate and best friend, but now that role was changing. The transition had been gradual over the previous months of their courtship and engagement, but now the finality of it hit me with full force. Apart from the knowledge that this was all part of God's plan for both of our lives, I could not have borne the thought of "losing" my sister. God ordained for her to take the next step of life into marriage and He ordained for me to remain at home, living with my family, and investing in the lives of the younger ones still living at home. I didn't know for sure how Nicole's marriage would affect our relationship, but I was pretty sure there would be more challenges, joy, and tears in the days ahead.

The early hours of the afternoon saw us back in our motel rooms, sharing the small mirror on the wall and squinting in the dimly lit light to fix our hair and put on our makeup. We snapped several photos before piling into the cars and driving over to the lake. A storm cloud blew in and drops of water began falling from the sky, threatening to ruin all of the carefully laid plans. In less than an hour, though, the rain passed and we were ready to proceed. I took my place at the digital piano, brought in for the occasion, and played an arrangement of a piece from the *Emma* soundtrack that Nicole loved and had asked me to play. Everyone was cleared from the backyard, and Nicole slowly made her way down the deck stairs to where Andy stood waiting. I provided the background music and God provided the breathtaking backdrop as Andy and Nicole spent a few tender moments together before the rest of the guests were ushered to their seats. Jennifer soon joined them to take some pictures of just the two of them before the rest of us assembled for family pictures. Then Nicole made her way back around to the front of the house where she waited until all of the guests arrived and it was time for the ceremony to begin.

Andy's Uncle Mark officiated and it seemed only a moment from Nicole's entrance until she and Andy were pronounced husband and wife and departed down the stairs to the dock and into the small speed boat that awaited them. They drove into the sun-streaked sky with the sign and streamers on the back of the boat announcing to the world that the special couple was "Just Married."

After a quick tour of the lake, Nicole and Andy rejoined us to cut their cake and greet the guests. A number of Andy's extended family members were in town for a reunion, so they joined us for the day, bringing the number of guests to just over seventy. We enjoyed a light dinner of sandwiches, salads, and cakes as we visited with each other. Part way through the reception, I realized that I had neglected to perform my duty of decorating the "getaway" car, so Nadine and I made a quick run to the grocery store and were able to track down some window chalk. Andy's sister and cousin jumped in to help once we got back and we completed our mission just in time. The bride and groom were saying their final fare-wells and emerged from the back of the house as we put on the finishing touches. And then Nicole and Andy were off, eager to enjoy their honeymoon week on the shores of the Great Lakes.

The clean-up was quick and I made it back down to the dock in time to watch the colors of the setting sun explode over the lake in brilliant array. I sat in the docked boat, reading until my eyes could no longer make out the words. Then I joined Dad and several others around the glowing fire pit until it was time to leave. The night left me in a nostalgic mood, wondering what other changes the future would bring.

Chapter 23

"Natalie always had a sense of maturity beyond her years. She was our regular sitter for weekly date nights for several years, and it wasn't until later that we found out she was only a few years older than our oldest! She became a part of our life and family—a great blessing to all of us."

The Kent Hobbs Family

building bridges

Nine-year old Joey walked out the end of the hallway and into the living room with a serious expression on his face. But as soon as he looked up and saw the smirk on Noelle's lips, he broke into laughter. Back into the hallway he went, where he regained his composure and again made his entry into the living room. This time it was Naomi who broke the silence by suddenly spewing out the air she had been holding in in her attempt not to laugh. All four of us burst out laughing for the second time as Joey was once more thwarted in his mission. Finally, after several deep breaths we made a valiant effort to resume the exercise in all seriousness. Joey entered the living room for the third time and this time captivated us as he assumed the voice of a sports announcer and proclaimed, "Oh my goodness! ASC's just scored another point leaving ESC's in the dust! ASC 65 to ESC 0. For those of you who just joined, ASC (Adult Stem Cell) and ESC (Embryonic Stem Cell) research is heating up. Even though ASC research is winning, the support for ESC research continues to strengthen. Why does support continue to grow even though there is evidence that ESC research is neither safe nor effective for human treatments?"

I was teaching a speech class for Noelle, Naomi, and Joey and Joey had chosen Stem Cell Research as his topic. He explored the difference between Adult Stem Cell research and Embryonic Stem Cell research and came up with a highly creative way of presenting the information to emphasize the incredible success Adult Stem Cell research was experiencing, contrasted with the dismal results of Embryonic Stem Cell research. Naomi and Noelle each presented their speeches on pertinent life issues and I was amazed to see their unique approaches to the topics and the way their personalities influenced their speeches.

When Joey was born, one of my greatest concerns was that I wouldn't be living at home long enough to develop a close relationship with the brother I had prayed for for years. I was sure I would probably be married and long gone before he was old enough to really remember things. But obviously, God had other plans! With Nicole and Nadine both moved out of the house, the "littles" (as we began calling Noelle, Naomi, and Joey from the time they were born, and we assure them that we will always retain the prerogative of calling them such no matter how old they are!) have become my students, close friends, and co-laborers. In addition to speech, we've studied Greek, European history and geography, spelling, Old Testament history, evangelism, and more. They share my enthusiasm for learning and are always up for joining me on some adventure or another!

Noelle was my first piano student, and Naomi and Joey followed quickly after her. From the time he was two, Joey would come up to the piano after my last student of the day was gone, reach his arms up and ask, "pwano wesson?" We started by trying to find the black keys and doing arm exercises, then slowly moved into tougher assignments. Eventually he became an official student and secured a spot on my studio schedule. I will always remember the day he arrived at his piano lesson with the words, "I love you Natalie" scrawled across the top of his assignment page. He was only seven at the time and I exclaimed profusely over the sweet comment. He looked at me and stated quite matter-of-factly, "Well I only wrote that because I didn't practice very much this week." So much for the sweetness!

At a young age Joey also had a rather distorted view of the process of aging. The two of us went on a walk together one morning and in the course of our conversation I asked what he wanted to be when he grew up. He paused for a moment and then began, "When I grow up, and I'm a girl..." Poor thing! With five older sisters, his only frame of reference was that one started out as a boy and eventually turned into a girl!

Naomi and I became roommates about a year after Nicole got married. Some of our family members prefer to say that she lives in a corner of my room. She graciously puts up with the lesser portion of the shelf and closet space, and even with me occasionally turning on the bedside lamp after she has gone to bed. Although we're rarely in our bedroom, we love to spend time together, whether it's doing our weekly Bible study, playing a piano duet, discussing current events, viewing pictures, or editing blog posts for one of our blogs. She has adeptly replaced both Nicole and Nadine as the fashion critic and is always sure to inform me if something I'm wearing doesn't look right. Although I have pointed out to her on several occasions that I would really rather not know that what I'm wearing doesn't look right if it's nighttime and I've already been wearing it all day!

If I could use one word to describe Noelle, it would be book-a-holic (that counts as one word, right?). She is a voracious reader and has the vocabulary to prove it. She's the only one in the family with whom I don't like playing *Race Scrabble* because she always uses obscure words. And then whenever I question her on them, she can tell me exactly what they mean! Much more introverted than any of the rest of us kids, it takes concerted effort to pull Noelle's thoughts and feelings from her, but in the end it's always worth it. She is very systematic and conscientious, and has a good perception of other people and life in general. One of my more memorable experiences with Noelle was teaching her to drive my manual transmission car. After a weekend trying to perfect the technique, I was inspired to record the experience in a short article titled, *Driving Me Crazy!*

This past weekend I taught my 14-year old sister, Noelle, how to drive my manual transmission car. I figure after a couple months of daily chiropractor visits I should be back to normal again. But until then, a couple thousand milligrams of Tylenol every hour should do the trick. It only took her about fourteen tries to get the car moved into action from a parked position without stalling out. And once the car landed back on the pavement, we probably made it an additional 20 yards or so before the forgotten-clutch-convulsions commenced. She still didn't quite have the hang of starting the vehicle, but we decided it was time to move out of the parking lot and wreak havoc on the road. I don't think the other drivers appreciated sitting behind us through several green lights, and no doubt they weren't very amused when we tried to entertain them by hopping through the intersection.

We had a great time, though, and found out new things about each other. I never realized Noelle had hearing problems—that explains why I had to rapidly increase my volume level while graciously reminding her to apply the brake when approaching a stop sign. I also began to notice symptoms of amnesia—Turn signal? Pedestrians have the right of way? That's what that DIP sign means? And all the while, my finest qualities broke forth with a radiant brilliance! "Pray without ceasing" became my motto for the day. And remarkably, as that beautiful chorus says, I found the things of earth growing strangely dim in the light of His glory and grace—unless it was a result of the minor concussion I sustained when my head hit the window... My faith was stronger than ever when I told the Lord that after this, I'd gladly endure any other form of persecution that He would have me experience. I figured things could only improve from here. And I experienced a renewed eternal perspective as I fixed my eyes above and prepared to drive right through those pearly gates.

Having had such a great experience on Friday, my sister was

at the wheel again on Saturday, for our longer trip out of town. Her animosity toward stop lights, stop signs, slow moving vehicles, and really, anything else that required her to bring the vehicle to a stop only intensified throughout the drive. By the time we were nearing our destination, she had had enough and decided to take the turn without the assistance of the brake. Though she did her best, and even went out of her way to pass through the nearest ditch, she was unsuccessful in her attempt to uproot the light pole on the corner as we exited the highway. Having enjoyed the experience so much the day before, she proceeded to hop through most of the town until we made our way into the parking lot. It was a nice trick on the street, but I had to tell her she had gone too far when she tried to jump the well-placed parking block. It took a few minutes to get the hang of walking again, but once the vibrations stopped, we did okay. I'm not sure who enjoyed the reprieve more—us or my poor little car.

By the time we made it home at the end of the day, my sister's driving skills had continued to steadily improve. It looks like we're only going to have a half dozen mailboxes to replace and we think we can just hammer out that huge dent in the garage door. Apparently my car was more severely traumatized by the experience than I realized and is currently on strike and threatening to sue for cruel and unusual treatment.

(Okay, so maybe I have slightly exaggerated the details in the above rendition of my experiences this weekend. I'm really not crazy...at least I didn't use to be...)

The poem, "The Bridge Builder" by Will Allen Dromgoole, has long been one of my favorites. Its timeless message never ceases to inspire me:

An old man, going a lone highway,
Came, at the evening, cold and gray,

To a chasm, vast, and deep, and wide,
Through which was flowing a sullen tide.
The old man crossed in the twilight dim;
The sullen stream had no fears for him;
But he turned, when safe on the other side,
And built a bridge to span the tide.

"Old man," said a fellow pilgrim, near,
"You are wasting strength with building here;
Your journey will end with the ending day;
You never again must pass this way;
You have crossed the chasm, deep and wide-
Why build you the bridge at the eventide?"

The builder lifted his old gray head:
"Good friend, in the path I have come," he said,
"There followeth after me today
A youth, whose feet must pass this way.
This chasm, that has been naught to me,
To that fair-haired youth may a pitfall be.
He, too, must cross in the twilight dim;
Good friend, I am building the bridge for him."

The Lord saw fit to make me the firstborn in our family and I consider it my solemn responsibility to set a godly example and build the bridge, as it were, for the sisters and brother who are following after me. I have fallen short of this aspiration time and time again, but I love Nicole, Nadine, Noelle, Naomi, and Joey with all my heart and would do anything to help them safely pass over the treacherous pitfalls that abound in this world. Indeed, in many ways I feel as though we are holding hands, cautiously guiding each other and taking turns leading the way as together we cross over the bridges that have already been lovingly built for us by Mom and Dad.

Chapter 24

"It has been a joy to watch Natalie grow up over the years. Her father's instruction, consistency, planning, and servant's heart have been expressed and lived out through the lives of his children. Loving discipline and focused effort have brought forth their good fruit. Many families, including ours, have benefited from John's unwavering commitment to his family."

Peter DeGraaf
Friend, Co-laborer, and Kansas State Representative

my father, my teacher

Dad grew up as an only child next door to a house full of boys. He attended a private, military all-boys prep school from first grade through high school and upon graduation was admitted into the Air Force Academy, which was all-male at the time. From there, it was on to Pilot Training, another all-male program and then into full-time service in the United States Air Force. Obviously, his life was rather devoid of female influence and friendship. He has always believed that God had a sense of humor to give him five daughters. We girls did not always share that sentiment. Growing up, we often felt like Dad's military style of leadership in the home was better described as "cruel and unusual punishment"!

In particular, Dad was a stickler for physical fitness. Our morning running routine was always preceded by Dad's favorite calisthenics—a combination of jumping jacks, windmills, push-ups and sit-ups. And this was not a casual time of warming up. It was every bit as intense as the running itself. We all gathered in the basement and sectioned off our little area where we stood to do the exercises. After we finished the jumping jacks and windmills, we would strategically wait until Dad began his set of push-ups and then race to finish our own required number of push-ups before Dad could watch and evaluate us for proper form. By the time we were finished warming-up, the last thing we wanted to do was go running. But, we didn't get a vote in the matter. As Dad so frequently reminded us, we were not living in a democracy, but in a dictatorship. A *benevolent* dictatorship, he was always quick to add!

We started out by just running the neighborhood block. Only Nicole and I were old enough to be subjected to Dad's regimen, so the three of us made our way into the darkness of the early morning three days a week, where we ran under the yellow glow of the street lights. Dad's stipulation was that he would set the pace and we had to keep up with him. Nicole was a better runner than me, so she usually did fine keeping up with Dad, whereas I often fell behind and found myself doing an all-out sprint to get to the end at the same time as Dad and Nicole. As we got older and Nadine joined us in the mornings, Dad devised a new system that incorporated maximum times. He designated a particular light pole as the starting point and bought each of us watches with a stopwatch. He staggered our start times and we were each responsible for timing ourselves as we ran the prescribed route. Our block apparently didn't provide enough of a workout, so the distance eventually grew to a mile, then a mile and a half, and then two miles.

Dad assigned each of us a maximum time. We were required to run under that time or else we would have to run a penalty lap. I had to run lots of penalty laps. Nicole didn't. Neither did Nadine. But not because she was a good runner, just because she had a way of devising the most ridiculous excuses and somehow always managed to get Dad to believe her. We will never let her live down the day that she got Dad to let her off the hook for not finishing the route because, according to her, her shirt was too tight!

The three of us girls commiserated together and often connived to get out of the running routine. We tried to encourage the scheduling of other activities on early Monday, Wednesday, or Friday mornings. We tried to get ourselves invited over to friends' houses to spend the night on nights preceding our running days. We tried to talk Dad into giving us the day off on holidays—you know, important days like Groundhog Day, Grandparents Day, or our birthdays. We tried to convince him that the weather was too hot, or too cold, or too rainy. But Dad was impervious to our pleas. Rain or shine, snow or sleet, we donned our running shoes and trekked around the neighborhood. Despite Dad's constant assurances that it was good for us and that we would appreciate it someday, we considered it an exercise in misery.

Physical fitness was not Dad's only area of imposed discipline. He was also adamant that we develop spiritual disciplines. When each of us was little, he started us on the Navigators Topical Memory System (TMS). The system consists of five packs, lettered A-E, with 12 verses in each pack. We were required to learn two new verses each week and review all the previously learned verses in the pack. On Sundays, we recited them to Dad and he would determine if they were satisfactory or not. Two verses a week seems more than reasonable now, but at the time we were hard-pressed to get it done. Almost without fail, Saturday night or Sunday morning found us kids scrambling to memorize our verses as quickly as we could. And then, on Sunday afternoons, we employed whatever stalling tactics we could devise to grant ourselves additional time before we had to recite them to Dad. Perhaps it was an extended trip to the bathroom, or some other pressing responsibility, or even a conveniently misplaced verse pack. But eventually, our turn would come and we would find ourselves seated on the couch with Dad next to us, holding our verse pack and looking at us expectantly while we fumbled through our mental records trying to recall a reference or an elusive word.

Occasionally Dad would give us a hint or "feed" us the next word of the verse. But this invariably led to his dreaded response after we had fumbled our way to the end of the verses. We knew it was coming when he would slowly lower the verse pack to his lap and look right into our eyes. "That was unsatisfactory," he would say, before issuing the consequence for our failure to perform up to the standard he expected and required. Most often our consequence consisted of working on our verses for the remainder of the day and then reciting them to him again before we went to bed that night.

Once we finished all five packs in the TMS, Dad moved us on to longer passages of Scripture. We started with Matthew 5-7—the Sermon on the Mount, then advanced to Romans 6-8, followed by the books of James and First Peter. After that, we were free to choose our own passages and I moved into the epistles, memorizing the books of Galatians, Ephesians, Philippians, and Colossians. We continued to learn two new verses each week and review one of the other packs or chapters we had previously memorized. Once we completed the last verses of a chapter, we were permitted to spend a week just working on perfecting the chapter for our official recitation the following Sunday. If it was satisfactory—no more than a couple of minor errors—Dad rewarded us with a payment of 25 cents per verse. However, while Dad never required perfection, he strongly encouraged us to work toward it. For that reason, he had a standing offer of a $3.00 bonus for any chapter that we recited word perfectly the first time. Obviously, the rewards were not exorbitant; nor were they an enticement, since we were required to do the verses anyway. But Dad thought it was important for us to receive a tangible return for our efforts expended in Scripture memorization. There were less tangible rewards as well, but it would be years down the road before we would begin to recognize them.

Dad's Scripture memory program was part of the training ground for another important life lesson: always strive for excellence. I learned early on in life that haphazard or mediocre work was not acceptable in our home. If I was given a task or assignment, it was to be done to the best of my ability. And even then, if there was room for improvement, I would be sent back to work to make the necessary changes in order to produce a higher quality of work. Which brings me to the Red Pen.

I vividly recall numerous occasions as a young girl when I proudly presented to Dad a paper I had written. I anxiously awaited his response, hopeful that he would "stamp" it with his approval. Instead, he would open up his desk drawer and retrieve the Red Pen.

After considerable time spent reading and re-reading my words and his editing marks, Dad would return my paper to me. It could easily have been mistaken for a blood-drenched piece of correspondence that barely survived World War II. After offering praise and encouragement for the work I had done, Dad went over his "recommended" changes with me. I often left his office in tears to re-write the masterpiece that had been mutilated before my eyes. Emotions of anger, self-pity and indignation flooded my heart and blinded me from appreciating the value of the important lesson that Dad was teaching me and the character it was forming within me.

For years, the painful process continued as paper after paper endured the strokes of the Red Pen. And little by little my writing improved, as evidenced by the increasingly less battle-scarred papers that Dad returned to me. I knew I had "arrived" the day he gave me back a paper and said, "Very well done." Period. I looked in astonishment at the paper before me, remarkably colorless. Not a single drop of red ink met my eye. After questioning his health and whether his supply of Red Pens had been depleted, I was satisfied that my paper really had passed Dad's rigorous review. To this day, much of my writing passes first across the desk of my forbearing father. And to this day, it is often met with the ruthless Red Pen. But I can honestly say I am grateful for every mark that it makes. Apparently the training has gone full circle now, too, because Dad regularly calls upon me to read and critique his correspondence and offer my input. And I don't hesitate for a moment to pull out my own Red Pen!

In addition to learning to strive for excellence, these tough experiences taught me to value criticism. Even though my work seemed good enough to me, once it came back from Dad, it was always better. In fact, I've learned that the end result is always better if the suggestions and criticisms of others are carefully weighed and duly implemented. It hit me years later that beyond helping me improve my writing skills, Dad was doing something far more important—something that every parent must do for their children. He was driving the foolishness out of me. He was training me to receive instruction and to accept reproof and correction. Many times since, I have been in situations where others have instructed, criticized, or corrected me. Were it not for the invaluable lessons God taught me through Dad, I am sure that I would have responded foolishly and missed many opportunities to learn and grow.

Whether given in love (as was the case with Dad) or harsh insensitivity, the criticism of others can be one of the most rewarding means of personal growth. While not all criticism should be taken to heart, I have found that it always serves as a tool to evaluate my own actions, attitudes, and motives, and to constantly look for ways to improve whatever project or idea I am working on.

Dad has been one of my best teachers. Not because he sat me down at a desk and stood in front of a classroom lecturing me, but because he took the time to walk with me through life, using everyday situations to help me learn skills and develop character. Above all, Dad taught by example. For as long as I can remember, Dad has made his daily quiet time a priority. A visit to his office any given morning would find him bent over the chair behind his desk, faithfully praying for the needs of his family and friends; or walking the perimeter of the room, reading the Bible aloud; or sitting at his desk with his geeky spare glasses on his face, studying and making notes.

Dad is the first one I go to with almost any question. I've often declared to others that he knows everything about everything! We love to sit and discuss various issues together, share information from the books we've been reading, or even engage in debates (friendly, of course!). I remind him that it's really his fault because he and Mom trained all of us to study and think for ourselves. That inevitably leads to differences of opinion on occasion and makes for plenty of lively discussions!

Although Dad was raised in a good home with morals and family values, it wasn't until he was a student at the Air Force Academy and became involved in a Navigators discipleship program that he became a committed Christian. Part of the impetus behind his rigorous attention to spiritual disciplines was a challenge he received from a friend during those years that he has shared with me on several occasions. His friend said, "What matters is not how much you are in the Word, but how much the Word is in you." Dad often reminds us that the Bible contains all that we need for life and godliness. And he has patterned his life after what the Bible teaches.

During their early years in the Air Force, Mom and Dad remained actively involved with the Navigators and developed many close friendships with families working full-time for the Navigators. Mom and Dad adhere to the command to give tithes and offerings to the Lord's work and became generous supporters of many of their friends. This led to another one of our family practices.

At the beginning of each week, Dad placed a prayer letter from a missionary family in each of our mail trays (these are a stack of paper trays that sit on a corner of Mom's desk and are used to distribute information and mail to each family member). It was our responsibility to read through the prayer letter we were given and identify specific prayer requests or praise reports to share with the rest of the family. On Sunday afternoon, after we arrived home from church, we all gathered in the living room to share the prayer requests and praise reports with each other. Then we kneeled at the couches and took turns praying for those requests. This practice broadened our understanding of different cultures and gave us an appreciation for the work God was doing throughout the world. And it was always thrilling to meet some of these families in person when they were traveling through our area, or if one of our family trips provided the occasion for us to visit them!

Although Dad is easily likened to a drill sergeant for his enforcement of discipline, he also gets points for creativity. He's not afraid to try something new and enlist the rest of the family in the experiment. By the time three "littles" came along, we exchanged the weekly prayer letters for a family character study. Dad worked up a schedule, pairing one of the older family members with one of the younger ones, and assigning each pair in turn the responsibility of preparing a lesson for a given character quality. Dad received training from the Character Training Institute to be a consultant for the Character First! program in businesses and thought the material would be beneficial to implement in our family as well. He provided us with the appropriate resource booklets each week and we put in the time and work to plan the specific details of the lesson.

In addition, each week one of us was assigned another family member whom we were to recognize for their embodiment of a specific character quality. After we selected the quality, Dad helped us design a certificate, and then we presented it to them the following Sunday during the lesson. I have good memories of our Sunday afternoon character studies as we learned to work together better as a family, were encouraged to recognize and praise the character we observed in each other, and were challenged to apply godly character qualities in our own lives.

Yes, we were sometimes resistant to Dad's efforts to instill discipline and character in us. But that's because being trained in godliness is not necessarily fun. The foolishness bound up in the heart of a child would rather feast on selfish, childish, attitudes and behaviors rather than be driven from him by the strict discipline of a loving father. But that is exactly God's program for bringing up children into mature adulthood. Dad is certainly not perfect and he would be the first to admit it. He's made mistakes in his methods and approaches, and God has obviously softened his heart over the years. But Dad has never slacked in his responsibility to be a father to us, his children. Time and time again, he has decided what he believes is right and best for our family, and then stuck to it. He does what he thinks is best for us, even if it brings temporary displeasure or dislike. He faithfully leads by conviction and doesn't cater to our whims and whines.

As much as I may have disliked the imposed regimen of my childhood, I find myself now rising each morning to begin the day with a physical workout. I find myself with my Bible in one hand and my journal in the other, studying and making notes as I pour over the pages of Scripture. I find myself charting a plan for Scripture memory and longing to hide more and more of God's Word in my heart. I find myself eagerly tearing open prayer letters from my friends on the mission field and including support for them in my monthly budget. I find myself kneeling before the throne of God, thanking Him for giving me a Dad who has given his life to teach and train me to be a woman after God's own heart.

Chapter 25

"Natalie vibrantly captures the essence of what it means to be a home schooling mom. Having been frequent beneficiaries of the Wickham family's 'open-door policy' we can attest to the truth of Natalie's vivid description of life in their home and the selfless nature of the Godly woman she calls Mom."

The Donny Williamson Family

my mother, my teacher

Crash...crash...crash...crash...crash...[long silence]...[peals of laughter]. At this point I came running up the stairs to find out what was going on. It was New Year's morning and most of the family was sitting around in the living room. Dad had gotten up and innocently pulled the cord to open the blinds on the windows. Apparently, the garland atop the window was tangled in the cord and was pulled from its place when Dad opened the blinds. Unfortunately, this set off the domino effect as the garland adorning the next window, which was attached to the first by a strand of Christmas lights, was also pulled from its place. This in turn caused the garland on the mantle to come slithering from its place, carrying with it a set of porcelain churches and trees that had been part of our seasonal décor for years. Everyone sat in stunned silence, watching the drama unfold, helpless to do anything to stop it. In the midst of hundreds of pieces of broken glass, Mom was the first to break the silence. Her lips parted to give way not to harsh words of anger, but to laughter. Soon everyone followed suit and they all chimed in in animated fashion to relay the details of the catastrophe to me when I arrived at the top of the stairs. Once the laughter died down, the vacuum cleaner and trash can were put to work as the shattered remnants of the displays were discarded. But no one seemed overly upset. After all, Mom was quick to remind us, those are just *things*.

That's not the only time Mom's perspective on life and things came out. Over the years, our home has seen many broken dishes, beat-up furniture, stained floors, dented walls, and torn books, but it rarely fazed Mom. And it never stopped her from opening our home to any and all. Our house would never make it into the pages of a home interiors magazine (unless it was the "before" picture!), but it has made it to the top of the list of one of the best places in the world to be for at least the eight members who have called it home. Our well-known open-door policy saw Mom welcoming people at all times of the day, expected or unexpected, inviting them in to sit and visit or stay for a meal. Quick visits often turn into hours as friends find a listening ear and understanding heart in Mom as they share with her their struggles or complaints. Mom has never been one of those people who is practically bursting at the seams to give counsel for any and every situation. Instead she listens patiently and empathetically, and helps shoulder the burdens of the weary and discouraged. All of us kids have spent hours at Mom's side, listening while she encouraged friends; or have eagerly entertained the children of those friends while our moms visited together.

You see, not only is home where we do school, home is where we eat meals, where we interact with people of all ages and backgrounds, where we play with friends, where we hold meetings, where we engage in animated discussions, and where we work day in and day out. In short, home is where we live life. Far from a house that sits empty all day, while its inhabitants attend to their individual responsibilities at work or school offsite, ours is abuzz with activity almost all the time. Children trample through the weed-strewn lawn outside while mothers visit on the well-worn couches inside as pleasant aromas waft from the kitchen where meal preparations are often underway. Ah yes, meals. Mom is a fabulous cook. Not because she cooks gourmet meals that take hours to prepare and require exotic ingredients. But because she does it every day.

By the time I was in high school, Mom had taught me how to plan a well-balanced menu, make grocery lists, shop for groceries, prepare meals, make recipe adjustments when necessary, and have a delicious meal on the table when it was time for dinner. She didn't sit me at a desk and talk in hypothetical terms about how to do these things. She showed me. She walked me through it by involving me in the process. She had me write actual menus for the family (and urged me to include meals other than tacos and pizza!). She guided me as I wrote grocery lists, taking into account the items we already had, and making note of items that were in the sale papers for the week. She took me with her to the grocery store where we walked up and down the aisles, collecting the items on our list. She taught me how to use the kitchen equipment and follow recipes. She encouraged my efforts and jumped in to help when necessary. She trained me in the art of homemaking, leading by example so that someday I might follow in her footsteps.

Mom's footsteps also led us to many a thrift store and garage sale. In her quest to provide for her family on a limited income, Mom employed creative strategies to clothe us and supply our household needs. This often led us through the doors of one of the local Goodwill stores to secure the needed clothing or shoes. The end of each season found us going through our closets and dresser drawers, bagging up the items that no longer fit, and passing them on to the next sister for her wearing pleasure. Occasionally we received a bag of hand-me-downs from other families and we eagerly tore into it, anxious to see what treasures it contained. Clothes we no longer needed were likewise bagged up and passed on to one of our fellow homeschool families with younger children. We never thought twice about buying or wearing used clothing. If it fit and looked nice, that's all that mattered. Now all of us kids are well-trained in the art of thrift-store shopping and we balk at paying retail prices for any article of clothing!

Ever the entrepreneurial spirit, Mom has encouraged us in all sorts of small business ventures. We've had booths at craft shows, gone door-to-door selling catalog items, set up lemonade stands on the corner, hosted too many garage sales, run concessions stands, bought and resold used items, and marketed greeting cards. Hardly a week goes by that Mom doesn't come up with some creative way to make a little bit of money on the side. Not all of the ideas get put into practice, and not all of the ideas are successful, but Mom has been one of my biggest cheerleaders as I've embarked on numerous business ventures. I can always count on her to share my enthusiasm and be ready to jump on board with any adventurous idea!

One year, our church implemented an initiative encouraging families to invest in the people in their neighborhood. Mom and I were inspired by the ideas presented and joined in by hosting a Neighborhood Ladies' Christmas Tea. Some ladies from church printed up the invitations and I walked the neighborhood distributing them and inviting almost 30 ladies to join us for the afternoon tea. As I introduced myself to the ones who answered the door and explained who I was and where I lived, on more than one occasion I got the response, "Oh, you mean the house with all the kids?" I always laughed and answered in the affirmative. Apparently between our own family and the many additional children that make our yard their home while our Moms visit or while they wait for their piano lesson, we've developed more of a reputation in the neighborhood than I realized!

While I handled the logistics of planning the event and put together Christmas gift bags for each of the ladies that would attend, Mom oversaw the time-consuming and labor-intensive food preparations. The whole family pitched in to make the endeavor a success by preparing the house, setting the table, trimming the tree, and all the other little details that contribute to an orderly household. In the end, only a handful of ladies attended, but we had a wonderful time getting to know each of them better. We invited a lady from church to share a devotional message with all of us as part of the event. The ladies absolutely loved all the scrumptious goodies Mom prepared and commented repeatedly on what a wonderful time they had. We were encouraged by the responses and have carried on the tradition every year since, always including the favorite tea treats on the menu, and adding some variety by putting together different gift bags and preparing a different devotional. Mom and I, and now Noelle and Naomi as well, love working on this annual event together and have learned to appreciate our different talents and personalities. We enjoy seeing how we can utilize our differences to be a blessing to other people and faithfully work together to advance God's kingdom.

When Mom began homeschooling us, she began her journey down a path that she never would have imagined. Her family became her career. Her teaching responsibilities became her education. Her children became her hobby. Mom was wearing so many different hats that she often felt like she was juggling a dozen balls at a time and dropping every one of them. How could she keep up with the laundry when she was supposed to be teaching her children how to add and subtract? And how could she teach her children how to add and subtract when she was supposed to be getting dinner on the table? And how could she be getting dinner on the table when she was supposed to be making sure her children received adequate socialization? And how could she be sure her children received adequate socialization when she was supposed to be at home meeting the needs of her husband? Indeed, the prospect of filling all these roles seemed overwhelming and impossible. It would have been so much easier to call it quits and send us all to school so that she could preserve her sanity! But Mom kept going. One day at a time.

Some days the house was a disaster. Some days we didn't get any schoolwork done. Some days we ate dinner at 10:00 at night, or fended for ourselves. Some days Mom took a nap while we watched the little ones or cleaned the house. Some days we looked back at the end of the day and couldn't pinpoint a single thing that had been accomplished. That's because Mom's biggest job was never a line item on a to-do-list. Her biggest accomplishment would never be recorded in a schedule of the day's activities. Moment by moment Mom was touching the hearts of her children, making investments that will return dividends for generations, indeed into eternity. Things we learned not because she stood in the front of a classroom and lectured us, but because she offered her life to let us walk alongside her every day. Whether she was listening to us recite our memory verses, or explaining how our wrongful actions were displeasing to the Lord, or praying with us over a difficult situation, Mom was caring for the souls of her children.

Truly, as William Ross Wallace so eloquently expressed in his poem, "The Hand That Rocks The Cradle Is The Hand That Rules The World."

> Blessings on the hand of women!
> Angels guard its strength and grace,
> In the palace, cottage, hovel,
> Oh, no matter where the place;
> Would that never storms assailed it,
> Rainbows ever gently curled;
> For the hand that rocks the cradle
> Is the hand that rules the world.
>
> Infancy's the tender fountain,
> Power may with beauty flow,
> Mother's first to guide the streamlets,
> From them souls unresting grow--
> Grow on for the good or evil,
> Sunshine streamed or evil hurled;
> For the hand that rocks the cradle
> Is the hand that rules the world.
>
> Woman, how divine your mission
> Here upon our natal sod!
> Keep, oh, keep the young heart open
> Always to the breath of God!
> All true trophies of the ages
> Are from mother-love impearled;

For the hand that rocks the cradle
Is the hand that rules the world.

Blessings on the hand of women!
Fathers, sons, and daughters cry,
And the sacred song is mingled
With the worship in the sky--
Mingles where no tempest darkens,
Rainbows evermore are hurled;
For the hand that rocks the cradle
Is the hand that rules the world.

Chapter 26

"My family sees the Lord in Natalie's daily life. She has used her gifts to bless others, and I believe homeschooling helped her learn how to make wise decisions. She is definitely letting her light shine for the Lord (Matthew 5:16)."

Dawn Bradshaw

looking $\mathcal{C}$o the future

Solomon, whom Scripture identifies as the wisest man who ever lived (except, of course, Jesus himself), summed up the whole meaning of life in one sentence, "Let us hear the conclusion of the whole matter: Fear God, and keep his commandments: for this is the whole duty of man" (Ecclesiastes 12:13). Solomon had more wealth, fame, and knowledge than we could dream of achieving and the book of Ecclesiastes is a record of his lifetime of experience and observations. It was Solomon who likewise wrote, "For the LORD giveth wisdom: out of his mouth cometh knowledge and understanding" (Proverbs 2:6).

We have the opportunity to take to heart Solomon's advice and develop an educational program for our families that will provide the maximum opportunity and environment for true success in life. But instead of learning from his vast experience and wisdom, we often prefer to embark on the same path of empty and vain discovery that led to his ultimate conclusion. We build our educational programs on a desire to pursue worldly riches by setting forth a high paying job as the ultimate object of a good education. Or we center our efforts on a desire to solve social problems by setting forth the acquisition of knowledge as the savior of mankind. But in the end, will we discover anything different from what

Solomon did? I dare say not. Why not save ourselves the hassle and heart-ache and just accept Solomon's advice?

This is the heart of my parent's commitment to homeschooling and it has become the passion of my heart as well. Homeschooling often results in a higher quality education, less exposure to negative influences, and a better-rounded social upbringing, but none of those are our primary motivation. Ultimately, my parents homeschool because they want us to fear God and keep His commandments. They want to fulfill their God-given responsibility to teach us to love the Lord with all our heart, all our soul, and all our might. They want to follow the pattern God set forth for His people by conducting this education when we sit in our house, when we walk by the way, when we lie down, and when we rise up (see Deuteronomy 6:4-7). They want to follow the pattern Jesus set forth when training His disciples by inviting us to walk alongside them day in and day out and learn from the daily experiences of life. They want to pass on a heritage of godly faithfulness and obedience that we in turn can pass on for generation upon generation until the return of the Lord Jesus Christ.

Mom and Dad didn't dictate every detail of our education, or initiate every opportunity that we experienced. Instead, they sought the Lord for guidance day-by-day and encouraged us to do the same. They embarked on the journey into homeschooling not because they knew what the end result would be, but out of faith, and obedience to what they believed to be God's calling for them as parents. The path has looked different for each one of us kids. And rightly so. Mom and Dad appreciated our unique personalities, and urged us to pursue the areas that interested us. The path will likewise look different for every family and every home-schooler. But as we keep our eyes fixed on the Lord Jesus, He will guide us in the right way. We can trust Him, the master Creator and Teacher, to customize an educational plan to perfectly suit our needs.

The prospect of homeschooling my own children someday, should the Lord so bless me, infuses me with passion and excitement. I long for the day when I can pass on to a new generation of children the godly heritage that my parents have given me. I am filled with hope for the future of our nation and our world when I consider the impact families can have for the advancement of God's kingdom on earth as parents faithfully train their children to love Him, fear Him, keep His commandments, and then do the same with their children. It's been eighteen years since I stood on our basement steps to have my picture taken, documenting my first day of homeschool. I had no idea what the forthcoming days and years would hold, but now I can wholeheartedly say that I wouldn't trade it for the world!

Acknowledgments

"Okay, so I have an idea." I began. The eyes of each family member seated around the table turned to me. We were just finishing up dinner and I had been busting at the seams all day waiting to tell everyone. "I think I'm going to write a book." I went on to share what the Lord had laid on my heart and what my idea was for the topic of the book. From that moment on, my family has supported and encouraged me every step of the way. They've let me bounce ideas off of them, proved themselves faithful in keeping the project a secret for months, endured my endless suggestions when I was trying to come up with a title, and served as my finest critics and editors. I am deeply indebted to *Dad, Mom, Andy and Nicole, Nadine, Noelle, Naomi, and Joey* in more ways than I can ever fully express.

One of the first non-family members that I told about my book was *Duane Strain*. He's the one who reminded me to keep God as the noun and myself as the adjective. His unexpected visits to our house are always a delight and his support of this project has been a tremendous blessing and answer to prayer.

This whole project would have probably been much easier were it not for my friend, *Jennifer Neef*. If it weren't for her, I wouldn't have ever attempted self-publishing! But her inspiration, energy, and example propelled me to reach for greater heights and to travel the more adventurous path. If I can achieve even a fraction of her success, I will be thrilled!

My family could only handle so much book and publishing talk at a time. For all the rest of the time, there was *Olivia Fletcher*. From the moment I told her about my book, she was on the job—e-mailing me helpful links, asking me questions, offering advice when I had questions, helping me spread the word, and more. I figured she was already doing enough work for me, so I might as well officially hire her to be my marketing manager! I couldn't have asked for a more enthusiastic, supportive, diligent, and thorough co-laborer in this project.

When I first set out to design a cover for my book, I figured I had an advantage because of all the graphic design work I've done through the years. I worked up a couple of ideas, but they were, in a word, pathetic. I knew I needed help. God providentially allowed me to renew my friendship with *Hannah Gleghorn* in the spring of 2008. Shortly thereafter, I happened to click over to her graphic design website and fell in love with her work. Every design was beautiful! After explaining the project to her and answering a few preliminary questions, Hannah agreed to do the design work for me. I sent her my initial designs just so she would see what I had been envisioning. The cover she designed and sent back to me looked nothing like what I sent her. Thankfully! I told her to forget that I ever told her I did design work. Hannah went above and beyond what I ever expected and you probably wouldn't be reading this book if it weren't for her (because the cover would look so bad, you'd never pick it up...).

Do you have any idea how much is involved in laying out the interior pages of a book? Me neither, thanks to *Tiffany Hiebert*. The prospect of purchasing and learning a new software program for the purpose of laying out the pages of this book was more daunting than probably any single other task. So when Tiffany e-mailed me to offer her services toward that end, I jumped at the proposal and made her sign the contract in blood. Okay, maybe not quite, but I was elated. Tiffany has employed her creativity and expertise to produce a beautiful layout that I just love!

Well over a dozen titles had already been vetted by my family and I felt like I was expending more energy coming up with title ideas than writing the rest of the book. So it was that eventually one week I pleaded with God to give me a title by the end of the week. That Friday night, I had dinner with *Rachel Wilkenson* and then we headed over to the bookstore. I was surveying shelves of books to determine what contributed to a good title versus a bad title. I came up with a few key principles to keep in mind, but still didn't feel any closer. Rachel began asking me questions about my book, why I was writing it, what the content was, etc. and then she suddenly blurted out, *Pajama School*! We laughed at the suggestion. But as I drove home, I became more and more convinced that it was the right title. As soon as I walked in the front door, I was greeted by Mom. "Okay, what do you think of this?" I asked. The moment she heard it, Mom exclaimed, "That's it! That's definitely it!" I was met by similar reactions from most of the rest of the family. That night the matter was laid to rest and I praised God for using Rachel to coin such a perfect title! Rachel also gave hours of her time to read through my manuscript and sit and analyze it with me. Her friendship and thoughtfulness is a treasure.

Crystal Paine is one of the most creative, productive people I know. Ever since our days working together at the Tea Room, I've been inspired by her tireless efforts to use her talents and resources to serve others. And her expertise in so many diverse areas is mind-boggling! So, I was thrilled when she said she had a thousand and one marketing ideas for my book and was willing to meet with me to let me pick her brain. I am so grateful for the hours Crystal spent helping Olivia and me brainstorm and organize our ideas to develop good marketing strategies (even if we did spend more time just catching up and discussing a plethora of other issues!).

When I suddenly realized one day that I needed a professional photo to use for the back of the book and other publicity materials, I knew exactly who to call—*Cori Brooks*. We've worked together on many projects over the years, and her constant desire to learn new things and maintain a standard of excellence is a tremendous blessing to me. We had a fun time venturing out into the drizzly weather one morning to snap lots of head shots!

Even though he was supposed to be working on his doctoral dissertation, *Craig Atherton* graciously agreed to serve as my copy editor. He fine-tuned my manuscript and prompted me to clarify my thoughts. As a result of his influence I am trying really hard to avoid long run-on sentences, and to use commas in the right places—if only I could figure out what those right places are...

Our family was at a backyard barbecue at the Baker's home when I met *Eric Miller*. In the course of the evening, the conversation turned to the book I was writing and Eric mentioned that he had done freelance editing for friends before and would be happy to look over my manuscript once I was done writing. I was amazed at the providential nature of our meeting and gratefully took him up on his offer. His thoughts were helpful as I finalized the editing process.

If everyone who reads this book is as sweet and complimentary as *Kelly Adams*, then I'll be basking in adulation for years. Actually, I'll probably just get a big head! Kelly agreed to read my manuscript and give me her impressions as a homeschool mother with young children. The Lord used her to help me overcome feelings of discouragement when I wondered whether it was worth it to even publish this book. Her godly insight and wise feedback were just what I needed.

There are countless others whose notes of encouragement, advice, and prayers have motivated me to see this book to completion. It is with a profound sense of gratitude that I acknowledge the many people that the Lord has used to teach me, correct me, challenge me, and inspire me to live a life that is pleasing to Him. I have such a long ways yet to go, but there is incredible joy in the journey! May the Lord be pleased to continue to allow us to travel the journey together for the glory of His name and the advancement of His kingdom.